A
BONFIRE
in my
MOUTH

A
BONFIRE
in my
MOUTH

Life, passion and the Rainbow Warrior

SUSI NEWBORN

 HarperCollins*Publishers*

National Library of New Zealand Cataloguing-in-Publication Data

Newborn, Susi, 1950-
A bonfire in my mouth : life, passion and the Rainbow Warrior /
Susi Newborn.
ISBN1-86950-468-2
1. Newborn, Susi, 1950- 2. Greenpeace Environmental Trust.
3. Rainbow Warrior (Ship) 4. Women environmentalists—Biography.
5. Environmentalists—Biography. I. Title.
363.70092—dc 21

First published 2003
HarperCollins*Publishers (New Zealand) Limited*
P.O. Box 1, Auckland

ISBN 1 86950 468 2

Designed and typeset by Chris O'Brien / PLP
Printed by Griffin Press, Australia

Duende
is an elusive Spanish term which can have
a number of meanings, including:

A secret hidden charm, an interior force, that only some
people have — an immaterial impulse that makes some people twinkle
or stand out through their presence alone;
the power to attract through personal magnetism and charm;
immaterial bodies or benevolent spirits that can inhabit a house,
causing noises and disturbance.

In my life, *duende* has all of these meanings.

Susi Newborn

1

I stood motionless, fists clenched, my knuckles turning white. I had closed my eyes in shock when he had first appeared in front of me, digging my nails into the palms of my hands as I held my breath. I pushed my back into the tree trunk and felt the rough bark against my pink mohair cardigan. I peeked quickly out of one eye. He was still there. He still had the axe.

'Do you think we should call the doctor?' My mother's voice broke the silence. It had a nervous edge as she joined my father on the front lawn of our house. 'Shall I call and see if he can suggest something? It's been going on far too long.'

I didn't understand. Why did she want to call the doctor? I didn't feel ill, just scared. But then I thought to myself, I'll tell him I don't want Father to chop the tree down.

Because I knew I was right. The fir tree had been there for as long as I could remember. It had been there before the house had been built, before the railway line at the bottom of the garden had linked the green belt to the city. It had seen the little humped bridge erected, brick by brick, over the railway line. It had witnessed the opening of the corner shop, on the other side of the bridge, with its steady stream of schoolkids buying their tuppenny bags of sweets.

'But what could the doctor do, *amor*? Surely she'll give in. She won't stay out here all night. She will need to eat. Surely?' They talked about me as if I wasn't there. Perhaps it was because my eyes were closed and they thought I couldn't see them. 'I'm sure that if we reason with her, she'll see sense and come in by the fire.'

I didn't feel cold, even though the sun was going down.

The day had begun as any other Monday. Pepita, our live-in nanny, had called me from the bottom of the stairs. She had already collected my younger brother, Edward, from his room, carrying him down the landing on her hips, and had gone to make a fire in the kitchen hearth. 'Susanita!' My name sounded melodious in her Spanish accent, much nicer than in English. Everyone adored Pepita, who sang Spanish nursery rhymes as she worked. Nothing complicated — songs about ironing, cooking and sewing.

My mother and Pepita would spend much of their days on the third floor of the old house surrounded by fabrics and sewing machines, cutting out dress patterns. Dresses for cocktails, dinners and parties, for Sundays and special trips to London. Gowns for balls and meeting the mayor of London, and frocks for tea parties with the queen of England. Miles of taffeta and silk and rayon — the latest craze. Nylon was considered vulgar. 'I hear that in Russia they have tablecloths made out of plastic! Can you imagine?' my mother would exclaim to Pepita as they hand-embroidered rows of coloured edging on my small felt dresses. I often used to creep up the last flight of stairs to the attic, the secret haven of haute couture, where I'd wander from room to room, opening cupboards and large wooden chests. I would marvel at the bodices with their ample bosoms, the pleating and the perfect shoulder pads, the small diamantes sewn to form bunches of flowers and the invariable belt with its discrete buckle — all stitched in place so carefully, pinned and pinked and oversewn. My mother would comment at the wonderful 'finishing off' of the hems of the garments she tried on at Harrods. I used to wonder what it was like to buy a dress in a shop.

The attic had its own particular smell — a heady mix of an amber liquid Mother kept in a chiselled glass bottle on her dressing table, cigarette smoke and make-up. The perfume bottle was always hidden when a certain friend came to visit, a young man I liked, who always told such good stories. 'He'll drink the perfume,' my mother said to Pepita as she hid the bottle in her lingerie. 'He'll drink anything he can lay his hands on. I've even seen him drink lighter fuel.' When I heard that I wondered if he'd be able to light fires with his inflammable breath. It certainly added to his mystique. I liked the way he talked to me, crouching down to my level and looking me in the eye.

The attic was out of bounds to the children, and I would hide in one of the cupboards when adults passed, among the rows of dresses, and emerge reeking of mothballs. One day when I was hiding in the attic I saw my godmother reflected in one of the full-length mirrors, sitting on the rocking chair reading a book and sucking her thumb. I didn't think adults did such things, but now, standing in front of the fir tree, I desperately wanted to suck my finger. Just a little suck, for comfort's sake.

When I opened my eyes my parents appeared distorted through my tears, and I remembered Pepita telling me a story about a statue of the Madonna in a small village that had cried real tears. I wanted to appear statuelike now — immovable, cold and hard, in control — but when I tried to wipe a tear away from my cheek the mohair cardigan snagged on the tree bark. I was annoyed as I tried to release my arm, carefully at first so as not to damage the cardigan, then with more force as my dignity became compromised. I remembered a trip to London to see *Swan Lake* and how nervous I'd felt, overwhelmed by the volume of traffic and people in Oxford Circus. We'd had to cross the road, and I'd charged in front of a line of blinding lights. Halfway across, in the middle of one of the busiest streets in the world, I'd had to stop and lean against the traffic island for support, and I'd been sick in front of everyone. My dignity had been compromised then, but I'd picked myself up, wiped my mouth with the lace handkerchief in my small purse and finished crossing the road.

'Tutu darling,' my father said carefully, 'we need to cut down the old tree to let in some light. It's just an old tree. Think how nice it will be to have some sunshine in the front room when our friends come to visit. It's dark and depressing in there now and you know how your mother loves to have friends over . . .' His voice trailed off as if he were becoming unconvinced by his own argument.

I tried to imagine the front room without the tree blocking the light. It was a room kept for special occasions, for visitors who, for some reason, couldn't be served tea in the kitchen. Pepita would wear a white lacy apron, and a trolley with hierarchies of cakes and sandwiches would be wheeled in, kettles busily transiting corridors, and silver tongs in the shape of animals' paws would be polished up for bowls of sugar lumps. Gold-rimmed chinaware would appear from locked closets, and delicate lace and linen doilies, exquisite in their detail, would be placed on individual Florentine side tables. It would take hours to prepare, and with everything 'just so' my mother would choose a fitting outfit and a selection of accessories: the gold charm bracelet with the miniature Eiffel Tower, Greek coins — charms collected on voyages overseas — the pearl necklace with the Toledo clasp adding the finishing touch. She would make her animated entrance when the guests had arrived, in a haze of perfume, sporting berry lips and touched-up nail varnish. Edward and I would be introduced, instructed to shake the men's hands and kiss the women's powdered cheeks, and wait nervously for our own cheeks to be pinched or our eyebrows smoothed by a gloved hand.

After the introductions and the removal of hats, gloves and coats, Pepita would take the two of us off to the kitchen until I was called on to give a piano recital. I hated this even more than all the pampering and pinching. My little legs couldn't reach the pedals, and I felt ridiculous, giving a small curtsey at the beginning and another at the end before leaving the room in silence. 'Oh, how delightful! How superb! *Bravissima!*' the women would exclaim. It would then be Edward's turn to perform a nervously quavering piece on his violin. The cakes, however, were delicious. There was always a grand selection — coffee walnut cake with its solid ersatz cream centre, ladyfinger cake with its individual Italian biscuits soaked in Dom Benedictine, baby meringues, chocolate rum truffles, vols-au-vent with ham and Gruyère. Just like the clothes, everything was home-made.

'The doctor is coming. He'll be here soon,' my mother said. I peeked again and saw my father had put down the axe, leaning it against the stone doorstep, its handle pointing skyward. I saw this as a sign that he was capitulating. If I held out long enough, I would walk away victorious. It was a matter of willpower, and he'd always told me one could do anything if one put one's mind to it. I was practising what he preached; he was bound to understand.

How could he not understand? I'd told him when he asked why I spent so much time alone in the forest. I'd described the sound underfoot, the tension of rubber boots against the sea of leaves, pushing through the undergrowth in a motion similar to skiing, the movement trans-forming into a dance, creating patterns in the leaves. How the patterns would move, opening and closing, teased by the rhythm of the breezes passing through the trees. I'd explained how I loved to gather up armfuls of foliage and make myself a bed, where I'd lie for hours, watching the squirrels chattering and jumping from branch to branch. I loved the way their little hands moved as they inspected the acorns, the way humans might examine a pumpkin or a pineapple at a grocer's. 'They talk to one another. I'm sure they know each other by name.' He'd seemed to understand.

I heard a car crossing the bridge in the distance, and when, closer to hand, I heard its door open and shut, another surreptitious glance revealed an older man carrying a leather bag. It had a curved top with a metal clasp in the middle. Peeking was no longer an option: I needed to keep my eyes open and my wits about me.

'So here's the little madam! Susan, would you like to tell me what's going on?' The doctor bent down in front of me, carefully hoisting up an expensive trouser leg. 'Your parents have told me you've been standing in front of this tree since this morning.' As my mother came closer he turned. 'She looks very healthy to me. Her eyes are clear, and she's not shivering.'

I looked up and saw how worried my mother looked, and suddenly I smelt the baking on her floured hands and felt exhausted and very hungry. I looked at each of the adults, who all seemed very concerned about me. But what was the point in talking to them if they wouldn't understand me anyway? I noticed my father had put away the axe. It was almost night-time — the street lamps on the other side of the bridge were already casting a pearled light through the fog — and it would be hard to fell the tree in the dark. He stood in his waistcoat with his shirtsleeves rolled up, his hands on his hips, looking at me, and I swear I saw him smile slightly. The doctor tugged at a silver chain hanging from his waistcoat pocket and a small round watch dropped into his hand. I couldn't prevent him from taking my pulse. My heart was pounding and felt like a racehorse in my throat. When his cold stethoscope touched my chest I uttered a small, startled screech. People never asked permission to prod, pinch or probe.

'Her heart is resonant, lungs and chest are fine. I see nothing wrong with her whatsoever,' he concluded, standing up with a slight wobble and closing his bag. He turned to leave. 'I haven't met many bold wee ones like her,' he said to my mother as she handed him his hat. I caught my father's eye for the first time since breakfast, since before he'd told me why he'd taken a day off work, before I'd run from the table in panic. He tilted his head to one side and smiled at me.

The doctor turned round one last time as he walked towards his car. 'Goodbye, Susan. A nice warm cup of Horlicks and into bed with you,' he said, trying to be jolly.

That's the last thing I want to drink, I thought. How could anyone possibly like something that tasted so foul? At school, everyone seemed to drink hot milk, and I was starting to realise how different my family was from all our neighbours and friends, who ate such bland food and rarely listened to music.

My father went inside and turned up a recording of a Bach cantata he'd put on earlier, a piece he often liked to play first thing in the morning. I could see my brother peering down at me from the window on the first-floor landing, and heard Pepita calling from the kitchen: 'Eduardo? Eduardo? Eddie? Gordito!' He always kicked the metal dustbin before letting himself in and invariably forgot to wipe his feet on the thick brush mat. My mother had told me how I'd put my newborn brother in the dustbin one evening, shortly after she'd returned from the maternity hospital. Perhaps this was why he kicked it — to remind me that I had to share our parents' love. I didn't mind; I'd grown to like him. I waved slightly with one hand and he nodded back, and I heard him hurry down the stairs to Pepita.

My father came back out. 'Tutu,' he said, 'I understand why you don't want me to cut down this tree.' We stared at each other for a while, two pairs of dark brown eyes communicating without words. He ran his fingers through his thick dark hair. '*A la pucha!*' he exclaimed. 'I don't particularly want to chop it down either, *chiquita*.' He sat down next to me.

'Dada,' I said in a soft voice as I moved closer. We sat together, backs against the condemned tree. I put my hand into the pocket of his thick corduroy pants and could feel at least two crumpled hankies. My fingers played with the embroidered initials — PN, for Pedro Newborn. He would dab a splash of cologne on his hankies before pocketing them, part of his daily ritual, like the cufflinks and the tie pin, and the starched white shirts which arrived from the laundry several times a week in a solid brown box secured with a belt.

'Come inside, and I'll read you *The Water Babies* and tuck you up in bed. Mama has made chicken soup, some polenta and an apple pie. *Por favor, chiquitita.*

'I tell you what,' he continued, 'maybe, if I just cut off a few of the bigger branches and clear some light, maybe Mama will be happy — I'll go inside and ask her. And then it's straight into a warm bath for you.'

He strolled back into the house and I heard them talking in Spanish, something they did when they didn't want my brother and me to understand, having forgotten that they'd spoken nothing but Spanish to us for the first years of our lives. We maintained a facade of total ignorance, naturally, but understood everything that was said. *Y claro!* My mother agreed to the plan. But of course!

Rolling down his shirtsleeves against the cool wind, my father stepped outside. 'OK!' he shouted to me from the step. 'We'll only prune the big branches and nothing else. It's a promise. You can come in now.'

I ran into the house, throwing my arms around his waist. 'Thank you, Papa!'

2

I was the daughter of a diplomat. I say 'was' because after my father's death I felt let loose upon the world, without a rudder, without an anchor. In the instant of his death I transited to another place — my security amputated, my best friend dead.

Being the daughter of a diplomat is itself a challenge. The expectation is that you will always behave with the best of manners, cognisant of the social graces expected at the endless functions one is obliged to attend. We travelled in cars with 'CD' on the number plate, and it seemed, at times, that even the police would be on their best behaviour as we drove past. On official occasions my father rode in cars as large as boats, with small blue-and-white flags fluttering on the prow. Men in suits faced each other in the back, on small stuffed chairs they pulled down to sit on. A wall of glass separated them from a man wearing a patent-leather cap, his hands in kid driving gloves around the wheel. The minister had brought back a pair of gloves from Buenos Aires for my father, lined with vicuña. The man with the cap was *El Señor Chauffeur*, the person who drove the men from function to meeting, from meeting to function, and they referred to him by his French title even when they were addressing him in Spanish.

The minister was my brother's godfather. We had a large photo of him holding my brother with my parents, Zoie and Peter (Pedro to his Argentinean family and friends), standing outside a Roman Catholic church somewhere in central London. The photo, in its leather frame, stood on top of the mantelpiece, and had been taken at my brother's christening. My brother had been christened Eduardo Daniel, but we all called him Edward, or Eddie. During the service I'd been taken somewhere nearby; there was a photo of me being rocked in my pram by the obligatory nanny. We kept photos of all the nannies, some in nursing uniform with a metallic cross proudly pinned to a lapel as if it was a medal won in the war to placate rebellious children. Others, from Paris, wore the softest cashmere suits and real silk stockings. They gave us giant chocolate eggs at Easter, elaborately decorated by hand, or gingerbread houses the size of tea chests.

We rarely saw our parents when we lived at 50 Tite Street, in Chelsea. They were always out at corps diplomatique cocktail parties, entertaining presidents at exclusive clubs or going to the theatre. Mother liked to tell the story of taking Eva Perón shopping in Harrods during a state visit by her husband. She described the Argentinian First Lady as vulgar, a woman who had used her sexual charms to advance her career. 'She has no taste in clothing either,' she added. Many years later she stormed out of *Evita*, the Hollywood version of Eva Perón's life, demanding her money back for the historical inaccuracy — Eva and Che Guevara together. What an insult!

Photos of Father and Winston Churchill, Father and the mayor of London, Father and Juan Perón started to appear around the house. When Edward and I were babies, our nappies would be collected by a laundry service and returned spotlessly cleaned and pressed. We would be pushed in our prams, by our nannies, along the banks of the Thames, past the maternity hospital where both of us had been born and back to the house, to be left outside sleeping on our hand-embroidered pillowcases.

One of my first memories is of lying in my pram, outside the house, by the wrought-iron fence separating a narrow strip of garden from the pavement. An old woman and man are peering down at me, covered in bright buttons which glow and sparkle in the sun. They are both wearing hats and seem very friendly, and are pulling faces at me. The woman has rouge on her cheeks and caked powder around her forehead. The man is chewing on a cheroot. They are singing a song: 'How much is that doggy in the window, the one with the wagg-er-ly tail.' Their voices are throaty and coarse and have an accent I'm not familiar with.

Oscar Wilde lived at 44 Tite Street between 1881 and 1884; today, the front of the house bears a blue plaque with his name on it. An architect had redecorated the brickwork 'aesthetically' in red, yellow and green. It was known as Keates House but Wilde dropped the 's' and the superfluous 'e'. Most of the houses on Tite Street looked the same, but not number 44.

One day, when I must have been about two years old, we moved out to the green belt. 'Too many peasoupers,' I heard my mother explain to a friend. 'The smog is just not good for the children.'

I have no recollection of the move, of saying goodbye to the pearly kings and queens, or the Chelsea pensioners, or even when Pepita arrived. But there I landed, in a three-storey house on Highfield Road, waking up to life as a two-year-old with a vague aftertaste of having been elsewhere.

My mother had a part-time job in the film industry, translating subtitles from English into Spanish and vice versa. She took the family car — small and modest compared to the Buick we had used in London — to her workplace, an old turreted mansion. We would go with her at the weekend, when she needed to collect something, and I remember the extensive garden was a small forest full of daffodils and bluebells. There were marble fountains covered in moss and gargoyles over the windows — horrendously foreboding creatures I desperately avoided.

My father would take the train into London every day. No longer with the embassy, he had accepted a job as a trade diplomat and had his own office in the city centre, with a secretary who answered the phone in both English and Spanish. He would leave in the early morning, my mother at the door to straighten his tie, hand him his case and hat and kiss him goodbye. He would pinch her on the bottom and she would giggle. She was a tall, big-boned woman, exceedingly handsome, with long dark-brown hair and hazel eyes. She had healthy, muscled calves, developed during weekend sorties with her gaucho friends on *la pampa* — the pampas — on horseback. Her legs looked stunning in black silk stockings and high heels, the black seams always perfectly straight. Her bottom was large and accentuated by her belted waist. She could rotate it seductively, rhythmically, and was a fabulous dancer. Her voluptuous bosom — I clearly remember snuggling into the cleavage for safety one taxi ride in central London when feeling faint — was contained and uplifted within tight, elasticised, skin-coloured corsets. She was gorgeous, and I knew she turned heads.

My father was equally handsome. He had thick, black hair, which he used to wear long in the front so he could sweep it back with hair cream. He was particular about his hands and manicured them regularly, buffing his fingernails with a small red velvet cushion he kept on top of his chest of drawers. He splashed cologne about generously, hissing as the raw skin burned. There was such a cocktail of aromas and perfumes in the morning as Pepita got us ready for the day, the adults disappearing in a flurry of activity, the smells of their toilette lingering. My father had dark eyes, which flashed with passion when he spoke about a piece of music, a poem or a book. Mother would describe how, at cocktail parties or dinners, all the women would gather round him, vying for his attention. She would describe the platinum blondes, the Marilyn Monroe lookalikes, with their high-pitched giggles and cheap perfumes. 'They have no idea how to have a conversation,' she would snarl, feigning disgust and probably quite jealous. 'And they haven't a clue how to cook a flavour-some meal!' Mother was adamant that the quickest way to a man's heart was through his stomach. I heard her telling Pepita this one day when they were discussing the 'Anglos' and their terrible food. They decided the sex life of the English must be just as boring and bland. 'Never wait longer than ten minutes for a man, Pepita,' Mother continued, issuing instruction on how to 'get a good catch' as if she were running a course for debutantes at a Swiss finishing school.

My mother was so haughty, so proud, yet very warm and friendly. She was born in Buenos Aires, the daughter of Cecile and Joseph Lezard. My grandmother was a well-known actress in Argentina, a contemporary of Valentino, while my grandfather, who was of French ancestry, made chandeliers for the tsars of Russia. In Argentina he developed an extremely successful refrigeration company and became very wealthy, and the family lived in an apartment in Buenos Aires with several servants, a housekeeper and a cook. My mother was driven to school in a Rolls-Royce with leopard-skin trimmings, in matching fur coat and hat. The family owned a couple of old fighter planes Grandmother Cecile had bought at a reduced price after the First World War — she was rather eccentric — and the pilot doubled as the chauffeur.

As a teenager, Mother would go on safari, travelling to Africa by steamship, with her father as chaperone. She kept a photographic record of the Zulu warriors she met, an open-air tailor shop in the Lebombo Hills and her encounters with wild animals in the Sabi Game Reserve. An older cousin, living in Natal, had built a house in an enormous tree. She had photos of the sea voyage there and back, of her father — the tips of his massive, snow-white moustache pointing skywards — playing quoits and deck tennis on the *Edinburgh Castle*. They joined the steamship in Madeira for the trip to Cape Town after travelling on the *Avila Star* from Buenos Aires via Montevideo, Santos, Rio and Tenerife. I still have the fertility belt a Zulu chief gave her on one of her visits, no doubt with a glint in his eye, and she often talked about the music in the African villages and the rhythm of their songs and dances.

Back home in Argentina, Mother would frequent the seedier side of town, near the docks, and go to the bars to listen to black American jazz musicians, or to dance the tango in the *milongas*, or dancehalls. Her father would return from solo journeys to the African continent with wild animals for her, transported in cages, to be kept within the apartment. Once she even had a puma she walked through the streets like a dog on a leash, until it was poisoned by a terrified neighbour who didn't know the poor animal's claws had been removed. When her gorilla bit off a friend's finger it was taken away to a private zoo outside Buenos Aires. This was at the place where my mother spent countless weekends and holidays — Don Torcuato, an *estancia*, or estate, of thousands of hectares of Argentinean grassland, owned by the parents of her best friend, China. The *gauchos* employed there to manage the huge herds of beef cattle lived with their *chinas* — their women — in a complex of houses and stables separate from the main residence. The latter was palatial, with a swimming pool and gymnasium, the zoo and an aviary, tennis courts, a chapel and private cinema. There was an Andalucian fountain in the indoor winter garden, Italian marble in the tiled bathrooms, and rows of candelabras in the big hall and the library.

In their area, the *gauchos* sat around an outdoor fire, drinking *yerba* — a bitter green tea made from the South American holly — through *bombilla* — gold-tipped silver straws — from a small dried gourd, called a *mate*. Half a cow would be strung up on a tripod ready to be roasted over the fire, the women sprinkling *chimichurri* — a home-made sauce of chilli peppers, spices, herbs, oil and vinegar — over the barbecuing meat. The *gauchos* would draw huge silver knives from elaborately worked silver sheaths hanging on their cowhide belts, and slice off pieces of meat. Everything was cooked and eaten: the *chinculín* — the most prized part of the small intestine — the huge tongue and the gonads.

My mother had underwear shipped from Paris several times a year — silk lingerie with handmade lace edging, as black as the chocolate bonbons her father arranged to have delivered to her, once a week, from the confectionery shop. She was an only child, the beautiful spoiled daughter of an acclaimed actress, and was nicknamed Perla, Spanish for 'pearl'. After leaving school, she worked as a journalist and then as a film critic — horror movies were her speciality. As she walked to work she dived behind stone columns to avoid the bullets of the real-life horrors being played out on the streets of Argentina. She boasted that in 1943 she had walked to work through a dozen revolutions in as many days. She always said she had no interest whatsoever in politics, a form of disassociation rather than a lack of interest, born of her direct experience of life under a series of military dictatorships. The only time I heard her comment on politics was much later, when she described the stupidity of Eva Perón's housing policy, accommodating the Indios from the north in the Buenos Aires suburbs. 'The poor people get moved from their tribal homes into prefabricated housing estates in the city, and when they start fires in the centre of their living rooms, as they did on their earth floors back home, they are criticised and called savages.' Wives of diplomats were not expected to have political opinions in those days. The only requirements were to look beautiful, never wear the same dress twice and be able to cook exquisite food.

As well as Don Torcuato, there was another *estancia* where Mother spent her weekends and holidays — Rincon de Luna. Mother described the men there as 'two-fisted, hundred per cent he-men'. And there, dressed as a *gaucha* — a female *gaucho* — she would ride on horseback for hours amongst Argentina's bovine wealth. Once, she rode through the night to get help when everyone else had eaten poisonous mushrooms and become extremely unwell. Years later, in a house in England, she dusted off her old leather *gaucho* boots, hand-tooled with a small heel, and gave them to a biker friend of mine too poor to buy his own footwear. I wore her baggy *gaucho* pants in the 1970s, pleated at the waist and gathered at the ankle in a buttoned cuff; the boots had always been too big for me.

My parents first met at a kindergarten in the centre of Buenos Aires, although I'm sure their mothers wouldn't have spoken to each other. My father's mother, Lottie Newborn, ran a hostel for young foreigners, mainly Englishmen, in Piedras, one of the less affluent streets near Avenida de Mayo. My father described his own father, Robert Henry Newborn, as a 'dark, swarthy bastard' of unknown origin, possibly Irish, a lawyer and a one-time diplomat who gambled away his money and left his home and young family to live in Brazil, where he worked for General Motors. He was never seen again. Lottie brought up the three children alone — Joan, Donald and my father — struggling to maintain her dignity in adverse circumstances. There are no stories of privilege or luxury from my father's side. He adored his mother and spoke often of his love for her, but there were also moments of great sadness as the children were farmed out to boarding schools.

As a child I identified far more with the stories of my father's up-bringing than I did with my mother's life of outrageous fortune. I never heard my mother express love or affection for my grandmother. She had been brought up by nannies as well, and had a governess. If her lace hankie dropped to the ground, she told me decades later, there would always be somebody there to pick it up for her, someone who wasn't her mother, someone who would never dare to call her by name, always *La Señorita*.

There was one story she often liked to tell about her father, one I could identify with. She had gone outside onto the main balcony of the family apartment and was walking along the parapet gazing down at the park around the building and the tiled fountains with their circular pathways. The apartment was several storeys up, and as she skipped happily around the perimeter of the balcony, oblivious to danger, her father caught sight of her from the lounge windows. With great emotion she would describe how her father saved her life, convinced that if he had rushed forward to grab her she would have toppled and plummeted to her death.

'See, Papa' she said, 'I am going to fly down to the park.'

'Hang on,' he replied softly, 'I am coming with you. Wait for me!' And with that he was able to approach and grab the hand she extended to him.

Zoie and Pedro met again as young adults, as amateur actors. It was love at first sight — in my mother's words, a *coup de foudre*. Being the daughter of a Thespian diva was a hard act to follow; she sought anon-ymity by taking on the stage name Carol Kent. Her first public performance was with the Buenos Aires Comedy Company when she was 19, in *Aren't Men Beasts?* Grandmother Cecile was hoping the young American millionaire frequenting the soirees at their apartment to gaze at her beautiful daughter would become her son-in-law. But by then Zoie was too busy mourning the death of her beloved father from tuberculosis to notice anyone except the dashing Pedro Newborn, and they were married in 1942.

Cecile boycotted the wedding until the last moment, then made a sweeping entrance with her new beau in tow, wearing an aigrette hat and carrying a bouquet of Talisman roses. How could she possibly condone the marriage of her Perla to a poor accountant from the wrong side of town? La Señora Salvadora Medina Onrubia de Botana — otherwise known as China, my mother's best friend — paid for the wedding lunch of caviar, salmon and pâté, turkey, petit fours, canapés, ham from York, brioches, bouchées, pastelitos, arrolladitos, medallones, timbales, tronquitos and empanaditas, croquetas and allumettes, and a cocktail strawberry fizz. Mother's going-away dress was of heavy blue georgette, trimmed with tucks, white edging forming a V to the elbow-length bell sleeves and at the neck. This was in the Jardín Chino, in Buenos Aires. Elsewhere, the world was gripped by war.

The newlyweds moved into a modest apartment with just enough furniture to make it comfortable, and my mother learned very quickly how to cook. After losing their first daughter — she was stillborn — they decided to pursue Thespian careers and applied to the Royal Academy of Dramatic Art in London, both winning scholarships. They took the next boat to London and graduated from the academy in 1948, when they joined the Royal Shakespeare Company and toured the country, camping or staying in cheap hotels. When my mother became pregnant with me, my father took up the post of press attaché at the Argentine embassy and bought a house in London, closing the door forever on their stage lives.

Charlotte Rebecca Thewles-Kay, my Grandmother Lottie, first arrived in Argentina in the early 1900s. As a young 17-year-old from Yorkshire, she left Southampton to travel to Hong Kong, and from there to Australasia and on to South America. It was a voyage not without several disasters. In Genoa, she survived the sinking of the SS *Annunciata*, which foundered with great loss of life, and her travel log describes a terrifying eruption of Vesuvius, during which, at anchor outside Naples, she watched the roofs of the public market place fall in and bury 300 people.

Lottie subsequently returned to York, where she met the enigmatic Robert Newborn. She had the most beautiful soprano voice and was now singing on stage. The couple travelled together to Hong Kong, where they were married in 1906. Robert had a post with the Foreign Office, in connection with which they travelled to Australia, where their first child, Joan, was born. They returned to York for the birth of their second child, Donald, before sailing to Buenos Aires. Here Lottie gave birth to my father.

Lottie was a woman with an extraordinary psychic ability. Once, when at the Teatro Colón Opera House in Buenos Aires with my father, a vision of one her clients at her *pension* appeared before her to say goodbye. She cried out in anguish and returned home to find the police investigating an apparent suicide — of the person she had seen at the opera. She died in 1963 with Donald, her eldest son, at her bedside, her ever-present lavender-filled hankie hanging from her bracelet.

My other grandmother, Cecile Lezard, with her 18-inch waist, was known as the Little Venus. She, too, was rumoured to be psychic and joined a spiritualist club, attending seances — very much in vogue at the time — on a weekly basis. She gave me one of her rings before she died. It had an aquamarine in the centre and was surrounded by diamonds in the shape of a pentagram. She told me it would protect me, and I would inherit her psychic abilities.

Cecile had also come to Buenos Aires as a young woman on a steamship from England, seeking adventure and fortune. She was never without a husband in tow, and was widowed several times. Prior to her death, in a hospital in Buenos Aires in 1965, she met someone she wanted to marry — husband number four — but he 'kicked the bucket' before she could 'tie the knot'. Lottie, on the other hand, survived in a world of men without one, relying instead on her own inner strength, her exquisite singing voice and the love of her children.

I have always regretted not spending much time with Lottie. I met some of her sisters, who had chosen to remain behind on the Yorkshire moors. Their father was a local coachman, and they often rode with him from Harrogate to Studley Royal. Lottie's younger sister, Gertrude, died in 1993 at the age of 109, one of the oldest women in Britain, and had famously raised the alarm during the hold-up of one of the coaches. 'I walked four miles to school,' she said in an interview shortly before her death. 'I always was a walker. Anyone one wants to live to my age should work hard and have an occasional drink. I like a sherry.'

One sister in particular I grew very fond of — Beatrice, although we called her Aunty Bee. As a young widow she had moved down to a small cottage near Basingstoke, in Hampshire. She had been a friend of T. E. Lawrence, better known as Lawrence of Arabia, and shared his fondness for motorbikes. She would describe riding pillion with him round the English country lanes, the wind in their hair. She made it sound so much fun. She lived in Winsome Cottage, the tiniest thatched-roof abode, with a pocket-sized front garden overflowing with wild flowers. I adored the place and would plead with my father to take me there. Even as a child I had to stoop to enter and be careful not to bang my head on the dark beams. A soft, diffused light came through the lead-paned windows, which were several hundred years old. Aunty Bee's long-haired cat would always be up on the oak table, lying in the warm sunshine, a kettle would be on the range in permanent whistle, calling everyone to take some tea, and the jam tarts and knitted tea cosy with its felt patches were straight out of *Alice in Wonderland*. The grandfather clock leaned at a slight angle — there were no straight lines anywhere — and a white-painted door with a latch led upstairs, to two tiny bedrooms with eaves and the sound of doves nesting in the roof. The toilet was outside, at the bottom of the garden path; upstairs was a commode with a cracked chamber pot.

Once a week, Aunty Bee would drag the cast-iron hip bath from the wood bunker, across the granite floors downstairs, to the small worn carpet in front of the range, for a thorough scrub and wash-down. She had a selection of pinnies she wore over her clothes, her thick stockings invariably rolled down around her ankles like socks. When she went shopping in the village she would put on small, buttoned, rubber boots, pin a hat to her hair and carry a wicker basket, swamped in a large wool coat.

Aunty Bee made judicious use of words — perhaps years of living alone had pruned away all unnecessary chatter. She would come and stay with us at the weekend, and when she wasn't there wrote brief letters on notepaper smelling of cottage flowers. Her spidery writing, in royal-blue ink — there would be separate letters for each child, addressed 'Master' or 'Miss' — always ended with 'God bless you child.' Aunty Bee was one of those people who could easily fade into the background on a family occasion, such as Christmas or a birthday, especially when a crowd of noisy Latin types was around.

One such Christmas, family and friends were gathered round the dining-room table for a sumptuous traditional feast — a huge turkey with chestnut and sage stuffing, bread sauce, roast potatoes and garden peas. Aunty Bee sat silently, eating helping after helping. The Christmas pudding floated in a sea of brandy, holly blazing, and was stuffed with silver trinkets individually wrapped in greased paper, with brandy butter heaped on top. Aunty Bee passed her plate for more pudding, again and again. No one noticed her suddenly lose colour and slump in her chair with the clammy look of someone who is about to be sick, before she leaned forward and, with a roar from her stomach, claimed everyone's immediate attention. I remember someone running from the room and throwing up in the hall 'in sympathy', as Mother swiftly gathered the corners of the table cloth and bundled everything — food, plates, spoons — into a pile, then rushed outside and threw it all into the dustbin. Aunty Bee was escorted upstairs. She was silent, her eyes apologising over the rims of her small, vomit-spattered spectacles.

Several hours later, Christmas tea lay on the same table, with a different tablecloth and a Christmas cake decorated to look like a snow-covered landscape with miniature robins and children on toboggans, along with mince pies and a *panettone*. Aunty Bee made her way slowly down the stairs. 'Have you seen my teeth?' she asked, gummy-mouthed, as she cleaned her glasses on the corner of her pinny. Rescued from the bottom of the bin by someone with a strong stomach and a pair of rubber gloves, the cleaned denture was returned to its owner and Aunty Bee was once again complete, once again replete, and fully sated with Christmas cheer. It was one of those occasions you never forget.

3

I attended kindergarten from the age of three and started school at five. Within walking distance of our house in Highfield Road, the school dated back to the late 19th century and occupied a fine Edwardian mansion. Originally started as a boarding school in London for just a handful of girls, it had since moved to Northwood and become both a day and a boarding school. It was run by a number of women who, rumour had it, had lost their fiancés in the Second World War. The gardener and the local priest, from the High Anglican church around the corner, were the only two males I saw there on a regular basis. The headmistress was a terrifying woman of German origin called Miss Worger. She was a theologian and placed great emphasis on religious studies, which became very confusing for me as I had been educated at home in a multidisciplinary approach to religion and spirituality.

Miss Worger's sidekick was Miss Lesser, a short dumpy woman with a blunt haircut. Miss Worger and Miss Lesser lived together in a house next to the school. They wore tweed suits, thick stockings and unflattering black shoes. Compared to my mother, and the constant cha-cha-cha of silk and perfume at home, these woman seemed rather dull. No doubt they were brilliant academics and were mourning the death of their beloved ones in action, but I grew to see them as sadistic control freaks from a dying culture, the last gasp of an imperialism drunk on patriarchy. *Nisi dominus, frustra* was the school's motto — 'Unless the Lord is with us, our labour is in vain' (Psalm cxxvii, 1. Vulgate) — emblazoned on shields that appeared on almost every item of clothing. There were uniforms for every occasion, including church both in winter and summer, and regulation underwear to go under the uniforms — no black bras allowed. There were also gloves for all seasons, and tunics for juniors and pleated skirts for seniors. Special paths within the grounds segregated our walking to class — 'Do not talk to those in classes above or below you; stick to your path!'

We wrote in italic script, even when we took dictation, with pen and nib, dipping into small ceramic inkwells on our wobbly wooden desks. I still have a bulbous growth on the third finger of my right hand from holding my pen tightly as I desperately tried to form the stylised letters.

I once thoroughly disgraced myself in class by peeing in my pants, too scared to ask to go to the toilet, the warm urine trickling down my cold legs to form a small pool beneath my seat. I will never forget the humiliation of having to mop it up myself in front of the class, as the teacher stood over me in total silence. When, years later, we moved from Highfield Street to a smaller house on the other side of the railway, I found a small pair of soiled pants in the roof of a dolls' house in my room. I can only speculate that I put them there as a child of three or four — another accident at school, perhaps.

It took only a few minutes' to reach the school on foot, but if I went the shortest way I had to pass the witch's house and the house where people had discovered oil in the bottom of their garden, and I was scared of both. I caught sight of the witch one day on my way home. She was at the front door when I passed: the obligatory mole with hair, a pointy chin, a crooked nose, black clothing, green eyes glowing. I ran home, my heart beating wildly, nervously chewing the elastic around my boater. 'I saw her! I saw her!' I yelled to my brother, who was firing arrows from the apple tree, his quiver on his back, aiming at his holstered and pistol-waving cowboy friend below. I commanded some respect after that — other, older, children hadn't seen the witch — but I never walked that way again. I had dreams of covens plotting to tickle me to death as I lay sleeping. I would lie absolutely still waiting for the torture, in a state of pure concentration. I would burn in anticipation, not quite awake yet not quite asleep, waiting for the witches who never came.

I was always relieved to return home to Pepita, my little terrier — Bobo — and my brother, who by now was attending an all-male public school in his own uniform. We had all travelled to London on the train to shop for our uniforms at Harrods, my first shop-bought clothing. 'How smart,' my mother commented as she scrutinised the light-wool tweed Sunday uniform the boarders had to wear. 'The tailored jacket is *très chic*. Shame the day girls can't wear this.'

I would run in from the street and charge upstairs, holding my breath as I changed quickly into my favourite clothes — pedal pushers and a jumper Aunty Bee had knitted. I wanted to join the boys in the garden for some 'cowboys and Indians' and assume my role as the hunted and persecuted Apache chief, climbing the apple tree to lie in wait. I had a headband and a leather waistcoat with beads and fringing, and looking at myself in the mirror I could see why I always landed the part. Dark-eyed and with olive skin, I looked more like an Indian than a cowboy or a cowgirl. I felt like an Indian too, climbing the tree without shoes, using my toes to grip the bark. I imagined riding horses bareback and jumping out of trees and rolling when I landed. I learned about stealth, how to creep up on someone without being heard — I rarely fired my rubber-tipped arrows, relying instead on the plastic dagger in my belt, which I used to scalp the enemy from behind. When the cowboys fired their small paper rounds of explosive caps they made loud snaps with a puff of blue-grey smoke. They wore large sheriff badges and red scarves and always had a hat dangling somewhere behind them. The cowgirls wore fringed waistcoats minus the beading, and always seemed to be called Jane. We rode around on horses made from mops and brooms, making clucking noises as we giddy-upped our wooden steeds.

I first met Athel face to face on horseback. He was a cowboy and I was an Indian. I had watched him from my bedroom window one summer afternoon when my brother had brought home some members of his school junior cricket team. When he had introduced me to the 'two von Koettlitz boys', I had run to my room in a moment of shyness. These were the first boys, other than Edward or family friends, to come into my home — the first outsiders. The fact that they were brothers added to their appeal, so I spied on them to gain a little insight before approaching.

A girlfriend from school — Ann, also an accomplished Indian — was with me at the time. I had started to make friends among the girls in my class, and having them come round made me more comfortable in their company. As we watched from the bedroom window, the two of us discussed ways in which to grab the boys' attention. I don't know whose idea it was, but Ann and I removed our regulation bloomers and chucked them down at the two brothers in the garden below. They watched the large blue pantaloons float down, put them on their heads and danced around. This intimate gesture immediately formed a bond between us, even if we didn't understand it at the time. The 'VKs', as they came to be known, were now part of my life — for ever.

We started going to the city quite regularly — to the theatre, or to visit Cecil Lezard, Mother's first cousin, who was living in a flat in Kensington with his new Welsh wife. He had also emigrated from Argentina, and was a brilliant engineer and my mother's favourite family member. Rumour had it he was training to be part of the British space programme, so he was a great hit with us kids. I had overcome my phobia of crowds and traffic and loved visiting his inner-city apartment, with its gold cage lifts and burgundy carpets. There were cigarettes and lighters on every table, crystal decanters full of ageing liqueurs, cocktails, soda water and silver ice tongs, and it was here I had my first taste of American jazz, part of the African diaspora that formed the musical score to my childhood. Cecil, cigar in mouth, drink in hand, would try out his selection of jokes on us. Another rumour, one I believed, was that he sold them to Christmas cracker manufacturers — they were that bad.

Edward and I used to hang over the balcony, chewing toffees and forming toffee-coated spit balls as we dangled from our waists, waiting for bald-headed targets to pass below. I remember the commotion and ensuing dressing-down when our one and only ever successful hit charged up the stairs, a sticky mess of chewed toffee wreaking havoc with his gloved hand.

'Enough of this liberal education!' I heard Cecil's wife admonishing my father. 'You'll spoil them for life!' A 'good spanking' was recommended by all and sundry, but my father didn't believe in physical punishment. 'The wildest colts make the best horses,' he would say, quoting Themistacles, from who-knew-when before Christ. The way he brought us up certainly raised a few eyebrows. In retrospect, however, I believe it gave us a solid grounding in conflict resolution, and the ability to self-critique and apologise and admit when we were wrong.

One day we went to see an animated film, our first-ever motion picture. Walt Disney's *Fantasia* was playing at a local cinema, so we took the double-decker bus, sitting on top as it wound its way through the old towns of Pinner, Ruislip and Harrow-on-the-Hill. The cinema was full and the air thick with tobacco smoke. My brother and I queued for an ice cream from one of the colourful usherettes, who wore a tiny pleated skirt and striped pillbox hat. She was standing at the foot of a stage, a large tray hanging around her neck displaying an assortment of drinks, popcorn and sweets. On the stage, in front of imposing velvet curtains with huge tassels, a man with a piano played an endlessly repeating repertoire of popular songs. As the lights dimmed and everyone rushed back to their seats, he disappeared into the floor and the curtains opened and a screen made its way down from above. Suddenly, from a speaker above the stage, a scratched recording of *God Save the Queen* started, and everyone rose to their feet. The execution of anthem and duty over, the lights were finally switched off. There was absolute silence in the smoky darkness — not even a cough. Then, in the middle of the screen, a pinprick of light appeared which opened up to the instantly recognisable rooster logo of *Pathé News*, in glorious black and white. 'Uncle Cecil designed their cameras in the US before he came out here,' whispered Mother, leaning sideways towards us in her beaver-skin coat, sleek and shiny like her hair.

My favourite book at the time was *The Wind in the Willows*, with Badger, Otter, Mole and Ratty. I was perplexed at how on the one hand adults anthropomorphised animals in stories for children, giving them personalities and bringing them alive in our imagination, while on the other they condoned killing them to make my mother's coat. It made no sense. In Bible studies at school they taught us to 'Hurt not the Earth. Neither the Sea, nor the Trees' (Revelations 7:3), yet no one talked about what was really going on in God's green land. Mouths and hearts were zipped shut, traumatised by the wars, perhaps, not knowing which words could be applied to describe the horror and deceiving children into believing the willow world really existed at the bottom of the garden.

So caught up was I in my first celluloid experience, I can't remember at what moment I realised what it was I was looking at, but suddenly the stark black-and-white images became skeletal people, with bulging eyes and grotesquely distorted bodies. Men with masks and uniforms were flinging bodies into a large pit one by one. As the bodies piled up, I saw naked women thrown in by their hair, and tiny children. I caught a glimpse of my mother out of the corner of my petrified eye. I didn't know what to do, so I froze, with my eyes shut. I could hear my mother's voice in the foyer demanding to speak to the manager: 'How dare you show such horrific images to an audience of children. Are you out of your mind?' On the way home, Mother gave us an anaesthetised version of the Holocaust, explaining the atrocities in a matter-of-fact voice. It made perfect sense to me that if humans could hurt animals and chop down trees, they were capable of hurting one another for no apparent reason.

♥

My parents took me out of school for one year when I was 10 so we could travel to Buenos Aires and meet our family there. The only relatives we had in England were various members of the Lezard family — Cecil and his wife, his brothers Julian and Selwyn, and his parents, Louis and Netta. Louis had been a lawyer in South Africa and was a director of de Beers, a man of great charm whose best friend was the king of Sweden, with whom he holidayed every year. Lezard Avenue in Salisbury, Zimbabwe, is named after Louis' cousin, Bertie, who was mayor there for a number of years and whose nephew, Hugh, married a relative of Queen Elizabeth II.

Mother used to say that if there was a plague and most of the people related to the royal family died, we would be in line for the throne. I tried to imagine Miss Lesser reading in the newspaper that I'd become her new sovereign. She would have to curtsey every time she clapped eyes on me, I thought. I hated having to show deference to those tweed-suited women, in their starched shirts and academic gowns. Miss Lesser was always telling me to brush my hair, smarten up my appearance, polish my shoes. Hours of playing in my forest dell had turned me into a creature of the wild; I wasn't concerned about dirt or fussy about my appearance. I'd long since given up playing with my doll and her immaculate handmade clothing.

When we started reading Shakespeare in Miss Lesser's class, I was always given the role of the freak. I looked like one, she said. I detested this woman and her cruel, stuck-up ways. The more sadistic she became, the more I would excel in class, becoming both an English and a Latin scholar, as if the pain she caused was fuel to the fire inside me. I was developing into an accomplished pianist, performing in local competitions and concerts, in places such as St Alban's cathedral. Every year, I climbed the steps to the entrance of the Royal Academy of Music, my hair oiled and firmly secured, and sat an examination in classical pianoforte. As I made my way up the rungs of the musical education ladder, I obtained excellent results in both theory and practice, a sense of rhythm always my best musical quality. It was assumed by all, except myself, that I would go on to read music or Latin at Oxford.

My second cousin, Julian Lezard, captained the Cambridge University tennis team and played tennis for England in the Davis Cup, and was known affectionately by the British public as 'Lizzie'. He married Lady Northlands and acquired a stepson almost his own age — the Earl of Ranfurly. Mother told a story about accidentally spilling Coca-Cola on the Ranfurly Persian carpet and 'never being invited to Court again'. She maintained she had blue blood anyway, from her French side — even though she was technically descended from a bastard of Louis XV — and therefore had no need to hobnob with the English aristocracy, who were all mad in any case. She told me that her stepfather — Cecile's third husband, Jack Delamain — had a title from the French aristocracy and that Cecile had become a marchioness through marrying him, and as a child I used to wonder if that entitled me to some step-granddaughter title. After all, Athel's father was a baron, and Alex, his older brother, was a viscount. I couldn't wait to try that one out on Miss Lesser. I was fed up with being called a freak. She would have to say 'Viscountess' instead of 'Newborn', in that awful tight voice. She would have to give me the part of a noble person in Shakespeare, regardless of how often I pressed her buttons. I mentioned all this to no one as I was never quite sure how tall my mother's stories were and I felt alienated enough already.

'If you take her travelling at such a young age, she will die an early death, like Mozart,' Miss Worger told my parents. 'Think of her education!'

By now I had a small group of close friends at school, with whom I felt safe. They forgave my family their unusual behaviour and Latin American customs, the parties in the back garden, the *mate*-drinking, guitar-playing friends. My mother felt very lonely in suburbia. She couldn't get used to the lack of emotion among the people she met, their awful food and how they cleared the table immediately after lunch or dinner. '*No hay sobremesa!*' she would say when describing their habits to folks back home in Buenos Aires. 'There is no *sobremesa*.' In Argentina, *sobremesa* is the time you spend at the table after eating, a very important aspect of any social gathering, and which can go on for hours.

Edward and I had to venture into the world of castles and hierarchy, *Rule Britannia* and Chaucer, every school day of our young lives. My friends' families would always comment on how different we looked from each other, he the lighter haired, blue-eyed, pale-complexioned one. My mother would make a joke about Edward's similarity to the Tite Street milkman, or say that I was a throwback to a relative from the Dark Continent — a distant one of course. For a while I harboured a suspicion I had been adopted, and thoroughly checked out all documentation I could find to verify my birth. 'In some countries, they throw stones at people with dark eyes like yours,' a girl said to me in the school playground one day.

31

My parents paid no attention to Miss Worger, and believing in another — richer — form of education, that of life experience, removed me temporarily from school. Mother, Edward and I left London in October 1960 on the SS *Libertad*, bound for Buenos Aires, where my father was to join us by plane. He didn't want us to undertake such a long journey by air as the route to Buenos Aires had only just been established and involved many stops and transfers, so it was decided the three of us would go by sea, as my grandmothers had done before us.

The SS *Libertad* was a small boat, with not many passengers, but quite comfortable. It had a small cinema and a gymnasium with a leather horse and wooden bars on the bulkheads. Edward and I spent hours in there, perfecting somersaults in gale-force weather. Mother was incredibly seasick all the way, so we had the run of the place. In the evening, we dined with the captain, and then we'd sneak off to see whatever X-rated horror film was showing, tiptoeing in after it had started. Because of a strike in Rotterdam the journey took much longer than expected, but we didn't care, we were having a great time. Those moments Mother was able to leave her cabin she devoted to playing canasta in the lounge, forming a partnership with my brother, and winning the cup after exposing the cheating incumbent, who had won by spying on his opponents' cards via a strategically placed mirror. Such was the scandal on board the SS *Libertad* as it made its way across the equator, the handsome Argentinian captain, dressed up as Neptune, officiating the raw-egg baptisms of those new to crossing the line.

From Rotterdam we sailed to Las Palmas in the Canary Islands, off the coast of Africa. Here we rode camels and visited Arab families living in caves. I loved the intense dry heat, which I had first experienced when we had stayed in a small Spanish village on my first voyage overseas. Pepita and the thumb-sucking godmother had been with us too; they had travelled by train and coach, the rest of us by car. Pepita had decided to return to her hometown of Madrid and had packed all her belongings into two old leather suitcases held together with string. We had stacked these on the roof rack, along with our own luggage, lashed down with rope and covered with a tarpaulin. It was the job of the person in the front passenger seat to keep a watchful eye on the tarp and make sure it didn't become loose and flap around as we sped down the French motorways towards Spain.

The mayor of the village came out to greet us when we arrived and showed us to the small stucco house we were to rent. We spent our days on the beach, being stung by jellyfish and eating freshly caught fish cooked on a grill. We were taken around in the mayoral car, which was big enough to seat everyone.

There was a walled military enclosure on a local hill — highly classified, we were told. The mayor drove us up there one day 'just to have a look,' and as we arrived, uniformed guards saluted and opened the grand metal portals. In we drove, and a line of officers, all in uniform and proudly displaying medals for their role in whatever civil or uncivil war, saluted in unison. A guard stepped forward and opened each car door. Taking my father by the arm, the soldier with the most medals, a general perhaps, guided him into the palatial building, pointing out details of strategic interest — models of weapons, aircraft and tanks, and maps pinned to cork boards. We followed dutifully, at the slow pace they had set, rather like the Gestapo high-step. A younger man in uniform suddenly appeared to offer my father the traditional *jerez*, or sherry, and cigar, served on a silver-filigree platter, with a small lace doily under the cut-crystal glass. Mother motioned to us that we should keep very quiet. The language we now spoke at home was a form of Spanglish, mainly English but with the odd Spanish word thrown in. She didn't want us to expose the terrible case of mistaken identity that had obviously taken place; this was the Spanish military after all, and there could be terrifying consequences. 'One cannot trust fascists,' I heard her whispering to Pepita when the brass were out of earshot.

Adept at playing the diplomat, suave and relaxed, my father behaved as any visiting dignitary would, although trying hard to cover up his South American accent. After being escorted back to our car — more saluting and more opening of gates — we drove off. As we made our way down the hill we passed an even larger, even blacker, limousine slowly making its way up. A small flag fluttered from the bonnet in the late summer breeze. 'Those must be the people they were expecting,' said my father, waving to them with a wry smile. Pepita anxiously palpitated her fan as the mayor accelerated dramatically in order to put as many miles as he safely could between us and the classified institution we had just infiltrated without killing anyone.

On our way back from this exciting holiday, we spent the night in Paris, my father booking us into a brothel by mistake. I remember the erotic frescos on the ceiling, and the comings and goings all night long.

My mother was not amused and admonished my father for getting it so wrong, never asking how he had driven straight there as if he had known the route by heart. I can't remember ever hearing my parents argue though, despite the fact that, as an animated household, we always talked loudly with a lot of gesticulation. 'It's our way of talking,' Mother would explain to friends, who wouldn't know quite how to take such spirited conversation. 'It's our hot blood!'

Crossing the Bay of Biscay to Las Palmas, we went through a terrible storm. My brother and I climbed up the tiny metallic steps to the foot of the radio mast, the highest point on the ship. In the howling wind and torrential rain, we straddled the antenna with our legs in an area the size of a boson's chair. From there we could see the bow of the boat nose-diving into the waves and the lightning-studded horizon. Mother lay in her bunk several decks below us, oblivious to our dangerous antics. She would mutter, 'I just want to die,' every time we entered the cabin, our compassionless souls unmoved. We didn't wish her a speedy recovery — it was far too much fun being unsupervised.

As we hung on to the mast for dear life, we broke into song, roaring in unison above the tempest: 'Joshua built the walls of Jericho, Jericho, Jericho . . .' We watched walls of water form and tumble down around the ship, like the walls in our song. We gave our rendition a contemporary beat by swinging from side to side in rhythm on the tiny seat of steel, drenched in water, our faces glowing in rapture. 'This is freedom,' I thought. There was thunder in the distance and we would be putting in to Africa within a day. Africa! Miss Lesser and Miss Worger couldn't touch me here. They belonged to another dimension now; they had no power over me.

We arrived in Buenos Aires in early November, when the jacarandas were in bloom. The *mateo* — the horse and carriage — was still around as a form of transport, and I preferred it to the *colectivos* — brightly decorated buses overflowing with people. My father was waiting for us in the inner-city dock as we sailed in. He had arrived in Buenos Aires unannounced, thinking he would surprise his mother. He hadn't seen her in a few years, since her visit to London when we were living in Chelsea. She was so surprised to see him when she opened the door of her small flat in Belgrano she was dumbstruck and it took her several weeks to regain her voice.

Cecile was also living in a small inner-city apartment, a widow now, and almost blind. She had been cheated out of her fortune by her 'companion', a woman who had worked for her while she was losing her eyesight. She had unknowingly signed over vast sums of money to this woman, who had disappeared into thin air when the theft had been discovered. Here was the diva, no longer beautiful, nor the centre of attention, on a modest pension, struggling to peel the potatoes for her evening meal. I felt sorry for her.

We remained in the capital for a few days before the real adventure began — the drive north with Father's older brother, Donald, the first real uncle Edward and I had ever met. We had been invited to stay with our other aunt and uncle in Argentina's northernmost province, Jujuy, in the foothills of the Andes. Donald worked for an American company that had built a natural gas and oil pipeline from Campo Duran in Salta, Jujuy, to Buenos Aires, and regularly travelled around the country. He suggested we accompany him. *'Es loco tu hermano,'* — 'Your brother is nuts' — I heard Mother saying in the large hotel bedroom we all shared, overlooking the famous Avenida Florida, as my parents discussed the proposal.

The city life outside our shuttered room never stopped, only quietening somewhat at siesta time and in the early hours. It was very different from London, where everything closed early. Here, there was so much vitality, so much warmth, and a bustling street life with shoeshine boys on each corner and newspaper vendors shouting out the day's headlines. The only downside for me was not being able to revert to my comfort zone of scruff. I had to get 'poshed up' every day in Buenos Aires. My uncle, however, reminded me of a cowboy — the kind I had seen in *The Lone Ranger*. Perhaps it was because he spoke English with a mixed American and Spanish accent, but in any case I immediately warmed to his relaxed style; without any formal training he played excellent jazz piano and didn't seem as concerned with elegance as the others.

We spent a day with Donald and his young wife, Mecha, as he drove us around the city. He steered with only one hand, his other arm resting on the open window as he leaned back into his seat at a slight angle. He turned and faced you when he spoke, only half an eye on the road he obviously knew by heart. I had never seen people drive like that in England. As we came up past Casa Rosada, or Government House, I started to sing a little Spanish ditty I'd heard my parents sing —something about the president having a large nose. Getting into the spirit of things — after all, this was where the large-nosed president lived — I sang louder, leaning out of the window in the hope he might hear me. I didn't notice the guards at the gate with their machine guns before I suddenly jerked backwards as my uncle jammed his foot on the accelerator. 'Do you want to get us all killed?' he yelled. The fear and anger in his voice made me realise how serious he was. We didn't speak on the way home, Donald checking in his rear-view mirror that no one was following. 'You must be very careful what you say and to whom you say it,' he said later. It would be years before I fully understood how dangerous my childhood prank could have been.

It took us five days by road to reach Calilegua, in Jujuy, where our aunt and uncle lived. We drove through eight provinces to get there, through *la pampa* and a salt desert, always on the same road. It was hot and dusty on the plains, and the salty air made us very thirsty. We slept outside under the stars on army-surplus camp beds, after eating *asado* — beef roasted on a tripod — with the locals. Donald was a great travel guide. When we ran out of drinking water in the desert, he plied Edward and me with oranges and then stopped so we could wash our sticky hands in hot water he siphoned from the radiator. He had his own methodology when it came to education. He believed wholeheartedly in life experience and had us standing over a dead skunk by the side of the road to breathe in the odour, claiming it would open up our eyes, ears and lungs. Like a dose of smelling salts, it certainly focused one's attention on the here and now, chasing out all mental chatter in an instant — a multilevel flush of the system. He recommended we sample *pisco*, a type of brandy, and smoke a cigarette; naturally, we complied. 'That'll put you off booze and tobacco for the rest of your life,' he said as we tumbled into our worn canvas camp beds feeling rather strange.

I was going through an initiation of sorts, transforming from a diplomat's daughter with an identity crisis into someone who had finally discovered her psychological roots. I felt as if I belonged in this space, and as we approached the Andes the feeling intensified. I would hang out of the window and breathe in the air deeply, an air thick with the spirit imbued in the place, filling my every corner.

Jujuy borders on Bolivia. Aymaran tribes, the Colla in particular, would come down to the flatter land of Jujuy to find work. My first encounter with an Indio was in the last one-horse town we drove through before arriving at Calilegua. There was only one street, where sacks of curious-looking vegetables and fruit, dried leaves and colourful spices lay outside the main shop, which also doubled as a café. Horses stood outside a bar waiting patiently for their owners.

A man wearing a turban and a jellaba greeted us as we entered the shop through swing doors. He asked, in perfect Spanish, what we would like to drink. *'Un te,'* I said, asking for some tea.

'¿Té de qué?' he asked back. *'¿Coca, yerba mate, limón o té de té?'*

'Tea of tea,' I answered, noticing the baskets of coca leaves everywhere and a man with long black hair scooping handfuls into a paper bag. On the counter, a lump of something I thought was calcified talcum powder sat on a brass dish being weighed on a set of scales. My uncle greeted the man in Guaraní, the lingua franca of the tribal region before the Spanish arrived. The man turned, and I saw an amethyst set into his chin. He looked at me and smiled — he had that twinkle in his eye all shamans have. He packed a wodge of coca leaves into one cheek and started chewing, offering some to my uncle, who declined. Using two fingers he spooned some of the white substance from the scales — it turned out to be lime — into the other cheek, so that he reminded me of my hamster back home, the one I had buried alive by mistake when he had hibernated in the winter. (By the time I'd realised my mistake and gone to rescue him he'd vanished — I hoped he'd woken up and excavated himself.)

My brother's blond hair fascinated the Indio. He walked around Edward slowly, taking in every detail of this nine-year-old English schoolboy. I half expected him to poke Edward to see if he was real. *'Qué rubio,'* he said as he stroked my brother's hair — 'How fair.'

Donald purchased a bag of coca for our aunt. 'She likes her coca tea,' he said, as we sat on small wooden stools drinking our *té de té*. We asked if we could buy some stamps for the letters we'd written to our parents, pages of descriptions of things we'd seen and people we'd met along the way, leaving out the *pisco* and cigarette of course — we'd save those and the skunk story for later.

The North African trader pointed to another shop across the road. As we left, we noticed him scurrying to the other side of the street and entering the building he'd shown us through the back door. *'Buenas días,'* he said as we came in, behaving as if we'd never met. And then, in perfect English, 'How may I be of service?'

'Aren't you the same shopkeeper we met on the other side of the street?' I asked.

'Oh no,' he answered with great panache, grinning from ear to ear and revealing a brilliant set of molars, a couple of them capped with gold. 'I am his brother!' Not only was this a one-horse town, it was a one-shopkeeper town as well, where a North African in the foothills of the Andes served coca to Aymaran tribes and adventurers from overseas.

'Calilegua is a fruit farm the size of the county of Middlesex,' I told the class on my return to school, almost a year later, giving the obligatory travel talk dressed as a gaucho. My uncle, married to my father's older sister, Joan, managed the farm. It grew all forms of citrus, bananas, mangoes, breadfruit, sugarcane, coffee, tobacco and avocados. Perhaps it grew coca too. I remember seeing plantations of coca on my return to Argentina as a young adult and was told they were some of the few legal growing areas in the world.

The road to my uncle and aunt's house was lined with tall bamboo, which leaned over and formed a tunnel. The sound of insects in the surrounding bush was hypnotic. Huge beetles called *coyuyos*, which hung from the trees like small bats, made an incredible noise at night, when it was cooler. Moths the size of birds, with fluorescent wings of blue and turquoise, would fly past in slow motion. Large, flat spiders would lie in wait on the walls inside. A tarantula was discovered under someone's bed the second day after our arrival and was shot dead. On our first horse-ride — everyone travelled by horse or jeep — we saw an anaconda stretched across the road. Our horses stepped over it nonchalantly, as if it were an everyday occurrence. With alligators, armadillos, anteaters and parrots also in abundance, the place teemed with bizarre-looking animal life.

I would get up at 4.30 in the morning, the best time for any activity, with the dawn air cool on the skin, and ride my horse bareback to a waterfall I'd discovered. Here I would salute the first rays of morning sun, in total bliss, the water cascading over both horse and rider. Joan was to moan later about all the animals Gerald Durrell, the zoologist-writer, put in her garage when he went to Calilegua looking for exhibits for his Channel Island zoo. He got everyone else to do the work, she said, and stayed at home drinking her gin.

The house had a large veranda, and a cooling breeze blew through it from the various fans. Edward and I accompanied our uncle to the plantations and watched the Aymaran people pick, clean and sort the fruit, chewing coca as they worked. There was a sugarcane harvest during our stay, with entire families working day and night, mothers carrying their young in slings on their backs. The cane was transported in colourful wooden containers by a miniature train, which snaked its way to the depot. We sneaked out one night to the harvest festival. We lay on the side of a small hill listening to the drums and the *quena* — the Indian flutes — and watching the dancing. An old man saw us and sat down beside us, pointing to something up in the sky. He spoke to us in faltering Spanish and told us to look at the donkey, look at the donkey, with its golden rein, its golden saddle. High on some hallucinogen, he spoke to us of visions, of gods. To a couple of small children he made total sense; although we couldn't literally see everything he was describing, we knew it to be true.

We started to spend more time with the Indios, in their simple homes with earthen floors and adobe ovens outside. The women showed us how they made their traditional bowler hats by mixing flour, water and alpaca wool together. They wore colourful skirts, one on top of another, and when the one closest to the body fell to pieces, another was added on top. They seemed wholly integrated with their environment, their highly tuned perception of other layers of existence giving them an understanding of life I hadn't encountered before. I wanted to take a photo but when the children suddenly dived under their mothers' skirts and the women raised their hands to their faces, I realised they'd never seen a camera before. 'You will take a piece of our soul,' they explained. 'We have heard about these machines. They are evil.'

Edward and I flew back to Buenos Aires for Christmas — several lifetimes, it seemed, since our arrival in South America. We flew a circuitous route, the only one possible, involving many stops, graduating from small planes with rattling wooden seats to the larger planes of the national carrier. Stepping out onto the hot tarmac of the capital's airport, I felt I had been altered at the very core of my being by my experience in Jujuy and the journey north. I had witnessed first hand the layers of existence, how perspectives changed according to belief systems, and was strengthened by the knowledge that I wasn't alone in the way I experienced the unseen, its movement beneath the surface of reality like a shoal of fish moving through the oceans.

I felt like an idiot standing up in front of the class a few months later with my silver-handled horsewhip and *boleadoras* — a lariat with balls on one end, which wrap the rope round an animal's legs when it is thrown

— my *gaucho* hat and pantaloons, trying to explain what the trip to Argentina had been like. We had returned to London by boat, a much faster trip this time. My father's work had transferred him to Italy, so we were coming back home to pack up and leave. My parents decided I should board at the school, and my brother at his, a decision I wasn't at all comfortable with. I was very aware of the ever-widening gap between the school system and myself, a huge hole at whose edge I stood totally alone.

I could see from the faces in the class that little of what I was saying made sense, or was indeed of any real interest. I felt more of a freak than when I had left, although one with some newly acquired powers for the likes of Miss Lesser, whom I knew I could turn into a donkey with golden reins whenever I chose. I didn't want to be left in these people's care: they were callous and incredibly boring, and I couldn't imagine how I would cope not being able to go over the days' events at home with my parents. My father's spiritual guidance clashed head on with the values of the public-school system. How would I manage when he lived thousands of miles away and I couldn't use him as a sounding board?

With additional uniforms purchased and all items tagged with my surname in red thread, I waved goodbye to my parents from the window of the school dormitory with a broken heart. The only music I would be allowed to hear from now on would be the church organ on Sunday or the pieces I was practising on the piano. Anything with a beat was considered threatening — I had already heard it referred to as 'Devil's music', and I was later to be called 'daughter of the Devil' by the house-mistress. Did such music remind them of the sex they were missing as war widows? It disturbed them that others could find joy and meaning in expression of any kind, of the *duende*, the soul that inhabits a secret place, or experience any depth of feeling. The more scared they grew, the more iconoclastic I became. I vowed to smash down their edifices of rigidity and control. I swore I would rebel against the patriarchal system that was perpetuating this nonsense, this split, this 'knowing the price of everything and the value of nothing,' as our famous Tite Street neighbour had put it.

Stuffed toys or any comfort item that reminded me of home would strangely disappear, and it wasn't until years later that I discovered the housemistress had removed them to her bedroom. When my birthday cake arrived, ordered by my mother to be delivered on the day from Lyons' Teahouse, I went to collect it from Miss Worger's study. I opened the lid of the cardboard box and noticed a slice was missing. The chocolate cream lettering — 'Happy Birthday Tutu, with love from Mum and Dad XXXX' — had been cut into either side of the words 'with love', and a generous portion taken. I noticed crumbs of chocolate cake on a small plate by the headmistress. 'Delicious cake, Susan. An excellent choice,' she said as she showed me the door, hand on my shoulder forcefully, making sure I wouldn't be staying to ask any questions.

'Is it true your father knows Lawrence Durrell?' a senior asked one day, immediately breaking a school rule. 'And Mahatma Gandhi, too?' She had a copy of *The Alexandria Quartet* in her hand. I'd seen the author, a tall thin man, at home a few times in the company of his shorter, stouter brother, Gerald, but only photos of the Indian leader when he had come to London and my father had enthused about him after hearing him speak. 'He's very quiet,' I said of Lawrence Durrell, 'unlike his brother.' I could see she wanted to question me further — she said something about my 'interesting family' — yet I was too caught up in my own isolation to want to talk with anyone. I had shut down almost completely since the cake incident, speaking only when it was absolutely necessary. I cried myself to sleep every night, howling into my pillow with such force that I ruptured small veins in my eyes. Every time I tried to write home, the tears would wash some of the ink away and I would tear the paper up and try again. I knew that no matter what I wrote, someone would read the letter before it was posted. I had contemplated running away, but was so emotionally exhausted I found everything a struggle and spent days in the sick bay staring at the ceiling. One morning I was found curled up under the bed. I had given up on life. I was waiting for the fairy hand to take me to the water and the wild, the world so full of weeping. But the hand hadn't arrived.

My parents flew to London before the end of term and removed me from the school. I returned with them to Italy, where I attended a local international school for a short while until my father was transferred back to England. Someone had written them a letter about my state of mind, but I never found out who — perhaps it was Cecil. It took me several months to recover from the experience and I rarely left my parents' side during that time, making up a small bed in their room at night. My brother, on the other hand, who had always been described as an 'easy' child, seemed quite settled in his school.

My parents had sold the house in Highfield Road before going to Italy, and we moved over the bridge to a smaller house, on a busier street, when we returned. I went back to the school. My old friends were still there, and as I could come home in the afternoon I felt able to cope. My parents purchased our first television set, and life seemed punctuated by international events watched in black and white on the 'goggle box': President Kennedy's assassination, the first landing on the moon. We were allowed to watch one or two programmes a week — *Rawhide* was my favourite — and I saved up my pocket money to buy the record of the theme song.

On my 13th birthday my mother took me with a group of friends to the 'flicks' to see *Summer Holiday* with teenage heart-throb Cliff Richard. I was wearing a pair of white shoes with tiny heels she had bought me as a birthday present, and a shift with matching headband she had made in secret, at night. I was beginning to feel my encroaching adolescence, checking out the boys at the cinema, eyeing them up to see if there were any as handsome as Cliff. I desperately wanted a bra — I'd seen other girls at school wearing them when we changed for gymnastics, and secretly bought one, stuffing it with socks every morning on the way to school, removing the socks on the way home and hiding it under my mattress at night. I would find any excuse to walk the dog, and instead of the forest dell my route would take me to the local park, the 'rec' where the 'yobs' would hang out and smoke behind the sports shed, portable transistors blaring out Gerry and the Pacemakers, the Shadows and Gene Pitney.

Puberty took over with a vengeance. The world of imagination in which I had found so much inspiration and comfort was bounced by an insatiable interest in the young male of the species, and I became a huntress. I still retained aspects of my tomboyishness and could muck out with the best of them, but another layer had been superimposed — the feeling of physical attraction to the opposite sex.

I started to inspect myself in the mirror and practised pouting the way I'd seen French actresses do in my mother's magazines. Like a lot of men, my father claimed he read *Playboy* for the articles. He'd gone to New York on a business trip and returned with a copy of the magazine, a pair of gigantic red sunglasses for me and some enormous chocolate dollars for my brother. Everything seemed to be huge — even the almost-naked women wrapped in the Stars and Stripes (that I saw when I took a quick peek) had huge breasts. Mother didn't seem to mind — maybe she read the articles too — but it would take some practice on my part to develop into anything as tantalising as that, I thought.

♥

We began going to the manor house at weekends when we were quite young. Coca, an Argentinian friend of my mother's, had married a very wealthy English businessman, and they had bought an old Sussex manor house, complete with ghost. I loved Coca like a mother. She was most entertaining, in her flamboyant Latin ways, and we all became very close. Like my mother, the inveterate hostess, she had a natural talent for organising wonderful parties.

Our music collection was expanding and growing more eclectic as Father travelled the world, and I was starting to buy records of my own. Music formed an integral part of any festive gathering, turned up loud for maximum impact. The manor house was in the middle of the country, but our house was a semidetached in a very densely packed street with several churches and a synagogue, and an old people's home opposite. At times, the heavy curtains on a second-floor window would part ever so slightly, and I would feel the disapproving glance of another rigid soul.

Coca would open the door as people arrived, a welcoming cocktail in her hand — I would collect their coats and bags — then usher them in to a room reverberating with a Latin beat. She would entice them into the room with samba or cha-cha-cha, her irresistible hip movements contained within the limits of her short black cocktail dress. When she clapped her hands above her head, bangles cascaded down her arms in time. She sang along in a guttural voice I heard men describe as 'sexy'. Her husband, an archetypal English gentleman, looked on dispassionately, not blinking. I never saw him dance, just lean silently against a piece of furniture with his pipe and tobacco pouch. Mother would run between rooms offering plates of food, or soothing the more staid guests, who were often taken aback to find themselves in the company of 'Negroes' or 'spics'. The prim and proper would be seated in the front room, drinking cups of tea and practising the art of polite conversation, while in the next room Coca would be leading a chain of pulsating bodies out of the French doors, across the patio, down the path and through the front gate. She would be singing the *clave*, softly at first then louder as they turned onto the street, the night mist cooling the flushed faces.

At the manor house things could get wilder, with the grown-ups behaving badly. There was always the justification of trying to frighten away the resident ghost — any excuse for an exorcism. People wore skeleton masks and dressed up in white sheets, and danced on top of the exquisite hardwood tables. I would fall asleep at night under the massive beams of the thatched roof, to the yelps and yowls of the pack below, dreaming of the young men I had met, in their tight pants. I tried hard not to notice the shape of their bodies beneath the stretched fabric, but it was difficult to have a conversation with them and keep one's eyes in check.

Coca's husband was often away on business, and weekends were always much quieter when he was home. We played games — croquet, Monopoly — or went for 'drives in the country'. The ghost remained impervious to all forms of expulsion and would return to haunt Coca when she was on her own, turning the radio on and off and throwing cutlery on the floor. She described the apparition as a drably coloured spectre of a woman, which disappeared through walls and doors, or, outside in the garden, floated an inch above the ground.

I saw her one night. She had climbed onto me on my bed, where I was sleeping next to my mother. I woke and saw this foul creature above me, with lank hair and glowing, putrid eyes, poking me furiously with her ossified translucent-green finger. I screamed, and as my mother switched on the light, the spectre dissolved into the predawn air. At breakfast that morning a similar event was recounted by a young male guest, who had whet my appetite and saturated my underwear the night before. I wish it had been me sitting astride him, I thought. The story went that unrequited love had resulted in a nobleman's daughter hanging herself in the west wing of the manor house, in the large room our family slept in. Eventually we learned to live with the ghost and accommodate its visitations, even to feel sorry for it at times.

One late afternoon in the early 1960s my father brought home our first Beatles record and we became instant converts. *Love Me Do* became the family anthem, and I fell in love with all four singers. A music impresario, who was also the uncle of a close school friend, gave us tickets to the 1963 Finsbury Park concert. I was now a regular shopper in London's Carnaby Street, my tartan hipster bell-bottoms with wide plastic belt and matching beret giving me an air of confidence as I strolled among the boutiques. I painstakingly sewed each Beatle name onto the black knee-length socks I purchased for the event along with a black plastic miniskirt. I never heard a thing at the concert, even though we had the best possible seats. I screamed the entire time, as did thousands of other pubescent girls, watching the suited, velvet-collared heroes shake their heads as they hit the high notes — ooooohhh!

I'll never know if it was hyperventilation caused by all that screaming, but when I left the stadium I felt thoroughly cleansed and buoyed by the expressive coming-together of youth. I felt invincible and able to challenge the duplicity and prejudice I saw everywhere.

I had been called 'wop' one day when walking down the street not far from school. Tensions had been mounting locally, especially among young males, with the arrival of immigrants from Pakistan, and anyone who looked or behaved differently became the butt of racial abuse. Nationalistic fervour was spreading like a plague. American soldiers on televised news openly referred to the Viet Cong as 'gooks'. From the odd comments and asides he made while watching the news, I sensed my father didn't approve of the war. I knew he identified with President Kennedy, with his relaxed style and with his attraction to women too, probably, but he was also critical of a number of Kennedy's policies, which he saw adversely affecting economic development in South America. Our neighbour, a young African-American lieutenant in the American air force based at Uxbridge, would come over for a whisky in my father's study. Here Father had his gramophone and records, a cocktail cabinet, his collection of antique books, old maps, framed copies of Renaissance oil paintings he had bought in Italy, and a ceremonial *mate* in silver and gold on the mantelpiece. He would sit in a large chair stuffed with horsehair and upholstered in a William Morris design. There were hand-embroidered, lace-edged linen covers on the arms and on the top of the back of the chair — to prevent soiling with hair cream, my mother explained. The embroidered insignia on these was that of the Botana *estancia* of my mother's childhood. A huge marble ashtray took centre stage on a leather-covered table next to the chair, with its companion silver Colibri lighter. Every week I would dust each item lovingly, oil the wood, polish the silver, and vacuum the thick pile of the crimson wool carpet and the large Persian rug Father had brought back from the Middle East. I would also vigorously brush the heavy blood-red velvet drapes, lined to keep out the cold. I would move slowly around the study, savouring the warmth and richness I felt there, my fingers tracing the vermilion velvet pattern repeated on the ivory-coloured wallpaper, a slight sheen shot through it like silk. From behind closed doors, I heard my father's laughter as he challenged the young lieutenant over the Vietnam War.

'It's shocking to think that fear of the atom bomb could do this to someone,' my mother said as she tried to explain to Edward why the friend he used to walk to school with every day was dead. The family lived just round the corner. I went and stood outside this house of death and stared; I wanted to understand. Our godmother had spoken of the bomb and described what had happened at Hiroshima and Nagasaki. She had been part of the organising committee for the first march on Aldermaston in 1958, to the heart of Britain's atomic weapons establishment. She had given me a small badge a few years later, explaining that the white-on-black symbol was made up of the letters N and D in semaphore (for 'nuclear disarmament'), contained within a circle which represented the womb, the unborn child. She told me it stood for peace, and that the black stood for eternity. My father often talked about Bertrand Russell, a man he respected immensely and who had won the Nobel Prize for literature the year I was born. He was chair of the Campaign for Nuclear Disarmament at the time of the first Aldermaston march and was imprisoned in 1961 for participating in a mass demonstration against nuclear weapons. Father would quote to me from various essays the Welsh philosopher had written, and what I heard made so much moral sense to my young mind I wore my black badge with pride, next to my school house badge, on my Harrods jumper.

'Take that revolting thing off, Newborn!' Miss Lesser glowered at me from behind her podium at the front of the class as I stood up to recite the Chaucer excerpt we had been given for homework. She pointed at the CND badge. 'See me at the end of class about detention.'

Had Edward's friend's mother known about this movement of people against the bomb converging on Berkshire with their banners, might she have stopped herself from placing a plastic bag over the head of each of her sleeping children? She might not have shoved one of her sleeping pills down her miniature poodle's throat before suffocating the creature with a cushion. When every other living thing in her house had drawn its last breath, she walked to the railway station to wait for the 7.45 a.m. train from Watford, and threw herself in front of it as it rumbled in alongside the platform, clutching her handbag.

She left a note in the hall, by the potted African violet, which said, 'Too scared of The Bomb,' and left it at that. I plucked a rose from our garden and laid it at the front door. I had passed the house every day on my way to school; I had seen the boys kiss their mother goodbye before racing up the path to the street. Something had come along and altered that forever, something so evil it had caused a mother to commit infanticide. 'How could a mother kill her children?' my mother sobbed. 'They were such sweet boys!' I never walked to school that way again.

4

I was in the school library copying out logarithm tables, squinting to make out the tiny numerals on the page in front of me, not really concentrating on the task in hand — after all, it was just another detention, one of many. It was 4.30 on a Sunday afternoon, and I was alone. The library door was slightly open, and there was an unsettling silence in the corridor outside. Everyone else was in the common room, writing home or chatting among themselves, playing Cluedo or making gonks to give as Christmas gifts. I could see the large staircase leading to the dormitories upstairs, and I looked around the library at shelves of reference books, *Encyclopaedia Britannica*, the collections — only the classics, naturally.

Each Saturday, boarders would line up in the library to show Miss Lesser the book they were reading that week. If it was a book that came from somewhere other than the school library it had to have a parent's signature in the front to show that it had been sanctioned as appropriate reading matter. I revelled in this literary line-up, waiting to see the look on Miss Lesser's face as I showed her my book. 'So it's Karl Marx now is it, Susan? Another one from your father's collection?' I had grown accustomed to her sarcastic tone and switched off. No offence to Marx, but I found *Das Kapital* very boring and was unable to get past the first two pages without nodding off. I had strategically placed the bookmark far into the book to give the impression that I was thoroughly immersed in the principles of communism. Miss Lesser didn't need to know how tedious I found it. Naturally I agreed with everything Marx said, but it would have been helpful if he could have summed it all up in a couple of sentences or a haiku or two.

I leaned forward to cradle my head in my arms and have a quick nap. Trying to focus on the tiny print had made me feel nauseous and I needed a break.

Poor Miss Lesser, she really didn't have a clue. I had argued with her in class about a phrase in George Orwell's *Animal Farm*, the one about all animals being equal but some being 'more equal than others'. She'd interpreted the famous line totally arse about face and I'd yelled at her and been sent out of the room. There was just no point in discussing anything in her class: there was only one correct answer to any question — hers. What did she think would happen if she let go and considered other ways of looking at life? I was immensely frustrated. I badly needed someone with whom to discuss my burgeoning politicisation and issues of spirituality, justice and sex.

My parents had returned to Italy and were living outside Genoa, in the small fishing town of Nervi, on the Italian Riviera, . They were renting a villa to which the only access was via a pathway of stone steps cut into the hillside. It had a beautiful walled garden of grapevines and gardenia overlooking the Ligurian Sea and the Gulf of Genoa, with a terracotta head of a young maiden spouting water into a pond. My brother and I had the lower floor of the villa, with a bathroom each. Mine was in pink marble. In the centre, between the bedrooms, was a large playroom with a table-tennis table, a stereo set and posters of the Beatles and the Rolling Stones. One wall was lined with bookshelves, and there was a black vinyl sofa under the windows.

I'd been given the choice of attending school in Genoa or staying on in Northwood College as a boarder. I was now 15 and the family felt I would be better able to handle separation. I also had a small group of very good friends at school, the closest of whom was also going to board, which cemented my decision to remain.

My father had left quite a collection of authors for me to read that term — Herman Hesse, Virginia Woolf, Anaïs Nin, Marcuse, Sartre, Christmas Humphreys (founder of the largest Buddhist organisation in Europe) — the idea being that I would send him comments about each. Miss Lesser had told him it was wrong to be feeding me books without Christian ideology at their core. He had asked that I be exempt from going to church. He told her we followed a theosophical path and adhered to no particular religious doctrine, and that he was studying Eastern philosophies and had become a Buddhist. As expected, the request was refused and I frittered away the time in church with a range of unholy thoughts, checking out the boys from nearby St Martin's and writing Bob Dylan songs in my prayer book.

A box of matches had been found under my bed when the matron and housemistress had conducted one of their weekly searches, and I had once again been escorted to the head's study. I waffled on about candles. In fact, a couple of us boarders would climb down the fire escape at night, when everyone was asleep, and go swimming in the school pool or sit under the stars and share a clandestine cigarette. At a prearranged time — messages passed in church under Miss Lesser's nose to the chosen few, more vandalised prayer books — we would wait for our suitors to arrive at the pool, strip to our underwear and dive in.

I dutifully documented each day's activity and each night's festivity in my diary, which I also kept under my bed. I wrote about losing my virginity in the back of a Mini, legs up, panties down, and the thrust-thrust of a young man from Wembley who had mentioned a sexy French au pair at home whom he fancied. He'd given me a box of Black Magic chocolates when I'd met him that night, parked under a street lamp not far from the school. I had gone down the fire escape alone; the date had been arranged by phone during a previous night's adventure, a call being made from the headmistress's study.

The young man thrashed around in the back of the Mini, the silhouette of his arched back and energetic buttocks projected onto the pavement, and everything was over in less than a minute. I felt nonplussed and wasn't at all impressed. If this was sex, I thought, forget it! Clutching my box of Black Magic with its red-ribbon bow, I sat at the window of my dormitory on my return, staring at the moon. I was a woman now, I told myself; it was supposed to feel different. But everything felt exactly the same, except for a slightly raw sensation between my legs. Chocolate after chocolate disappeared into my mouth. I ruminated as I munched. I had been conned, bought by a bloody box of chocolates and the threat of the older, more experienced au pair. Tears spilled over, dribbling down my cheeks to my chocolate smeared mouth and streaking my chin. I felt immeasurably sorry for myself. So I wrote it all down in my diary, every last detail — the smell, wiping myself with one of my socks, checking my undies for blood.

I heard the stairs creak and raised my head, eager for some company. But it was the housemistress. As she came down the stairs, I noticed she had a box of matches in her hand. This puzzled me. She was a self-confessed pyrophobic and, when the matches had been found under my bed, had described family members burned to death in a terrible fire.

She didn't notice me and quietly opened the door of the headmistress's study and went in. She came out shortly after, and quickly disappeared down the corridor with a haunted look on her face. I wondered what she was doing and why she looked so strange.

Then I smelled the smoke squeezing its way out from under the door, gently at first, then billowing spectrelike. I have no idea how the alarm was raised, except that suddenly the housemistress returned and ran screaming into the study. 'Fire! Fire!' she yelled, grabbing a fire extinguisher from the wall and covering the place in foam. She seemed animated and flushed, her haunted look replaced by one of excitement. I watched from the door as the fire engine arrived and completed the job. From what I could hear as I stood at the door of the library, it had been a paper fire, seemingly targeted at that year's GCE O-level examination papers* — the very papers I was about to sit.

Miss Lesser arrived, bustling in through the front door, and saw me standing in the library door directly opposite the scene of the crime, and in that moment I knew from the look she gave me who would be implicated.

'No one will believe you, simple as that,' Miss Worger said when I told her the story several days later. There had been an emergency meeting of the board of trustees the day after the fire. Most of the O-level papers had been destroyed and I was being blamed. The question was what would they do with me? My parents were telephoned in Italy and told to come and get me — I was going to be expelled. A high-ranking member of the Anglican church was on the board of trustees, and when details of the fire, my loss of virginity and my philosophical challenging of the status quo were exposed, he immediately requested I be expunged from anything which might link me to the school. I had been given the lead in the school play, a public performance for parents and the community, and I had just won a cup in an intercounty equestrian event. I never acted in the play, and my name never made it onto the oak and walnut panelling inside the entrance foyer where sporting achievements were recorded. I was allowed to complete my exams, a teacher seated on guard outside the examination room waiting for the moment I put down my pen, before being removed while the ink on my last sheet of paper was still wet. My

---

* GCE: General Certificate of Education; O level: Ordinary level. Usually taken at the age of 16, although since replaced by another qualification.

parents were waiting in the headmistress's study.

'Where's your eiderdown?' my mother asked as we packed up my things in the dormitory. I knew where it was. It was on the housemistress's bed, along with all the other things she'd stolen from the boarders.

'My, that's a lovely shawl, Miss,' I had commented one Christmas as I was waltzing around the gym with another boarder.

'She stole that from me!' my partner whispered as we twirled around. 'My parents gave it to me for Christmas. It's hand-spun and comes from Northern India.'

'Hand-spun, you know. Comes from India,' the housemistress echoed as she wrapped the soft cream-coloured garment tighter about her. 'A friend gave it to me.'

Luckily my eiderdown still had my nametag on it, giving the game away. She hadn't thought to remove it, nor the names on the other objects she had collected and stacked in her room. She would leave her door open, flaunting her kleptomania, and, urged on by the other boarders I would go in to look for items of sentimental value that had disappeared from their lockers, earning myself the nickname Borney-Balls. Most items were gifts from the parents of some of the younger boarders who lived in Africa, Australia or India and only went home once a year. A letter from the school had already been written to my parents complaining about my visiting these younger children — seven- and eight-year-olds — in their bedrooms at night. I would hear them crying themselves to sleep and would read to them, or just talk. I knew just how they felt. In the letter I was described as wearing 'a transparent nightdress'. 'What exactly are you insinuating?' my father wrote back.

I whisked the eiderdown off the housemistress's bed, my mother watching in stunned silence. 'How did you know it would be here?' she asked.

'I just did,' I said.

In Miss Worger's study I had tried to explain what had happened regarding the fire, I knew I had been falsely accused and that they had considered me the Devil's daughter even before they had found out about my sexual escapade, yet at some fundamental level I felt genuinely sorry for the housemistress. I could see Miss Worger was in a difficult position having to acknowledge that the woman was obviously not well, my mother having recounted the eiderdown rescue to her.

'I'll make you head girl,' she said, outlining a resolution she thought might appeal. She would keep it all in-house, retire the housemistress and refer her for treatment. 'But you will have to compromise some of your beliefs and principles.' I looked at my mother, wanting her to decide.

'Thanks, but no thanks,' my mother said as she stood up, proffering her hand to Miss Worger. 'And you know what they say,' she said, looking the headmistress in the eye. 'Better the devil you know. Goodbye.'

I knew that expression on my mother's face. It was animal in its fierce protectiveness. I'd seen it once before in Genoa, as we were walking along a narrow cobbled road. A car almost hit my friend and me as it veered out of an alleyway. My mother yelled something to the driver in Spanish and hit the bonnet with her handbag. The car stopped suddenly, and the driver got out and walked menacingly towards her. Within seconds a circle of dubious-looking characters was closing in around us. My father said he saw the glint of flick knives.

'Would the *signora* like to repeat what she just said?' the driver asked as he swaggered up.

'Listen you young whippersnapper,' my mother said in Spanish — she still didn't speak much Italian — 'you see that pile of shit over there?' She pointed to a pile of dog faeces. 'I'll hit you so hard with this handbag it'll send you flying head first into it.' And with that she spun her black leather Gucci bag around her head a couple of times, like a *boleadoras*.

'Fuck me,' a young man said. 'She's one of us!' And with that everyone nodded and left, the driver apologising.

A taxi was waiting as we marched defiantly out of the school. The driver had already collected my suitcase from the bottom of the stairs.

'I must talk to you about contraception,' my mother said with a slight grin as we drove off. 'Miss Worger told me about your diary.'

Where was the diary now? I hoped it had gone up in smoke along with the examination papers. It had never been returned although I'd asked for it back. I regretted listing all the girls in my class who were no longer virgins — that had been a bit slack, I thought, a breach of confidence. I wondered if they would be lined up outside the head's study and castigated, one by one. As we boarded the plane to Genoa I felt sad that I hadn't been given the opportunity to say goodbye to anyone.

Being the teenage daughter of a diplomat living on the Italian Riviera was genuine, unadulterated Fun. I chose to study for my A-levels* by

---

*A level: Advanced level. Usually taken at the age of 18.

correspondence. I was determined to lift my game and show my family I could still be a committed student — that male pheromones hadn't entirely scrambled my brain.

Every day, I would dutifully work at my window desk, gazing out at the lapis lazuli seascape and the curvaceous coastline when I needed to give my eyes a break from the printed page. A couple of days a week I attended a Swiss school in Genoa, where lessons were conducted in various languages. I liked the place and immediately felt at home. The principal would lie with his feet up on his desk, playing guitar. Philosophy was taught in Italian, biology in French, literature in English, and physics, chemistry and mathematics in German. This was how a place of learning should be, I concluded, where they treated you like an adult, not an aberration. I soon had a circle of close friends, and life took on a completely new dimension — one of *joie de vivre, la dolce vita*. I cruised up and down the Riviera in friends' convertibles, to nightclubs in Portofino, and a *trattoria* serving the best *gnocchi al pesto* in the world in Camogli. I would dance until the early hours of the morning, then walk along a pier in yet another small coastal town, eating homemade ice cream from a *gelateria*, listening to the waves of the Mediterranean breaking against the old stones.

Our home help in those days, Mirella, came from a village in the mountains behind our house. Her life of simplicity and her strong, almost pagan, religious beliefs fascinated me. We spent hours talking, for by now I was fluent in Italian and had an understanding of Genovese as well. I learned from her about the walled asylum a few kilometres' walk into the mountains, the leper colony on the other side of the river, and the people dressed as monks crawling their way to Rome in thanks for prayers granted. When she told me about local dishes in which song birds were cooked in delicious sauces, I tried to persuade her the practice was wrong, but failed completely. She drew maps for us of walking tracks through the mountains, showing us where we could eat in rustic peasant kitchens.

This would be a weekend adventure with Dad. We'd set off together, clad in shorts, walking stick in hand and carrying a backpack with Mirella's map, a canvas water bottle and a Swiss Army penknife. Our goal would be to reach the designated eating place in time for lunch. My mother would remain behind with Coca, who had come to live in Italy after the death of her husband. She'd bought an old villa not far from us and turned it into a small pension for her circle of eccentric friends — still any excuse for a party.

Mother and Coca would drive to a predetermined location, a spot on a country road near where the track passed, and we would stagger out of the wilderness, full of wine and garlic, olives and cheese, and be driven home, snoring in the back seat.

During the lead-up to my A-level exams I realised that, inadvertently, I had missed out on a large component of the French paper — the study of a certain number of French literary classics. Not having the time to read all of them, I decided on a plan of action: I wouldn't sit the French exam, and instead would concentrate fully on my other two subjects. I decided to do this without telling my parents, even though the omission had been a genuine mistake. I didn't want to cause them any further disappointment, and I also felt embarrassed about the slip-up.

Remembering conversations with my father when I was younger, I set out to stage an appendicitis attack on the morning of the exam. My father had often stressed that mind was all and matter nothing, that one could do anything if one put one's mind to it. In his exploration of different spiritual paths he had been reading some of the writings of Mary Baker Eddy, founder of the Christian Science movement, and been inspired by how she had reduced Christianity to a simple system of divine metaphysics. He taught me to observe my thinking, and the impact this had on the way I felt — how feelings affected my physical state.

I read up on the symptoms of acute appendicitis in the local library, and one month before I was due to sit the French exam began my training. Every lunch time, explaining that I was having a short siesta, I would lie on my parents' bed and imagine my appendix becoming inflamed, repeating a list of symptoms I was to display over the ensuing weeks. I was to sit the exams at the British consulate in Milan, and arrangements were being made with family friends for me to stay with them for the duration.

A week before I was to travel to Milan, my mother started commenting on my appearance. 'You look a bit pale,' she said. 'Are you sure you're OK?' I felt fine, yet I could see in the mirror that I was beginning to look pasty, and even started running a slight temperature. Luckily for me, the French exam had been scheduled last, allowing me to plan my medical crisis in detail without it impinging on the two exams I was eager to complete. Although I implicitly believed in the potential of the mind to influence matter, I didn't have total faith in my ability to succeed. Consequently, I approached the day of the French exam with mixed emotions, resigning myself to the fact that I would go in, sit the exam and just do my best. I was confident I would pass the language section, and perhaps that would give me a high enough percentage to scrape through.

E-day came tumbling down the black tunnel of time like a bowling ball heading towards a kingpin, and before I knew it I was sitting in our Fiat 1500 and being driven to Milan by my parents.

We cruised along the *autostrada* from Genoa to Milan, and queued up to pay the toll. I was sitting in the back of the car, staring out at the Lombard plains, madly trying to come up with a counterplan. Thoughts were rushing through my mind — better luck next time, perhaps — and I concluded I hadn't quite reached the spiritual level necessary to complete the task.

As we drove up to the large apartment block where I would be staying, near the *duomo* in central Milan, I decided to accept my situation, and then promptly forgot about the whole thing as I started to enjoy my week in the city. I confidently answered exam questions about Giacomo Leopardi et al. in a beautiful hall with a couple of young nuns who were also sitting the exam and a young consulate employee officiating at a desk in front of us.

Then, suddenly, it was the night before the dreaded day. I panicked, and collected my French books and got everything ready for the morning. My clean clothes were pressed and hung over the chair. I had handed over responsibility for the outcome to a greater power, to Creation (I never identified with 'God'), and abdicated from any involvement in the decision-making, feeling quite liberated and relaxed. I was still running a slight temperature, but, as my mother had declared this to be hormonal, no one was very concerned.

The people in whose flat I was staying went to work early in the morning, usually waking me on their way out. That morning they banged on my bedroom door, wished me good luck and left, the sound of stilettos on tiles fading down the hall as my hostess ran to catch her bus. I got up, feeling fine and remarkably refreshed. I pinched myself all over and looked in the mirror. Nothing unusual. I put on my long, pink silk dressing gown and made my way to the bathroom. I leaned over as I brushed my teeth, and then found myself thinking, Why am I lying on the floor? as I tried to roll from under the basin. A woman's voice, somewhere out in the hall, was saying something to a man in uniform. Someone was trying to lift me up, their arms under mine. I couldn't see the person, but he was murmuring reassuringly as he lifted me onto a stretcher. I recognised my hostess in the hall as I was carried out. *'Meno male che sono ritornata!'* she said to me, waving her hand as the stretcher passed. 'It's a good job I came back. If I hadn't, I can't bear to think what might have happened.' She had returned to the apartment to collect something she'd forgotten in the morning rush. *Meno male* — thank goodness.

I was taken to a nearby hospital, where it was very soon determined that I had acute appendicitis and needed to be operated on as soon as possible. I was driven, very carefully, back to Genoa to be operated on by my father's close friend and Italy's best neurosurgeon, who would perform the operation in a small, private Catholic hospital in Genoa. I heard the explanation through a fug of hospital smells: 'You have had an acute appendicitis attack, *signorina*. You passed out in the bathroom, clutching your stomach.'

I can remember protesting as I was carried down the stairs on the stretcher, wanting to leave so I could go and sit my French exam. I tried to get off my portable bed — I had no pain, I felt fine . . .

' . . . and he's sewn you up in black silk, darling. It won't leave a scar.' My mother's voice drifted toward me through the haze, like a Jewish harp expressing itself in words, twanging in and out of my consciousness. I was lying in a lovely room with an oil painting of the Madonna on the wall at the foot of the bed. If I tilted my head slightly, I could see a crucifix above my head. Maybe I was dead, but then what was Mum doing here? A nun came in, dressed in white. She bowed her head and scurried around. I realised there were others in the room. Someone heavy was sitting on my bed. The brain surgeon handed me a small jar with something floating in it. *'Un gatto rabbioso,'* he described it. 'A raving cat,' I thought, translating. My appendix.

As he stood up, the mattress sprang back into shape and I felt a sharp pain in my side. So, they had cut me open, severed a piece of my intestine and sewn me back up with black silk. I was catching on fast. I imagined wearing my bikini on the beach, small lines of black silk holding me together as I strutted my stuff along the sand.

'How long will I be here?' I asked the surgeon, feeling very sorry for myself.

'You can leave as soon as you can fart,' he said, 'as long as you don't go skiing or laugh too much and you let your mother take good care of you.'

The chicken broth was excellent, with freshly grated Parmesan, and *pastine* at the bottom of the bowl. There was a hunk of sourdough bread on a small plate next to it, and a glass of sparkling water. A nun shook out a linen napkin over my lap as another helped me sit up to eat my first post-op meal. They pointed out the Bible to me on the bedside vanity. Dad had left the latest *Time* magazine and a copy of a book by P.G. Wodehouse I had requested to cheer me up; the nuns had put both in the drawer. Someone, somewhere, was having the last laugh and I didn't want to find out who. The last thing I wanted was to look at anything related to a god of any kind. I wondered if the nuns would cross themselves every time they came into my room if they knew what had happened. Jeeves made me laugh, and as I held onto my wound trying not to pop the stitches, I strained and farted. I had learned my lesson. Never, ever again.

Convalescing on the settee at home, I watched my mother walk down the corridor throwing her black velvet cloak around her as she prepared to leave for a function at the American consul's villa. I noticed something small and pink dangling from the back of the cloak, rather like a pig's tail. She had been sitting on a chair in the lounge, painting her nails, before getting up to leave. I looked at the chair, and there it was — the empty jar, a wet patch on the upholstery and the smell of formaldehyde. I had brought my appendix home after being discharged from hospital with compliments for making such a speedy recovery from the nuns lined up at the door.

A friend had come over and I'd given him the 'raving cat' to look at. He turned the jar round and round in the warm morning sunlight. 'Funny-looking thing,' he said. He lifted off the rubber seal and poked the fleshy content with his silver Parker pen. I couldn't bear to look at it — it reminded me far too much of what had happened. He popped the container onto the seat as he stood up when my mother walked into the room. 'Here, *signora*, you have my chair. I am about to leave,' he said, blowing me a kiss and walking out of the room.

'Such beautiful manners,' Mother said as she sat down.

As I stumbled down the hall, calling out for her to wipe her back, my appendix hitching a ride to a cocktail party, I nevertheless assumed a state of passivity. Father had recently been introduced to the I Ching and was quoting it extensively. He'd spoken of the ebb and flow, of Yin and Yang, and I'd been thinking about it all for myself. If this was another message, I'd got the picture. I accepted full responsibility. I was very Yin about the whole thing.

I can still see my mother clutching the severed appendix in her hand, squeezing it like a raw sausage. She threw it at me, horrified, the cloak following closely; I was praying the chemicals hadn't ruined it. My father waited patiently while Mother changed her clothes. 'I can smell it everywhere!' she exclaimed, and Dad and I shared a quiet giggle in the lounge. He'd scooped the appendix off the floor and flushed it down the toilet for me.

A couple of days later the whole family laughed when I retold the story at a dinner party at the surgeon's home. His wife had made ravioli to commemorate my first hesitant steps from my sickbed, and he'd broken open a vintage bottle from his *cantina* under the house. There's nothing quite like humour to help one find resolution, to help one move on.

I had been made captain of the school swimming team back in England, and at one stage had been in daily training for the Olympic Games, with one of the fastest times in backstroke for my age group. But my experience of swimming in the sea had been limited. Now I went swimming in the sea every day, jumping off the rocks with my mask and snorkel and spending hours exploring underwater, engrossed. I learned how to dive with tanks, and was selected for a water ballet company which performed with the Italian Olympic swimming team, part of the performance being underwater.

I preferred the simplicity of mask and snorkel. I would strap a knife to my thigh, adding a weight belt and flippers if I wanted to dive deeper, my faded bikini bottom tied together on one side, the elastic too worn to keep it decent. I rarely wore a top. I usually went swimming alone, in secluded areas accessible only by boat or by climbing down steep hillsides. I was skinny and flat chested, and with my hair cut short I probably looked like a young boy to anyone who may have seen me.

I started working with a group of people from the University of Genoa's marine mammal department. One of the lecturers had written a book about sharks, called something like *My Friend the Shark*. My job was to dive down and look for sharks' eggs — tortoiseshell-like pods with a yoke inside and tentacles enabling it to cling to rocks underwater. I'd been told not to dive if I was menstruating, and had thought what considerate people they were, giving me time out at that time of the month. I never equated those plastic-looking pouch things with sharks; it never crossed my mind that I was spending a lot of my working day in 'shark-infested' waters. No wonder I nearly always worked alone.

I loved every moment underwater, savouring the peace and solitude. I retrieved Etruscan amphorae with octopus stowaways — I suspect they were subsequently smuggled out of the country to museums elsewhere — and, as our Zodiacs returned home, I lashed the mouths of barracuda with rope as their wriggling, writhing bodies thrashed against me. I was obliged to carry a harpoon at all times, its small tripod head machined to lethal sharpness. It made me feel uncomfortable and I rarely used it, but it was compulsory. The boss had bled to death in a quiet corner of the Ligurian coast, his leg severed by one of his 'friends' a few days after the launch of his book.

I had a boyfriend, the son of a local shipping magnate, who would take me skiing in the mountains and dress me in fabulous clothes. Sex was becoming more enjoyable, in a Mini again — I had the positions down pat — parked high on a hill, with a view of Genoa's night-lights in the distance, or in a dedicated fucking apartment, the rent of which was shared among a group of male friends who didn't want to leave home, which would have meant leaving *Mamma*, home cooking and all the perks of a cosseted existence.

When I was 17, my parents left Genoa to return to London for my father to take up a new post as European representative for the Argentine National Meat Board. I decided to stay on and live on my own, and found an attic flat in an old apartment block in the centre of Genoa. There was no lift and I had to walk up several flights of stairs to my front door. My parents helped me furnish the place with some of the items from the villa in Nervi before they left.

Mirella was told to keep a watchful eye on me and would pop in once or twice a week and cook a delicious pasta sauce, clean the floors and collect my laundry.

In 1967 I flew to Rome on my way to Buenos Aires, travelling with my parents. Mother had made me a special outfit for the occasion — a miniskirt and jacket with matching waistcoat. As soon as I stepped out of the plane I realised the material was far too heavy for Rio de Janiero. Sweat broke out and dribbled into the tiny cup of strong black coffee my father ordered at the airport bar.

I had just spent a couple of weeks in Rome as a guest of a friend of my father, who owned an estate outside the capital, and whose brother would soon be taken captive by the Red Brigade, mistaken for him. I knew Dad had some important friends, and I could tell this guy was one of them. Once, my father had flown to Rome to have lunch with a prominent businessman. He had stood up to say his goodbyes and leave, as lunch had dragged on a bit and he had to catch the plane back to Genoa. The businessman asked him what he was doing. 'The family are expecting me home,' he replied.

'Sit down, Pedro, you will catch your plane.' The man, immaculate in silk cravat and perfectly pressed suit, gestured for my father to sit. He then called the waiter over and whispered something in his ear. A phone was ferried to him, a long cable stretching across the carpet, the waiter kicking it out of the other diners' way. A call was made. 'Here, Pedro, let us finish our cognac in peace and my man will drive you to the plane.' Not wanting to appear rude, my father sat down and finished his meal. He smoked the cigar he was offered, waited for his coat and scarf to be brought to him, shook hands, and departed with the man who had been summoned to drive him. After a typical Roman car journey involving short cuts up one-way streets and much honking and swearing, my father was deposited metres from the runway. There was the plane, passengers, pilots and ground staff waiting patiently. My father ran down the corridor to the boarding gate. '*Buena sera, Signor* Newborn,' the flight attendant said, almost saluting. 'We have been expecting you.'

My parents had a very loving relationship; I never once saw them angry with each other. Sure, they expressed their emotions assertively, but it was never done in an aggressive way. When my father travelled abroad on business, my mother would insert little love notes in clothing in his suitcase, in his underpants or socks. Dad would invariably write a letter home on the letterhead of whatever hotel he was staying in. Waving goodbye to my father at Heathrow, my mother would cry — she hated being separated from him. His favourite city in Europe was Lisbon, where he stayed at the Hotel Ritz.

Although the closeness of our family made up for the fact that we rarely saw our relatives, it didn't prepare me for the shock I felt when I realised how atypical we were, that few people were brought up amid such love and devotion. My upbringing worked against me at times — I hadn't developed a protective veneer and was unable to handle any form of aggression. Nevertheless, I am immensely grateful to my parents for allowing my childhood to remain intact, for not short-changing me of those precious years by fast-tracking me into adulthood. My father always said the most important thing in life was love — simple as that — and I believed him completely. I still do.

Arriving in Buenos Aires my mother and I decided we would take a trip north, by train, to visit our family in Jujuy. The journey would take a few days, and we would stop at many small towns along the way. It was very hot in the capital and I was looking forward to spending time by the open window in the train compartment, cooling down.

The British built the railways in Argentina, a necessary arterial link between small towns and villages throughout the country, and the trains reminded me of the ones in old cowboy movies, their carriages linked by a covered veranda and with gas lamps swinging at night. There was a dining car with a bar, and travellers from Buenos Aires to Salta always dressed up for the evening meal.

It was Sunday. My mother didn't like to travel with her back to the front of the train, and I didn't want to give up my window seat, so we were sitting next to each other, facing the empty seats on the other side of the compartment. We could see the bells ringing in the belfries of small brick churches, swinging from side to side, summoning the faithful, as the train moved slowly through the villages, the driver on the lookout, waiting to be hailed should someone need to get on.

'It'll take forever to get there!' My mother was wilting in the heat. She fanned her face with a small fan and clicked open her compact to tidy her hair and reapply her lipstick. Her cousin Cecil hated her doing this in public; on one occasion when he took her out for dinner, at the table in a full restaurant, he produced a mirror, brush, razor and an aerosol can of foam and proceeded to shave.

I had my feet up on the slightly faded upholstered seat opposite, and shut my eyes, breathing in the smell of miles and miles of flat, dry earth. I was savouring every moment, feeling the slow motion of the train under my buttocks.

The train slowed to a standstill and I could hear people climbing on board. A small congregation was making its way to the next village for

Sunday mass. I heard the door of our carriage open and shut and the sound of someone sitting down on the seat opposite. I quickly removed my feet and opened my eyes. Mother had often told me, as she brushed my hair at night, that the gauchos were the most handsome men in the world, the most skilled horse-riders. She had always spoken of them with a glazed, vacant look in her eye, her head slightly tilted as if reliving a memorable encounter.

Sitting opposite me, his knees almost touching mine, his legs parted, was the most exquisite man I had ever seen. He was dressed from head to toe in the best gaucho tradition, polished boots glowing, spurs strapped on and shining, silver knife, whip and boleadoras tucked into a wide black leather belt with a silver-plated rastra — a large ornamental attachment — in the centre. His black cotton bombachas — loose trousers fastened at the bottom — fell in pleats around his powerful thighs, and his smocked shirt was unbuttoned under a black waistcoat. I could see the indent at the base of his neck, and some hairs from his chest peeking out from beneath the spotless white shirt. He wore his poncho pampa folded over his shoulder, and a scarf knotted under his chin. His hair was jet black and straight and had been bluntly cut to just above his shoulder. A full moustache, black hairs perfectly trimmed, rimmed his top lip. He had a sheen to him, like a healthy animal.

I looked at his hands. They were large and very strong. The nails had been cleaned and scrubbed. As he breathed, his nostrils flared like those of the horses he undoubtedly rode most days of his life. He acknowledged our presence by leaning forward slightly and touching the brim of his hat with his right hand. 'Señora, señorita,' he said, looking at us individually as he addressed us, with ebony eyes and a clear, direct look.

We said nothing as we adjusted to his company and the train resumed its sluggish progress, Mother pretending to read a book, I fiddling with my clothing and trying not to stare at the gaucho, already rehearsing what I would tell my girlfriends — 'drop-dead gorgeous', 'God's gift to women' and so on. Our eyes met occasionally and I blushed. I desperately wanted to leap onto him and kiss that soft dip in his neck, lick it, open up his shirt and stroke my hands along his tight body. I wanted to saddle him and ride, ululating through la pampa, orgasm after orgasm, as I rocked myself astride him, galloping under the hot sun. I could feel the perspiration making its way down my inner arms, a certain hum between my legs, and my mouth beginning to pout.

I couldn't let him go, I thought. This was a once-in-a-lifetime chance. I fantasised about dancing with him, of breaking the male-only rule for dancing the *malambo* — I would even get off the train and go to church with him if that's what it took. But he never spoke to me again, just stood quietly when the train started slowing down at the next village and left without saying a word. Perhaps I'd made him feel uncomfortable, checking him out like that, my eyes running up and down his body, tarrying in those areas it is important for a young woman to assess.

The train slowly gathered momentum and my mother's voice brought me smartly back to earth. 'Phew! Thank God he got off when he did,' she said, stretching out her arms having sat statue-like throughout the encounter, book immobile on her lap, never turning a page. 'I wouldn't have lasted another minute sitting opposite such a divine specimen. And now I am so hot and sticky' — she pulled her lime green polyester shirt away from her skin — 'and quite wet with perspiration.'

'Yes, I'm quite sweaty too,' I said, and then, to myself under my breath, 'Boy, I could have done him some damage.'

'What's that, darling? And anyway, only horses sweat — men perspire and ladies gently glow.'

I didn't want to glow — I wanted sweat! I wanted it to pour off me, to drip down my legs, smelling of cows and horses, of *mate* and worn leather. I wanted that thick moustache to caress my inner thigh, the nostrils to flare in between my cracks and crevices, mouth sucking, tongue lapping. I wanted to arch my back and fling my legs around his neck. I wanted to sweat and sweat and sweat!

The train resumed its monotonous pace in three-four time, a couple of blasts on the whistle cutting through the Sunday devotions and the calls of people waving goodbye. I watched, in a state of lulled sensuality, hypnotised by the rhythm of the passing landscape, the motion of the train, and the passion I felt within me. I was trying to remember a D.H. Lawrence poem about an encounter in a tramcar — a sulky woman with a violet fan, the poet, a flare, a spark kindled 'instantly on my blood' — and was getting nowhere, when I heard a kerfuffle. A dark man in a loose-fitting pair of white cotton pants and a moth-eaten poncho was being pushed off the train by one of the guards. The man dived head first, ungraciously, over the railing outside our compartment, bellowing obscenities about the guard's mother. He was clinging onto a leather satchel, which the guard was desperately trying to retrieve as he shouted,

'*Bandido! Bandido!*' The satchel contained the takings from the ticket collection. The guard didn't want the stolen amount deducted from his wages, so it would be a fight to the death to get it back. He leaned over the railing and managed to grab the satchel just before the *bandido* leapt off the train. The man rolled over as he hit the ground, and I saw him get up and run off, back towards the village, still shouting obscenities. The guard straightened his jacket, smoothed his hair and resumed his ticketing, smiling as he passed our compartment.

'*Fue un bandido!*' he said, gesturing towards the horizon on the other side of the railing.

'Even on a Sunday,' I chortled back. Well, he hadn't been the only one to commit a sin today, I thought later as I fell asleep in my railway bunk, the landscape starting to change, a backdrop of mountains now silhouetted in the moonlight.

When we returned to Genoa, I looked through our library for any book I could find on *la pampa*. I leafed through the pages searching for an image of a gaucho — any gaucho, the archetypal gaucho. I found one, a watercolour of one sitting on a small stool, staring back at the artist.

Months' later, Mirella found it under my bed in my attic flat when helping me pack to return to London. I told her about the Sunday on the train. 'Aren't you going in the wrong direction then?' she asked.

My father had telephoned to say London was becoming a very exciting place to live, especially for the young — there was 'something in the air'. I knew about hippies, from the 'summer of love' and my mother's flower transfers and big plastic daisy earrings. My father's Japanese friend, the one who had turned him on to the I Ching, with his waist-length hair and grass-smoking habit, had been described as one.

I gave most of my belongings to Mirella as I stuffed my boyfriend's Mini with the essentials for the drive to London. My boyfriend had given me a Seiko watch as a token of his love, a gift I felt somewhat ambivalent about. I had returned from Argentina with a writing-case full of letters he'd written while I was away — an outpouring of romantic declaration. He'd even followed me to Rome and turned up unexpectedly one morning at my hotel room, convinced I didn't care for him in the same way as before. He was right — I was looking for a reason to break it off. He'd taken me home to meet his family, and I knew I'd blown it completely when I'd complemented his mother at the dinner table. 'Superbly prepared bollocks, *signora*,' I had said, mixing up the Italian word for 'kidney' with the one for 'gonads' and pronouncing it so clearly, with such conviction, in my best local accent.

We crossed the English Channel in silence, the familiarity of the cliffs of Dover welcoming me back. I knew as I stepped ashore I was about to begin an entirely new chapter of my life. I had no inkling, however, of the tragedy that lay ahead in the new decade we were entering.

5

I was lying on the mattress in my room, smoking some hash in the kif pipe I'd brought back from Morocco a month earlier, when the phone rang. The small house in Fulham was full of people — residents and various hangers-on. My old friends Cathi and Athel and I rented the house, which had become a crash-pad on the international traveller's circuit. My mother's voice at the other end of the line sounded detached, empty. 'Come quickly, your father has had an accident. He is in Mount Vernon Hospital. They are trying to resuscitate him.' It was a Saturday in early January.

An hour earlier, he and I had been chatting on the phone. We'd met up for lunch the day before and gone to a vegetarian restaurant — his favourite — where we'd eaten nut burgers, then strolled through Harrods' record department.

I'd teased him about a comment he'd made in the Andes, when we were crossing through the Quebrada de Humahuaca, travelling from Calilegua to Bolivia in one of the farm jeeps. We'd climbed higher and higher into the mountains, winding our way through an expansive valley gorge with its striped landscape of coloured sand. The only person we'd seen on the journey was an American uranium prospector wearing an oxygen mask. He'd waved, and spoken to us through its nozzle, sounding like a Dalek. My father and I had stood at the edge of a canyon, as magnificent as any in Arizona, looking across the miles of bare stone and sand. 'Can you imagine blasting Pink Floyd out here?' he'd said, making a sweeping movement with his arm across the horizon. 'Imagine two gigantic speakers . . .'

My father had his ear to the ground when it came to the latest in rock music but I thought the idea of electric music in that sacred space vulgar and inappropriate. I gave him heaps in the middle of Harrods as we flicked through various records, he pointing out some new recordings of his Bach favourites, I reading the small print for him as he'd left his glasses at home. He invited me to come back that evening and check out his new stereo, which he'd had imported from Sweden. He'd been busy making a cabinet for the speakers — the timber had been specially cut and he was about to return home to assemble it. 'Come over with your friends,' he said as we strolled out of the shop. 'You guys can smoke your hash and I'll drink whisky and we'll make an evening of it.'

He was quite a hit with my friends, so hip he made me look straight. He had bought us front-row seats at the infamous Frank Zappa concert, the one at which Zappa was attacked by a jealous fan and biffed off the stage into the orchestra pit. We had mistakenly presumed him dead when we saw the trickle of blood from his mouth as he lay unconscious on the hard floor.

People were always dropping by to see my father, to turn him on to some new album, or just to chat. He would discuss their psychedelic trips with them in great detail, finding spiritual analogies and challenging them to undertake the quest nonchemically. He was practising yoga on a regular basis, studying Buddhism at the Theosophical Society in London, and planning to go to India. I felt humbled by his practise of raja yoga, his striving for that neutral and open space in his own mind, thinking no evil of anyone, feeling entirely connected. I would complain that I couldn't get as far as the bus stop without feeling irritated by someone. He would laugh and encourage me to keep trying.

As we left Harrods, pausing slightly on the pavement outside before going our separate ways, he blew me a kiss. I watched as he walked confidently down the busy street.

> A river of vehicles and people flowing between us. It was five o'clock on an ordinary afternoon. How was I to know that that river was Acheron, the doleful, the insuperable?

The words of the Argentinian writer Jorge Luis Borges, describing the memory of a parting, thinking it to be false while 'behind that trivial farewell was infinite separation', bring that moment back to me with powerful poignancy.

When my father phoned the next day, he was about to start his late-afternoon routine of asanas, and we discussed his belief in my generation's quest for a deeper meaning to life, our abhorrence of violence and war. It was his valedictory, although neither of us knew it at the time. 'Follow the path,' he said, before putting down the phone.

Our last meal together at home, a week or so before, had been strange as well. I had asked him to consult the I Ching for me. I needed advice on whether or not I should give up my job. I was working as an assistant editor in a publishing company in the centre of Bloomsbury, my boss was the wildly entertaining creative director, and I was earning excellent money. Yet I felt something was missing — I was unfulfilled by my hedonistic and egocentric lifestyle.

My father looked across to me as he held the thick oracle in his hands, peering over his small, round, wire-framed spectacles. He was a big fan of John Lennon, and in particular of his criticism of the Vietnam War. He had wept openly when the Beatles had sung *All You Need is Love* one Christmas on television, and had even considered purchasing one of Lennon's erotic pen-and-ink drawings, which were for sale in a gallery next to his office. He had come back with a catalogue of the show one evening and I can remember Mother making a joking comment about him having 'lost it'. He'd also bought a copy of Yoko Ono's poetry book and given it to me. I hadn't the heart to tell him I thought it was crap, all that minimalist deconstructionalist bullshit. His National Health optical freebies reflected a kinship with the musician he probably felt he could only express discretely, but were nevertheless an outward sign that he was 'one of us'. It was rumoured photos of revolutionary fighter Che Guevara had been handed out at a Beatles' concert, and being anti-American was a thoroughly dangerous position to adopt when one's employers were part of a fascist dictatorship.

'Whatever you do from now on, it will be for the good of the world.' He spoke his own words, having read what he needed from the book. 'You will dedicate your life to protecting Creation and you will be involved in great change. There will be people, however, who will wish you harm, who will not want you to succeed, who will be jealous of you.' I listened attentively, remembering how strongly I had felt after the earthquake in Skopje in 1963. I had put my name down as a volunteer to go there to help the victims, and had been turned down, not yet 13. When I was even younger, I had desperately wanted to become a nun, go to Africa and work in rural hospitals; becoming an aid worker would be even better as it didn't involve religion. Fun had got in the way between then and now, and I knew I needed to re-evaluate my life. I was bored, and I was contributing nothing to humanity.

Athel held me close as the taxi drove from Fulham to Northwood, a journey of 45 minutes. I was alternately sobbing in the back seat, leaning forward and urging the driver to go faster, talking to my father in my head, and telling him to hang on as I was on my way. I burst in through the hospital doors, heart thumping rapidly in my ears, mouth suctioned dry with fear. My eyes darted around, looking for someone — anyone — to guide me through the next moment, direct me through the experience I was about to have. I heard the sound of a woman sobbing and followed it into a sterile room with pink swing doors at either end. My mother was sitting at a table, her head in her hands. A torrent of information made its way to my ears — electrocuted, stopped breathing, brain dead, DNR . . . do not resuscitate . . .

'Your father is in the next room should you wish to view the body,' a gentle voice said, a hand against the small of my back. 'Perhaps you would like a cup of tea first, dear? We've just made a pot. Your mother is having one.'

The thought of seeing my father's dead body and drinking tea was too much for me. I ran out of the room screaming, in utter despair. Athel was sitting on a bench outside and caught me as I threw myself on the ground, pounding my fists at whatever surface they found, trying to break through the material veneer of life and bring my father back. If I saw the body, if I saw him dead, there would be no redemption. This way there was still a chance.

Later, when the undertaker called him 'the deceased', I had to sit on my hands to stop myself from slapping him. I held onto Athel all night, as he rocked me back and forth. My mother was taken to a friend's house, where she stoically refused medication and meticulously planned her life as a widow. Come Monday, she was back at work.

Edward was away on tour with a theatre company. He'd been acting professionally since the age of 10, and would recite from plays such as *Under Milk Wood* in the toilet in the early morning, family members crossing their legs as they waited their turn outside — Richard Burton booming from within the bog. After training at the Webber Douglas Academy, he worked with the National Welsh Theatre, the Theatre Royal in York and in rock musicals in London's West End. He was told of his father's sudden death during a show, in the interval, and had to return to the stage.

When we all met up at our home a day or two later, the police were inspecting my father's study. He'd been drilling some holes in the wall for attaching the cabinet that was to house his new stereo. The extension lead for the electric drill he was using had been plugged into a wall socket near a metal gas pipe. The wires leading into the extension socket had been connected incorrectly, and the earth wire in the wall socket had been cut back, severed with some form of sharp instrument — a knife or a pair of scissors. Other wall sockets in the room had also been tampered with. A live current had passed directly through the electric drill he had been holding, and when he had toppled and held on to the metal gas pipe along the skirting, his heart had stopped from the massive electrical shock he had received. He had fallen onto his Persian rug, dropping the drill. My mother had heard a slight noise and gone into the room. She had seen him lying on the mat on his back, with his eyes shut, and, thinking he was finishing his yoga routine with the asana known as The Corpse, had quietly left the room. She had waited for him in the kitchen, reading her latest copy of *Woman's Day*, waiting for him to complete his routine so they could watch his favourite TV show together. When he hadn't appeared, she had gone back into the study. Deprived of oxygen for over 20 minutes, he had turned a grey-blue colour.

Just before I had left to go on a hitchhiking holiday around Morocco with Cathi in 1973, my father had called me at work one day. I was at my desk overlooking Russell Square, designing book covers, when the phone rang. 'There's a family crisis. You are urgently needed at home.'

'Do you mean right now?' I said. 'I'm at work, Dad'.

'Right now!' was the reply. The journey took just under an hour, and by the time I walked in the front door I had mentally prepared myself for an announcement that my parents were getting a divorce. Instead, my father handed me an official-looking telegram from the President of the Junta requesting our immediate return to Buenos Aires, giving us 36 hours in which to pack up and leave. My mother was sitting silently on the couch, stroking her arm as if to comfort herself. 'What's this about, then?' I asked.

'Well, they want to keep an eye on me, I guess. What do you think I should do?'

It was over five years since we had been back to the Argentine, and in that time there had been extreme political unrest, with military coups and dictatorships resulting in thousands of deaths and disappearances.

Friends there had had their house destroyed by a bomb thrown in through the living-room window. We'd spent a joyous weekend with them, our last in Buenos Aires, before flying back to Rome, and I found it hard to imagine the place destroyed, with windows blown out onto the street and body parts among the rubble. Another friend, a newspaper editor, had been shot on the Argentine–Bolivia border. Artists and writers were fleeing the country, seeking refuge in Europe. My uncle had written a chilling letter. He had trained his seven-year-old son, the young cousin I had met for the first time as a baby on our last trip, how to get out of the boot of a car, just in case.

'Tell them to stuff it up their proverbial!' I said, screwing up the telegram and flinging it onto the floor. I was incredibly naive. I knew very little about what was really going on in South America. This was September 1973, and Salvador Allende, the socialist president of Chile, had just been assassinated in a military coup. Juan Perón had returned from exile in Spain and been re-elected president of Argentina. Latin American armies were being backed by the CIA, and thousands of activists were being butchered in acts of state-backed terrorism. One evening my father had received a phone call from the Argentine ambassador in London, mentioning the arrival of a well-known dissident South American poet. The ambassador warned my father he was not to be seen at the public meeting the artist was due to address; his presence at other such functions had been noted and had caused the government some distress. I had occasionally accompanied my father to gatherings of exiled intellectuals, and had once sat on the floor of a packed hall almost directly at the feet of an old man. By that time totally blind, Jorge Luis Borges was considered by many to be the greatest literary figure of the 20th century. A lover of freedom, he had recently resigned as Director of the National Library of Argentina. He stroked my face after we had been introduced and I kissed his cheek. The folds of skin hanging down his face, like the flews of a bloodhound, were cold and translucent, and he smelled of musk. His wisdom transcended politics; he could make government and civil servants look stupid with the brilliance of language, not needing to insult, merely describing the truth.

I watched carefully for my father's reaction to my outburst. He reminded me of photographs I had seen of fellow Argentinian Ernesto 'Che' Guevara, nine years his junior. Cuban photographer Alberto Díaz 'Korda' had taken a photograph of Guevara in early 1960, the negative of which had been given to an Italian publisher and activist, Giangiacomo Feltrinelli, seven years later. When Guevara had been assassinated in October 1967, Feltrinelli had had 100,000 posters of the Korda photo printed with the caption 'Che Lives', giving birth to an icon that has since become one of the most reproduced images in history.

'OK then, I'll do just that,' came the reply as my father retrieved the telegram from the floor and ripped it into small pieces.

My mother fiddled nervously with the hem of her skirt, still saying nothing. She seemed scared to express her opinion, as if others might hear what she said and hold her to account.

'So it's sorted,' I said, irritated by the interruption and getting up to leave. I wasn't going to let any old South American dictator get in the way of my life — there were concerts to go to, chillums to smoke. And anyway, these people were thousands of miles away — how dare they try and interfere. What could you expect from someone who lived in a pink house? Bugger the lot of them. Who was Perón, anyway? Rumour had it that my father had had to leave Argentina for being anti-Perónist. He was once attacked in the street by a gang, who asked him why he wasn't wearing the mandatory Perónist badge on his coat. 'Because I wear it in my heart,' was his reply. It saved his life. 'Perón's wife screwed her way to the top of the Republican ladder,' I said later to Athel as I explained why I'd taken the afternoon off work, remembering my Mother's uncharitable description of the dictator's wife.

My father had a *guerrillero* seductiveness similar to Guevara's, a comparable expression in his eyes. Several grieving women, in mink or astrakhan coats, large sunglasses hiding their doleful eyes, were inconsolable at his funeral. 'I have no idea who they are,' my mother whispered to me just before the service started. The undertaker had ignored our request for a live guitarist to perform Spanish classical music in the crematorium, and the priest refused to read from Kahlil Gibran instead of the Bible. Dad should be burned on a pyre in our back garden, I thought, as I sat in the front row of the ghastly mausoleum-like chapel. Mother could sprinkle *chimichurri* on him as the flames took over his flesh, a gaucho could read from *Martín Fierro*, and there'd be an accordion player in the corner on a stool, with someone singing *Mi Buenos Aires Querido*.

I returned to Fulham and stomped around my bedroom for a couple of days, trying to make sense in my head of what was happening, until life in London in the early 1970s took over again. I was back, barefoot and beaded, grooving to the music, smoking dope with William Burroughs, listening to the Grateful Dead playing *Dark Star* in festival mud for hours on end, the collective consciousness of a generation astral-travelling to the furthest reaches of the universe in search of peace. We genuinely believed we were part of 'the Revolution', a middle-class dream fuelled by excessive use of drugs, while in other areas of the world people were being thrown out of helicopters, murdered for writing beautiful cantos, and tortured for knowing someone who knew someone who might possibly have been a member of the Communist Party. We even sported the famous Korda photo on our T-shirts, or on posters on our walls. 'He looks a bit like your father, Susi,' friends would say, and I would feel so proud, not fully realising at the time who had been paying my father's salary. It was only when I saw the word *junta* in the *Guardian* newspaper one day — my early-morning reading on the tube on the way to work — that the penny dropped. I remembered the logo on my father's business letterhead with the words 'Junta Nacional de Carne' at the top, embossed in shiny red and black ink. I saw it superimposed over the printed word in front of me and gasped. This was serious shit. No wonder they had wanted to keep an eye on him.

I thought about my young cousin in Buenos Aires, a seven-year-old trained to escape from a car boot just in case. I looked at the seven-year-olds on the train, going to school, with their rough knees and rosy cheeks. They chatted innocently about the games they played, their teachers — everyday conversations untouched by fear. Was it possible to live through a nightmare and leave the children untouched? My eyes filled with tears. I couldn't bear to think of so much suffering, of places I knew and people I loved traumatised by uniformed militia, the depravity of torture, the perversity of power.

Athel took me for a walk along the River Wye, in the Chess Valley. We sat down in a place I had often gone to with my father. Then, we would spread a tartan blanket under the same weeping willow. It was a perfect spot, in that English kind of picture-postcard way, and I remember running through long grass picking wildflowers. We climbed over stiles and ran some more until we fell over on top of one another, a soft bed of clover cushioning us as we rolled around, wrestling and screeching, before we stopped to gaze at the clouds. 'I named you Susan Alice because of this place,' my father said when he first took me there. It had something to do with Lewis Carroll, but I never got the full story.

Twice in my life I've been horrified to witness the construction of a road. In Calilegua, I saw the impact of the Pan American Highway on the local people, the sewer of the Western world regurgitating its filth in the name of progress. Who wanted it anyway? Certainly not the Aymaran tribes. Then, as I climbed out of Athel's dune buggy that day, I noticed a big scar across one of the hills in the distance.

'What's that?' I asked him.

'I think it's a motorway,' he said, in his lovely soft voice.

My stomach turned. It was happening again, it was falling apart, I was roaring inside. 'Fuck the motorcar,' I yelled. 'Fuck progress!' I kicked the wheels of the buggy. 'What are we doing to this place?'

Grief is an intense emotion, and bereavement an almost sacred state in many cultures. In this altered state of consciousness experiences are lived in a state of total detachment or total absorption. The shock of my father's sudden death both illuminated and destroyed me. When I saw that motorway slicing its ugly mechanistic way through the gentleness of the landscape, I became radicalised, changed fundamentally and forever. I was no longer innocuous, no longer the 'make love not war', in-with-the-in-crowd dope-head or whatever I had imagined I was. In that split second I reinvented myself as an antihero, a guerrilla fighting for Creation, a warrior powered by *duende* — that which the spirit hath moved. Consensual reality needed adjusting — small wonder people were going mad trying to figure it all out.

I paced around my bedroom again. I knew I was driving Athel nuts. He'd been ferrying me back and forth between Fulham and Northwood so I could keep an eye on my mother. I was convinced she was going to flip out. My brother had returned to his theatre company after the inquest had revealed no fault in the Black and Decker drill Father had been using the day he was killed. No one had discussed the earth wire or the electrical box that had been tampered with. 'We rented this house out for ages, when we were in Italy,' I had heard Mother say to a policeman as he took notes. 'I certainly don't want to pursue this any further.' As she had shown him out, they had both brushed past me in the hall. 'And anyway,' she had said, drawing in close to him, 'it would be like opening a can of worms.'

A conversation I'd had with my father after the telegram incident and shortly before his death made more sense now as I watched my mother try to conceal from herself the reality of the situation. 'I can no longer confide in her,' my father had said. 'She would worry far too much.'

'Do you remember me chucking my knickers at you the first time you came over to my house?' I asked Athel on one of our trips to Northwood.

'Mmmm, schoolgirl knickers. If only I'd known at the time,' Athel said, winking at me, and we both laughed.

We'd lost touch when Edward had moved to another school, what with all our travelling around, until one evening, in a country pub, I'd noticed these two young men by the lead-pane window, and in particular their handsome, chiselled looks and long dark hair. One was wearing an old fur coat, the other had shiny yellow boots and a singlet made of material that seemed to move three-dimensionally. It took me a while to get over my shyness when I realised they were the VK boys, and I didn't speak to Athel at all until much later. We went back with them to the family manor house, after the pub closed. The baron was upstairs somewhere, in a little room at the top of the building, taking apart old radios and looking at the stars through a telescope. The baroness was busy downstairs with sundry aunts, preparing supper.

The boys lived apart from the main house, in converted stables. Alex was a budding photographer and had a small darkroom there. Athel's room was painted black with stars on the ceiling and was above the garage. We took turns sitting in the middle of the room, surrounded by the quadraphonic speakers he had positioned in each corner, and playing our favourite Hendrix track, cranked up to the max. Someone had made a chillum from part of a silver Yamaha flute. A piece of silk soaked in whisky was wrapped around the base to keep it cool as we drew in huge lungfuls of Pakistani hashish mixed with tobacco. Slabs of the stuff, branded in gold and kept in small calico drawstring bags, would appear as chillum after chillum was prepared and lit, Hendrix's guitar wah-wahing from one speaker to the next. In came the aunts —they always knocked and waited patiently for someone to open the door. We could just make them out through the haze of hash and cigarette smoke, their identical aprons visible before their faces. They carried a tray full of munchies, scones, sandwiches and a pot of tea. 'We always know how hungry you get up here,' they chirped in unison.

We drove past the manor house now. 'You know those old Peugeots Dad likes to buy?' Athel chuckled as he spoke. 'Well, when he's finished with them, he buries them in the courtyard. Flattens them and then covers them with bitumen.' The baron had spent some time in Tibet and kept a prayer wheel beside him at the long wooden dining table. People would appear from various rooms to take their seats beside this slab of oak, young men with leather-fringed boots, tunics and long hair — it felt almost medieval.

'Quick!' Athel had said one evening, in possibly our first real exchange. 'Pretend you're my girlfriend.'

I'd dropped by for a visit and had run into him bounding up the stairs to his room. A young woman in a Rolls-Royce had turned up at the front gate and was asking after him, saying that she'd come to take him out, that they had a date. She was the daughter of a local businessman, a man who had made a fortune collecting rubbish.

'So nouveau riche,' Mother had commented one day, describing the family to me. 'She walks a black panther around Moor Park while he takes off to work in a helicopter.' She had obviously forgotten her own past. 'They have an underground swimming pool with a jukebox. No breeding whatsoever! Have you heard the way she speaks?'

Obviously, the most eligible bachelor for their daughter would be one whose father was a nobleman, someone with a coat of arms and a bit of ancestry and history to their name. In the case of the VK boys, there might even be a castle or two somewhere. I felt quite sorry for her as I hung off Athel's shoulder, hamming it up, enjoying the role-play. 'Nice car,' said Athel as he looked down at the Rolls from the stable window, watching her drive off.

Alex and I had had sex one night against the sink in his darkroom. Pissed and stoned we had fucked crazily, not bothering to take our clothes off, knocking over jars of photographic chemicals. Led Zeppelin had added more horsepower to the grinding and grunting as Athel had tried to sleep in the next room. Afterwards, I had sensed this incident had changed something in my quiet relationship with Athel, as if there was a third person present when we were alone, standing between us yet drawing us closer through some magnetic attraction.

He turned to me now when he'd assured himself the Rolls had finally left. The girl had looked quite upset seeing us together, my hip angled into him coquettishly.

'That felt quite comfortable, you and I, like that,' he said.

It was the bashful way he looked up that decided my future. He was right: it had felt comfortable, something more than just sexual attraction.

All the screwing, all the different partners, had been getting to me. We lay down and made love in the middle of the room, removing each other's clothing bit by bit — the bell-bottoms, the velvet jacket, the paisley scarf, the beaded choker. *Foxy Lady* was playing on the stereo as we played air guitar with our bodies, me on top, riding him like a bucking bronco at a rodeo. We lay on the carpet afterwards, smoking a cigarette, our bodies tingling all over. He still had his patent-leather Chelsea boots on. I whipped them off and we sat with the soles of our feet touching.

'They say this is the way souls communicate,' Athel said, laughing and wriggling his toes between mine.

'I don't think I can repeat what yours is saying to mine,' I replied, trying to pull him back towards me with my feet. Souls and soles thus entwined, we became inseparable.

No one was really discussing what had happened to my father. We all knew he had been electrocuted, but no one seemed to make any connection between his death and the telegram he'd received three months before. Perhaps there was none to be made, yet why had he been stripped of his Argentinian nationality when he had declared he wouldn't be returning to Buenos Aires? Why had he started taking out life insurance policies for the first time ever — not one, but several.

'See that man under the street light?' he had said once, indicating a stereotypically dressed secret-agent type — trench coat, collar up, cigarette in mouth, pretending to read a newspaper. 'He's been watching the house for a few days.' He drew back the curtain a little so I could get a better look. The man looked so much like a character out of a Bogart movie that I had a hard time taking the situation seriously.

'You're bloody joking, Dad.' I watched as the man rubbed his hands together vigorously before putting them back in his pockets. It was freezing out there. Early morning, early January. Who would want a job like that? 'You told them to fuck off, didn't you?' I asked. I was so naive.

'Well, yes, I did, and I no longer have a job, nor a nationality. Luckily, the British have given me a passport but Mum is still freaking out because it says "Born in Buenos Aires". When the weather improves and the snow has melted in Europe,' he continued, 'your mother and I will go travelling. We're thinking about going overland to India in a VW bus. On the way back, we'll stop in Tuscany and see if there are any old farms for sale.'

By the time I awoke that Friday morning, he'd gone into town to collect the last of his possessions from the office. I phoned him there and we arranged to meet for our nut-burger lunch.

Athel visited me dutifully several times a week in those first months of grieving, as I kept watch on my mother's mental health at home during the week, returning to Fulham at the weekends. I had handed in my notice at work and spent the weekdays in my father's study, listening to Bach, staring at the wall, having endless conversations with myself as I tried to cope with my mental anguish. There was no way I could bring up the subject of my father's death with anyone: I was the only person he'd confided in, and when I tried to raise the issue of the telegram and his death, I was told I was imagining things.

Mum had started to stockpile food and other items, including hundreds of rolls of toilet paper, in the attic. She had become increasingly paranoid about world food shortages since the United Nations Conference on the Human Environment in Stockholm, in 1972, had revealed critical global ecological problems, and was treating me incredibly hurtfully, even though I was her only real support at the time. 'Everyone forgets a widow,' she told Athel bitterly when he came to pick me up one day. Was she angry at herself for not having gone back into the study sooner, for not knowing how to administer CPR properly? Whatever it was, it manifested in some cruel behaviour towards me, which I've learned to forgive over the years, telling myself it was due to trauma.

My father's study was full of gifts I'd brought back from Morocco: a prayer mat from Taroudannt, silver jewellery from Tiznit, some soapstone from Ouarzazate, a pigskin water carrier from Tafraoute, beads from Goulimine. Cathi and I had hitched through the Tizi-n-Test pass on our way south from Marrakech, with Cathi the object of much attention on account of her Nordic good looks. She'd disappeared in the Marrakech medina, getting out of the car with one of the Algerian men who'd picked us up on our way back to town. The two remaining men, in the front of the car, started discussing in French what they were going to do with me. They decided to take me to a hotel and rape me, not knowing I understood every word they were saying. I waited until we were near the hotel Cathi and I were staying in before opening the door and throwing myself out. I bolted across the road and ran as fast as I could to the hotel, ran to my bedroom, pushed a heavy wardrobe up against the door and waited. I'd heard the car brake suddenly and the sound of doors slamming but hadn't dared look back. That night I dreamed of Cathi hanging from a meat hook the way I'd seen carcasses in the medina. I waited until the evening of the next day before creeping out and making my way to the post office to phone home for help.

The two men were waiting on the other side of the road. They smiled when they saw me and fell in behind as I walked at a brisk pace, following me all the way to the post office. The place was crowded when we got there, and I stood in line for over an hour to book my call to the UK. As the hours wore on, the place emptied, until it was just me, the two men and the telephonist on duty. It was getting late now, almost closing. I approached the telephonist and whispered across the counter to him, in English, 'Those men are following me.'

'What can you expect, young lady? I would be doing the same if I were not here working.'

I started panicking, and sat down at the table in the centre of the room, rummaging around in my shoulder bag, looking for my knife. It had been removed at the airport by some official and handed back to me by an air stewardess as we flew into Marrakech. It was a hunting knife I carried for cutting up fruit or raw vegetables. I wanted to show the bastards I had a weapon and would use it if I had to. I took it out of my shoulder bag, sliding it out of its sheath, and showed it to them, turning it round slowly for them to see. I steadied the tip of the blade with the top of my index finger, gripping the hilt tightly as I tried to make eye contact. I spoke to them in French, quietly at first, and then loudly as I felt my indignation rising. 'You fucking leave me alone or I'll use this,' I said. I was so scared I'd wet myself, and I hated their guts for ruining my holiday.

When the telephonist threw me out of the post office, the would-be rapists had already departed abruptly with apologetic mutterings: '*Excusez-moi, mademoiselle,* we didn't know you could speak French.' I got back to the hotel, feeling sick to my stomach, and found Cathi there. 'I had the most wonderful time,' she said. 'I lived with the beggars in the medina for two days. Come on, I'll take you there.'

I needed as much light relief as I could get, so I followed her flowing cotton dress through the alleyways and up and down flights of steps, until we came to where she'd been staying. I should have sold her to the old guy sitting on the floor, I thought later. He wanted to buy her for his son, the one who'd taken her there a few days earlier. He had some goats he could give me in exchange, and some American dollars. I'd bought a beautiful pure-wool jellaba, edged in silk, from a very old Berber in the Atlas mountains and had paid the equivalent of US$4 — he hadn't wanted any more. I doubted the amount of money the old guy wanted to give me for Cathi would have covered a phone call home, and what would I do with a herd of goats? I hadn't eaten meat for years.

My father laughed when I told him the story, showing him how to put on a turban the way Berbers do. Perhaps if I hadn't gone to Morocco he would still be alive today, I thought, looking at the prayer mat I'd bargained for in a market. It would have been so easy to walk round the back of the house, and the shed where the tools were kept hadn't even been locked. They'd been keeping an eye on him anyway, so they would have known what he was doing in the study. It made absolute sense to me. Everyone else thought I'd gone mad.

Several decades later, in a suburb in Auckland, New Zealand, my mother threw a copy of an Argentine newspaper onto the kitchen floor. 'All it's good for is the litter box,' she exclaimed when I asked her why she wasn't going to read it. I paused as I wondered whether or not this might be a good moment to talk with her about my father's death. She had never remarried, despite being courted by a rich Italian landowner we knew, who had flown her to Rome for dinner one weekend a year or two after my father's death. She just couldn't bring herself to get involved with anyone again, saying she enjoyed living on her own too much. She eventually followed my brother and his wife to New Zealand in the early 1980s, having no family to speak of in England.

When I asked her why she'd never considered returning to the Argentine, she said, 'Because it still says "Born in Buenos Aires" in my British passport.' I was expected to understand, and there could be no further questions. So great was her fear of the fascist oligarchy that she wouldn't deal with her mother's estate or a possible legal challenge against the person who had defrauded Cecile of substantial amounts of money. She stubbornly refused to believe democratically elected government had finally returned to Argentina and wasn't interested in discussing anything political. She was impenetrable in that respect. In her final years, she found some enjoyment translating love letters between young Kiwi women and the handsome Argentinian sports heroes they met in New Zealand. She also gave private classes in Latin American Spanish pronunciation for Auckland University. Just before her death she decided to look at issues around which she felt fear, and joined a group called Feel the Fear and Do It Anyway. I like to think she was getting ready to talk.

I got off the tube and looked at my *London A–Z*. Poland Street was a small street running parallel to Wardour Street, in Soho. I was looking for no. 9, and when I walked in I found a young woman sitting at a desk, her feet up on a table. The place was chaotic — books and files everywhere, a Gestetner copying machine in the corner, coffee mugs, merchandise falling off shelves. In the back office I could hear the animated voices of a number of people with different accents — Canadian, American, Australian, Cockney. The last was the loudest. There was an incredible feeling in the place; it was alive, and positively hummed with energy. I'd found the address in *Alternative London* and had jumped on the train in a spur-of-the-moment decision. I was burning up inside from all the unresolved issues — my father's death, the destruction of the planet, pollution, war, nuclear weapons. It was all so urgent, something needed to be done *now*. I was going to offer myself for the front line; I was going to become a volunteer in the fight for the planet's future.

The 26 principles proclaimed at the 1972 Stockholm Conference had spelled it out. Good, I thought. If everyone agrees this is what should be done, there won't be too much of a problem and I'll be out of a job in no time. I'd pinned a copy of Chief Seattle's speech to the wall of my bedroom. It began: 'Every part of this earth is sacred to my people.' Well, that's how I felt too. I'd felt that way all my life — an intrinsic feeling of belonging, of being part of the earth and it being part of me. From somewhere deep within my bloodline, a voice was making its presence felt and a battle hymn was being sung.

'Can you type?' A young woman by the name of Joanna had welcomed me into the Friends of the Earth (FoE) office and immediately made me a cup of herb tea. I rambled on about things a bit too much — an outpouring of grief, my willingness to work, to do anything. Years before, my father had sat me down at an old typewriter. He'd covered up all the letters, and methodically, a day at a time, had taught me to touch type. 'You can find work anywhere in the world if you know how to type,' he'd said.

'We have all the campaigners' manuals to prepare and send out to our local groups,' Joanna continued, 'and we've lost one of our team. Can't pay you very much, though; no one gets well paid in this job'.

Leaving the office later, I looked up at the building I was to come to know intimately — a place that housed a number of excellent nongovernmental organisations (NGOs), with Troops Out of Ireland and Social Audit among them. I felt immensely proud to be part of such a dynamic group of international activists — people who were taking on the nuclear industry, the West's obsession with the motorcar, the construction of motorways, all the rubbish that was being created by a lifestyle based on consumption, and the killing of endangered species. The London office of FoE had been opened in 1972 and already had a reputation as a leading environmental campaigning organisation.

I had listened attentively as another young woman had spoken movingly of what was happening to the great whale species, of how they were being hunted for use in the cosmetics industry. She had a beautiful book on whales, *Mind in the Waters*, a collection of stories written about cetaceans compiled by Joan McIntyre for an NGO called Project Jonah. It opened with a poem by D.H. Lawrence: 'They say the sea is cold, but the sea contains the hottest blood of all, and the wildest, the most urgent.' Something about those words would follow me through the next decade, permeating — to paraphrase Joseph Conrad — all my acts, my passions and emotions, and become the backdrop to my life.

'What are these?' I asked, holding up some silk-screened banners of whales I'd found in a box in a corner shortly after I'd started.

'They were made in a San Francisco by a group called Greenpeace, who sent them to us to use in our "Save the Whale" campaign,' Joanna replied.

The name of the organisation rang a bell. I'd been skimming through *Time* magazine one lazy summer afternoon in 1973 and seen a black-and-white photo of a man being beaten by French commandos on a yacht which had sailed into the French nuclear-testing zone around Mururoa atoll in the South Pacific. The yacht, *Greenpeace III*, had sailed to the zone the year before to protest against the nuclear tests, and had been rammed by a French minesweeper. The black-and-white peace symbol was painted on its sail. Another symbol stood out above this, a circle with a line through it, which I later found out represented ecology.

Joanna told me Greenpeace had witnessed first-hand the slaughter of sperm whales off the coast of California, capturing the whole thing on film. Small inflatable craft, powered by outboard motors, had been launched from a boat the crew had chartered for the first Greenpeace Save the Whale campaign, and had been positioned between the whaling boat and the whales, denying the harpooner a clear shot. It was brilliant — so simple and powerful. And the principles underpinning Greenpeace's actions were ones I could totally relate to from a spiritual perspective — nonviolence, accepting responsibility for injustices of which one was aware, the Quaker philosophy of 'bearing witness', and doing something about what one disagreed with. I already felt an old hand at the game. The Greenpeace people had also sailed to the American nuclear tests in the Aleutian Islands, and consequently had gained the respect of the native people of north Vancouver Island and the adjacent mainland, the Kwakiutl, who had gifted them a totem, which they had used as a logo on T-shirts and badges.

Among the group were a couple of young men who had worked as paramedics during the occupation of the village of Wounded Knee, on the Pine Ridge Reservation of South Dakota, in 1973 — a powerful protest by Native Americans over the US government's failure to honour treaties granting them land and self-government, and the brutality of police and government agencies towards them. The two men had been among the very few non-natives given access to the occupation, and had since been made honorary members of the Lakota nation. It was truly inspiring. It was a coming-together of people, a movement without ego, based on a love for Creation. I knew the moment I unfurled those banners and saw the distinctive silk-screened images that I wanted desperately to be part of it. I had an image of Mahatma Gandhi in my mind, a black-and-white photo of him sitting next to his spinning wheel. These long-haired men, standing up in their rubber boats, acting as a human shield between the whale and the harpoon, had taken his principle of satyagraha and adapted it to their own purposes. How could anyone not be moved by images of a whale thrashing in agony? The 'great heaven of whales in the waters, old hierarchies', butchered, so women could enhance their appearance; hunted as they rocked 'through the sensual ageless ages on the depths of the seven seas' for short-term economic profit. An eco fighting force was needed to capture humankind's destruction of the planet on film for the world to see, and to protest about it totally nonviolently. The juxtaposition of two such divergent paradigms — satyagraha and media savvy — appealed to me. It smacked of something totally new, something that could work.

I dozed off on the tube on my way home from work. Athel and I had gone our separate ways, although we still remained very close friends, and I'd moved into a squat in Fulham. The trauma of my father's death had resulted in some promiscuous and rather self-absorbed behaviour on my part. I'd had a number of affairs, cold-heartedly moving on from one to the other, so blasé about sex I'd even fucked an American Vietnam War veteran on the floor of what we called the Magic Bus as I travelled with a group of friends from London to Athens, on my first trip to Samos, in the Greek Islands, in 1976.

I felt as if I'd been touched by magic, surrounded by these amazing people who were engineering such a profound response to the destruction of our planet. They were people who believed life was precious, and stupid as this may sound, I felt as if I could hear them approaching as they all gathered momentum. My father had been right, I thought. I was now part of something huge.

6

A hand opened the tent fly and snatched the polystyrene cup that was on the ground. There were two cups there but it was the one with the red lipstick imprinted on the rim that the young man wanted. 'It's for my grandfather,' he mumbled apologetically, trying not to trip on the guy rope as he stuffed the cup into his padded jacket.

The woman opposite me smiled. She was extremely beautiful and looked good in her zippered 'zoot suit'. I felt positively scruffy and stinky by comparison, after days of sweating inside a space blanket and not washing. Here I was, miles from anywhere, on a frozen rock at the edge of the Atlantic Ocean, surrounded by ice, with Brigitte Bardot in my tent.

'Where do you go to the toilet?' she asked innocently, in that yummy French accent. Her eyes were rimmed with black pencil and she had the lipstick pout I'd been practising unsuccessfully for years. I felt a little twinge of sadness that she used so much make-up — perhaps she didn't know about the whales. I liked her and knew she'd be beautiful without any camouflage. To get to my tent and ask me questions about the toilet, she would have had to journey on a small plane and then a helicopter, not in some private jet, or with VIP treatment on some national carrier. She would have had to leave her Yves St Laurent and Armani outfits behind and prepare herself physically and mentally for subzero conditions.

'Well,' I said, 'if it's night-time, you pee in this jar in your sleeping bag.' I showed her the jar by my rolled-up sleeping gear. 'Guys are luckier — they just piss in bottles. It freezes overnight,' I continued, 'but we do have a toilet for use during the day. It's over to the east of the camp, on the other side of the ridge, a tripod with a seat on top — nothing fancy. Be careful when you sit on it, though. A crew member from California had an upset stomach, and when he sat on it, it collapsed. He's still wearing the same clothes, poor guy.'

She had come with her lover, a Sygma photographer, who suddenly appeared in the tent. He was extremely handsome, and younger than his famous girlfriend. I could see immediately what she saw in him. I was about to hand her the bog paper when there was a blinding flash as he took a photo.

'You are so brave,' she purred, stroking my face, removing some straggly bits of hair from my eyes. We chatted for a while, about just this and that . . . I admired the fact that she'd insisted on coming all the way out to Belle Isle to cheer us on. Gutsy lady. Shame about the face paint.

I couldn't remember how long we'd been on that ice-covered rock when she flew in to see us. It seemed as if it had been forever and we were a lost Arctic tribe who'd just been discovered by European explorers. We'd been chopping massive blocks of ice each day to melt for water; it was important to rehydrate often, as the air was so dry and rarefied. It was March 1977, and I was sharing a small tent on the ice of this New-foundland island with three others.

'Call me when you return to London. Come and stay with me in Paris.' She removed her glove and scrawled a couple of numbers on a piece of toilet paper. The world's most drop-dead gorgeous woman was inviting me to stay with her, giving me her home phone number. I couldn't pinch myself — I was wearing too many layers of padded fabric. 'Please don't give these to anyone. They are my private numbers,' she said, leaning over to kiss me goodbye. I could smell expensive perfume, the musk notes mingling with her own pheromones. Should I tell her about the sperm whale, I wondered? Someone opened the tent fly again, this time to summon Brigitte back to her helicopter.

'A storm is on the way, ma'am, and we need to get you out of here.' The man looked at me as if reprimanding me for spending so much time with her. I was holding the piece of paper with the phone numbers, trying to figure out where I should put it, knowing the fact I had Brigitte Bardot's private numbers would be round the camp in no time. There would be pressure put on me to hand it over, no doubt — for the sake of the seals.

Years later, in a small café in Aghios Konstantinos, on Samos, I found the phone numbers tucked away in my notebook. An old man was sitting by the window of the café, gazing out to sea, drinking ouzo and eating a small piece of fish. He had sat there every day for as long as I'd been living and working in the village. He had no teeth, and the whites of his eyes were yellowing and bloodshot. He survived on the mezes served at the café and the odd pomegranate handed him by passing village women. Every now and then he'd bring out a crumpled magazine photo of Brigitte Bardot, carefully iron it out on the small wooden table with his arthritic hands and look at it lovingly, before folding it and putting it away.

Breaking my promise — I felt she would have understood — I wrote the phone numbers down for him at the top of the photo, which was falling to pieces as quickly as its owner. It was the day before he died. There was only one phone in the village, at the rival café a few doors down. I explained whose numbers I was giving him and he just looked at me as if to say, 'Yeah, right,' a trace of a smile in his eyes. The next day his body was laid out on the small table in the café. He hadn't finished his last ouzo and had lolled forward onto the table. Passers-by thought he was sleeping. His mule tethered outside the café waited patiently through the night for him to wake. He most certainly took those phone numbers with him to the grave.

Several months before, I'd been sitting in the spacious living room of the Battersea Gardens flat I'd moved into, a place my flatmate Annie and I shared with yoga teachers, acupuncture students and some travellers from New Zealand. I was enjoying life, feeling fulfilled by the work I was doing at FoE, and at peace with myself. I cared deeply about some of the people I worked with, people who have since gone on to become world leaders in their individual fields; I enjoyed hanging out with them in the pub after work, or in their homes. One of my favourites was a shy American called Amory Lovins, a consultant experimental physicist with degrees from Harvard and Oxford. From his belt hung an array of items, a bit like a carpenter's apron, except his tools were a slide rule, a compass, a penknife and a glasses case. When he needed something, he'd remove it from its personal holster like a cowboy reaching for his gun. I was fascinated by the white-bread-and-jam sandwiches he ate for lunch: was his brilliant brain fuelled by sugar, fruit and processed flour alone? He was your typical nerdy-looking geek, but with a mind far sexier than that of any hunk I've ever met. He and Canadian Walt Patterson were taking on the nuclear industry.

Anyway, there I was, sitting in the sun in the living room when the phone rang. 'I've lost my copy of Lovin's *World Energy Strategies*. Can you bring me a copy? Come for breakfast tomorrow.' Jackson Browne's voice sent a prickle rush of heat to my skin. I motioned to Annie, mouthing his name and fanning myself as if I were about to swoon.

This is crazy, I thought. A week before we'd been listening to Jackson Browne's new album, singing along, sitting cross-legged on the floor after our mung bean pie with sprouts, sourdough bread and lassi. There had been a smell of mugwort and Tibetan sandalwood in the air, and a visiting Buddhist monk in saffron robes had lain beside us in a pool of sunlight. I'd forgotten he was there, which then made me feel I'd exposed myself, that I should have been more composed and not so seduced by the material plane. Most of us had gone to Jackson Browne's concert, and I'd sat up near the front, on the passageway floor, trying to get a better look. When he dedicated my favourite song to FoE and our antinuclear campaign, just like that, I was convinced the entire place saw me blush.

I felt terribly embarrassed when I arrived outside the hotel, a copy of *World Energy Strategies* and a small jar of miso — my breakfast — in a woven shoulder bag. Two black stretch limos were parked in front and a man in a uniform watched my every move as I cycled up. I looked around for a place to lean my bike. I'd covered the patches of rust with FoE campaign stickers and thought it was quite cool, but it looked positively trashy next to the luxurious cars and I contemplated pushing it around the corner. I tried to enter the hotel inconspicuously, aware my op-shop wardrobe might not go down too well with the paying guests. I made my way over to the reception by walking around the foyer hugging the walls, rather than diagonally so everyone could see me.

'Hi, you must be Susi. I could tell by your clothes. Follow me, please,' an American voice said. It belonged to a huge man, dressed in black leather with a bandanna around his head, who was leaning against the front desk.

One of the receptionists was polishing surfaces with a chamois. 'Hiya, Prince,' he yelled out boyishly to a man who was coming down the main staircase. 'He's Prince Rainer,' he said, looking over at me. That accounted for the second stretch limo. 'A real live prince, man. Can you believe it?' Get a life, I thought, hoping the prince hadn't noticed me.

I recounted the day's adventures to Annie as we lay on my bed. 'He told me I reminded him of Joni Mitchell,' I laughed.

'I'd run away from home for a guy like him,' she said. 'Why don't you follow him to Morocco? You can put up his tent for him.'

'It's not like that,' I said, truthfully. I'd warmed to Jackson immediately;

89

he'd seemed genuine in his concern for what was happening to the planet, chatting away comfortably as he had his breakfast. The cup of hot water I'd requested had been brought to me on a silver tray by a man in a white tuxedo: 'Madam's hot water.' I could tell the waiter was being sarcastic. Jackson told me about other rock stars in California who wanted to dedicate some of their immense wealth to helping the environmental movement. 'Trust me, Susi, we're going to get in behind you guys. You're our heroes.'

I'd spent the day with him and his bodyguard, sitting in the back of the stretch limo and shopping at Harrods, madly hoping I wouldn't bump into anyone I knew. Reading my mind, he asked me to race him up the internal staircase rather than use the lift so no one would see us. We were trying to shake off the bodyguard as well, who insisted on pacing around checking out the surroundings, thereby announcing Jackson's presence to the nonplussed shoppers — very uncool. I felt sorry for Jackson. He'd wanted to go camping in Morocco after his tour but had been prevented by his legal team in case he injured his hands erecting his tent — hence Annie's suggestion.

'I've got his phone number.' I smiled, waving it under her nose. We cackled like two old witches as she chased me round the apartment trying to snatch it out of my hands.

I put my foot in it, though — several times. I wasn't up with the play. A musician called Graham Nash phoned the office to talk with someone about making a substantial donation from a fund he had established to save the world, and Muggins here cut the guy off, not once, but twice, thinking it was some hoax caller. In the pub that Friday, as we mulled over the week's events — what it had been like in the House of Lords for the reading of a particular bill, how a certain campaign was developing — and strategized over a couple of pints of bitter, I told my story about the nutter on the phone posing as a rock star. I realised from the stunned silence and the look on people's faces that I'd cost the organisation thousands in potential funds. 'Trust me,' the so-called nutter's friend, Jackson Browne, had told me in the stretch limo. He'd gone back home to the US and had obviously spread the word, just as he'd said he would. I'd spoken to him on the phone one evening after plucking up enough courage to dial his number in California, spurred on by Annie, who was keen to keep the story on the boil. 'Trust me, Susi,' he'd said again. Well, they wouldn't trust me now, would they? Not bloody likely.

I explained the situation to a young woman who was staying in the Fulham squat — a Yaqui Indian. We stayed up all night and talked, and I told her about my experiences in Jujuy. I felt a great sense of kinship with her, sharing the pain of having her culture destroyed by the same paradigm that had extended its genocidal tentacles further south. An African-American woman had given me some peyote a few months' earlier, and in a potlatch of my own I had come to the conclusion that the only way to stem the crackling of the holocaust was to meet it head on. And now, both in my home and at my place of work, I was with people who were doing just that. We were all converging on the epicentre, drawn together by an unknown force. 'Follow the path with heart,' the Yaqui woman had said, smiling and sounding like Don Juan.

Funny how things work out. In the Poland Street office I met David McTaggart, the skipper of the yacht that twice had sailed so bravely into the Mururoa nuclear-testing zone, the person I'd seen being beaten up in the *Time* photo. He was using the FoE office as a forwarding address while taking the French navy to court over the 1973 incident, in which he had been injured by French commandos. He was also writing a book about the experience with a Canadian journalist friend, Bob Hunter. A friend of Bob's, a New Zealand cetologist called Paul Spong, who lived and worked with orca in British Columbia, was also in town, looking for a place to stay. I'd found him a spare room in a Hammersmith squat. After all, these two guys, Bob and Paul, had been the ones who'd had the idea of placing small rubber boats between whale and harpoon gun. They deserved maximum respect.

There was a knock at the door. Annie and I had been advertising in *Time Out* for a vegetarian flatmate and were expecting a Canadian by the name of Allan, who'd phoned earlier. I'd explained the flat was near the Battersea power station — 'You know, where Pink Floyd's huge pink pig balloon broke loose after the photo shoot for their album cover and sailed across the channel.' He'd seemed like a nice guy. Beautiful voice. We had one of those peepholes in the door, and Annie and I took turns peeking at him before we let him in.

'Mmmm,' said Annie, 'not bad, eh?'

I caught sight of a familiar decal on his jacket, in yellow canvas oversewn with green cotton. 'Are you part of Greenpeace?' I asked once we'd opened the door.

'How the hell do you know about Greenpeace?' came the reply. 'We're a bit thin on the ground in these parts.'

I rattled off a litany of names, adding that a couple of them still owed me for a phone bill.

'Isn't it amazing,' Allan said later as he moved into the flat, 'that in a place as big as London —'

'It's meant to be,' I replied.

One evening, David, Allan and I went to an Irish pub someone in Troops Out of Ireland had recommended. Allan was in the UK to drum up support for a second campaign on the ice fields of Canada's east coast to protect endangered seals from overhunting by the Norwegian sealing industry. In return for being allowed to bludgeon several hundred thousand seals to death, Norway had agreed to recognise an extended Canadian fisheries jurisdiction. I knew by now that David wouldn't be into it: he wasn't convinced there was sufficient evidence that the seals were endangered and he resented the fact that 'cute animals make good press'. Allan already had the support of the International Fund for Animal Welfare in the US and a Swiss animal conservation foundation, and was getting ready to raise public awareness in Britain.

David kept looking over his shoulder, jiggling on his bar stool. 'I'm paranoid, man,' he said, lighting yet another cigarette. 'You can't trust the French. They'll have had their guys keeping an eye on me since I won the ramming case. I'm sure they're following me.'

'Relax,' I said. 'Most people here are in the IRA and they've got far more reason to be concerned about their safety than you. And anyway, have you ever seen a Frenchman drinking Guinness?'

David showed us a letter he'd received from a woman called Denise Bell. She ran a local FoE group in Harrow and had attended an FoE whale rally in 1976, which had inspired her to raise funds to buy a boat to, as she put it, 'visit the Norwegians during their whaling operations in the North Sea and to attempt to prevent them from killing whales'. I recognised her name from the list of groups at the central FoE office and smiled at my vision of her trying to disrupt the Norwegian whaling fleet. 'I say,' I imagined her saying in a posh English accent to a grizzled Norwegian whaler, 'would you mind ever so not doing that?'

David had already met Denise and said he'd nutted out a budget for her — a 'reality check' as to how much money she'd need to raise. I was intrigued by his description of her: I'd got her wrong. 'She lives above a laundrette. I think you guys should go see her, perhaps give her a hand. Maybe she'd be interested in joining us,' David said, looking around to see if anyone was listening, which of course they weren't.

He'd asked if we would be interested in establishing a Greenpeace office in London when we returned from the 1977 seal campaign in Canada. He'd heard about a group in London also calling itself Greenpeace, and wanted to make sure we registered the name officially before they did. The London-based activists had also been campaigning against French nuclear-weapons tests in the Pacific. They had used the name Greenpeace in 1971, in a broadsheet published in *Peace News*, a newspaper founded in 1936 by individuals involved in War Resisters International. By 1972 the name was being used by a coalition of individuals and groups in Britain, an autonomous network with little connection to the Canadian organisation, which, based in Vancouver and at that time called the Don't Make a Wave Committee, eventually became the Greenpeace Foundation. The London Greenpeace was far more political, with links to animal rights activists who'd damaged vivisection laboratories and immobilised sealing boats. I felt uncomfortable about David's rather imperialistic approach and thought it only fair that we consult with the London outfit before opening our own office.

'They're all goddamn anarchists,' spluttered David. 'There's no way we could work together.'

I watched in horror as a man with an ice pick and a snot-covered moustache rammed the point of his weapon into the skull of a harp seal. The animal looked up at its executioner, never once losing that classic beatific look in its ebony eyes, even with blood and brain tissue splattered over its white coat.

Paul Watson, one of the two Wounded Knee paramedics, had stayed with Allan and me in Battersea. He'd come to Europe looking for support for the 1977 Greenpeace seal campaign he was organising, had recruited a couple of Norwegian women as crew, and had had a few days in London before flying back to Vancouver. He was a quietly spoken, intense man with incredibly strong determination. I could see he wouldn't give up easily and I liked that. With a borrowed projector and a sheet hung in our living room for a screen, he had shown me film footage of the harp seal hunt he and Bob Hunter had tried to disrupt the year before. It was the most gruesome and bloody thing I'd ever seen — seals skinned alive as their pups watched.

'Count me in,' I'd told Paul, already knowing Allan would be going. 'I'll come along as a FoE rep.'

I had been shocked to the core. And here were these two brave guys, Bob and Paul, standing right in front of the sealing boat. I saw the split-second 'Fuck me' look on Bob's face as the sealing boat moved forward, just slightly, and wondered if I would be that brave in his position. It wasn't about animals, I figured. It was about Creation, full stop. It was about man's destruction of the planet for the satisfaction of short-term greed. Hungry for power, the biggest dick wins. It was the patriarchy having a wank. I felt incredibly angry.

'That lichen's hallucinogenic,' Walrus said, pointing to a white rubbery-looking plant I could see through the ice. He'd been one of the activists at Wounded Knee. 'The native people dry it and smoke it.'

I stopped in my tracks. We'd been drinking water from ice containing this lichen all week. Could that be why we'd all been feeling so happy, playing the flute and juggling when the sun came out, ice as far as the eye could see? We'd developed into a tribe of our own, telling our stories late into the night and curling up close to each other in our space blankets to sleep, beanied heads sticking out of the top. A crate of brandy had arrived by helicopter, after the first tents had gone up. I'd been busy trying to find a spade, irritated that all I could find in the equipment tent was piles of socks and plastic measuring jugs. I could hear the others getting very drunk, very quickly, on the brandy, and then came a crash as the radio operator fell on top of his tent. 'Over and out,' he said, before hitting the ground.

I looked across to Allan for reassurance — he was always so professional, organised and focused. It had been quite farcical so far and I was having second thoughts about my involvement. We'd all gathered in Montreal several days before for a campaign briefing. I'd made sure I had enough miso for the entire campaign — Allan and I had stocked up before leaving and brought our chopsticks along as well. At the briefing someone was looking at an aerial photograph in that morning's paper of Norwegians hunting harp seals off the coast of Labrador. 'We'll have to alter our plans,' someone else said. 'The sealing ships aren't anywhere near Belle Isle.'

There followed a flurry of activity as people raced around, looking at maps and making phone calls. No one got much sleep. I was puzzled. The seal hunt wasn't due to start for a couple of days, so I thought the photo must be archival material. Pathetic really, but I couldn't bring myself to speak up. I felt such a newcomer — a novice, the greenest member there. They'd even given me a green padded suit to wear and allocated me to the Green Squad, which was going to spray the seals green, thereby rendering their pelts worthless.

I finally forced the words out. 'Don't you think you should check when this photo was taken?'

Silence. I'd never been anywhere you couldn't open the windows before and I felt claustrophobic. I was hermetically sealed in with a group of crazed activists, champing at the bit to get out and disrupt the grotesque slaughter of thousands of harp seals for their soft fur coats. In the ensuing hush it seemed as if the room hummed with some kind of malevolent energy. I knew I'd get sick if I stayed in there much longer.

'The editorial staff at the paper say they used a photo from last year's hunt,' a spectacled young man said, putting down the phone. 'The boats are off Belle Isle.'

Dan McVermott, from Willowdale, Ontario, weighed 84 kilograms and was travelling at between 80 and 95 kilometres per hour, sliding down towards the ice overhang as I was making my way up. I was almost at the top. I remember falling back when he hit me, tumbling down the ice slope, over and over like a snowball gathering speed, then a couple of strong arms picking me up and dragging me back to my tent. My neck hurt like crazy but I wanted to go back and have another go. It was such fun, sliding down the steep slope in our padded suits, taking off from the overhang, flying through the air and crash-landing into soft snow.

'You were knocked unconscious, Susi. We need to monitor you in case you've suffered internal injuries,' a voice said, as someone peered into my eyes with a torch. 'If your pupils start dilating, we'll need to get you to a hospital.'

I wondered where the nearest medical centre might be. Blanc Sablon, on the mainland, where some of our crew were stationed to handle the international press who were arriving in force, didn't seem to have much more than a small hotel. There were no doctors among the crew, but there was a vet. At least he might know how to put me down if the going got particularly rough, I thought. What a way to go. I was hoping like crazy it was nothing that serious.

There had been a storm the night before, and when we had woken everything had been covered in a thick blanket of snow. Our campsite had looked entirely different and we'd had problems getting our bearings, disinterring the kitchen and locating the cooking utensils. I was glad I'd brought my chopsticks as most people had lost their spoons by now. I kept them hidden in my suit, and one of them had snapped during the fall, piercing me.

None of us had got much sleep during the storm, and one of the Norwegian women had panicked inside her tent, screaming for help as one side, weighed down by the accumulating snow, had closed in above her head. A few of us had pulled on our cold-weather suits and braved the elements to help, but it had been impossible to stand upright in the wind, so we had crawled along the ground as best we could, feeling around for something — anything — we could use to dig. We had found a couple of aluminium saucepan lids sticking up through the snow, but they had buckled under the freezing weight we were trying to shift. We had been able to hear the poor woman whimpering underneath, softly at first, muffled by the snow, and then louder as we had got closer. She had been absolutely terrified.

Several days later, when we were finally evacuated one helicopter load at a time before a predicted worst-ever storm, the same woman lost it again when she realised she wouldn't be one of the first to leave, the departing crew having been chosen at random. With that uncommon strength people seem to acquire when highly distressed, she charged towards the helicopter and heaved me out of the seat I was in and threw me onto the ground. Jumping back in, she strapped herself into the seat and looked down at me, jaw clenched. I felt sorry for her — she was obviously terrified — and it didn't matter to me when I left. Hell, I didn't even want to go. I had no desire whatsoever to vacate the newly declared sovereign territory of Freelandsea. Walrus and I had just finished writing up our Declaration of Interdependence. It went like this:

> We, the people of Belle Isle, do hereby declare our independence this day the 19th of March 1977 (Christian reckoning), Year of the Snake. We declare our sovereign territory to include the islands of Belle Isle and its environs, including all waters and ocean bottoms and air space extending 200 miles from the coastline of Belle Isle, except where our

I asked, pointing across the river to some high-rise office blocks.

'Naturally,' he said. 'Otherwise what's the point in doing all this?'

I was shaken. Surely an effective movement rose and then fell, its job accomplished; it was designed to become obsolete, not to create structures and systems which mimicked those of the oppressor. I'm sure I saw it all far too much in black and white, but the idea of a corporate Greenpeace disgusted me at a profoundly philosophical level.

The door above the laundrette in Harrow was opened by a woman in a fake-suede brown coat covered in stickers. Some were peeling off, the glue stains like patches of dried-up semen. An old Labrador called Shandy was by her side and followed her everywhere she went.

'You must be Allan and Susi. Very pleased to meet you.' She shook our hands and I felt comfortable with her immediately. She had a wise face, like the faces of native American chiefs in my photo collection, and her long dark-blonde hair was parted in the middle. I noticed some expensive jewellery on her hands, and as if reading my mind she said: 'I was involved with a rich geezer and he bought me these. We've broken up.' She had a sexy, throaty voice, with a Middlesex accent — a touch more refined than the 'Sowfeast-Ender' accent of my FoE colleague Pete Wilkinson.

'Who was that tough guy at FoE?' David had asked me once. 'The one you told me about who's really good at campaigning. A working-class guy.'

I could see he was scheming again, head-hunting the perfect collection of activists. 'That's Pete Wilkinson,' I said.

David looked at me. 'How do I get him? How do I get the guy to come and work with us?'

'Take him to a football match and then to a pub,' I replied. 'He's working in the Halstead post office. What a waste. It'd be great if he joined us. He could run the nukes campaign.'

It had been Pete's voice that had carried most from beyond closed doors when I had first entered the FoE office — the voice of a genuine working-class hero among the mellower tones of all of us middle-class toffs. He shone among us like the rough diamond he was, combining in-yer-face demonstrations with humour and a good slogan.

'Excuse the mess,' Denise said, leading us into the lounge. 'And the dog hairs everywhere.'

While I could tell she was older than us, she had one of those timeless faces imbued with the silent dignity of souls blended together through the ages. David, at 45 the elder statesman among us, had said she'd run a business and knew how to keep the books. He was going to join us later. Denise pointed out his Navajo rugs in the corner of the room. He'd obviously been dossing down there as well.

It took me a while to stop castigating David in my mind for putting himself about like a tomcat and to focus on why we were there. Denise had persuaded three bands — Medicine Head, Jenny Haan's Lion and Strife — to do a benefit concert for 'Save the Whales' at the Marquee Club in central London's Wardour Street. She was getting T-shirts made and had written up some information on whales and whaling to hand out at the door. She asked Allan, who'd already carried out extensive research on whaling in the North Atlantic, to check her facts. I said I'd help sell the merchandise and spread the word. There was a good feeling of cooperation, of a team. When David was around he tended to get in the way, trying to direct things the way he thought they should go rather than letting the process find its own way forwards. He always wanted to interfere, to criticize or change things so he could be involved; he had a prima-donna complex, yet at the same time hated being in the spotlight because it made him paranoid. Without David in the office, it was much quieter. We got on with the job in hand, going with the flow, and he seemed to resent us for this, although I never really understood why. Perhaps it was because he was never at ease, always pacing the square and looking for a way out.

Denise, Allan and I all shook hands again at the door. Denise had agreed to become part of Greenpeace Ltd provided there was a strong commitment to saving whales. I can't remember who suggested we go to Antarctica to see what the Russian and Japanese whaling fleets were doing — rumour had it they were killing blue whales — but I do remember covering the walls of the newly opened, newly scrubbed office with navigational charts of Antarctica as we meticulously charted fleet positions and their movements over the years, trying to find a pattern. We calculated how much fuel we'd need to voyage between various locations, and worked out where the stopovers would be; we looked at whale migration routes, questioning people from the British Antarctic Survey. The story of the orca that played ball with an old stomach same time same place every week touched me immensely. I knew we needed to get down there as quickly as possible and save those magnificent beings from the barbarity of the whaling fleets.

lots of wood and brass everywhere. She'd been built in the early 1950s —
a Scottish fishing trawler called the *Sir William Hardy*.

Denise filled me in. 'The Ministry of Fisheries was using her for research
with the Torrey Research Station. She's up for tender. They've left her in a
bit of a mess — it's difficult to see exactly how much work there is to do
inside without lights. Who can we get to come down here and tell us
how to get the generators going?'

I knew immediately who to phone. 'Would you know how to get the
lights going in this old boat we've found?' I was speaking to Athel from
the phone box right in front of the boat, making a very bad job of trying
to describe her. 'You know, a boat — a fishing boat. A big one — I think
Den said she's around 145 feet long, 425 tons.'

Athel was a qualified mechanic who could get anything going. I smiled
as I thought of him lying on his bed in Fulham, his hair still in the net he
wore for working under cars, asleep in his grease-covered overalls. He
loved machines, especially powerful motorbikes. He'd bought one for
me once, a smaller version of his own. I, on the other hand, had never
developed a relationship with the mechanical world — it had a lot to
answer for, in my opinion — and tried to sell the bike on the sly,
unknowingly without the engine, which I hadn't even noticed had been
removed. Athel was definitely the man for the job.

It's funny how a story changes over time, how people try to rewrite history,
self-mythologizing, putting themselves in positions of power and giving
themselves roles they never had, claiming successes not rightly theirs. I
deeply resented, and resisted, the impetus I could see in certain people's
personal desire to profit from what we were doing. It disgusted me. I
abhorred hierarchical, hegemonic structures intent on domination. The
exaggerated assertion of masculinity on the world stage troubled and
offended me. I had this niggling feeling that the potential for a mass
movement, for a spontaneous uprising of eco warriors, would be
jeopardised by a continual need to chase media coverage of spectacular
stunts. I couldn't get my head around it. Careerists in the environmental
movement have come and gone; some have stayed, others have become
wealthy in their paid positions as 'protesters'. There are those who have
become traitors to the cause, jumping the fence because the pay is better
on the other side. Fortunately, there are others who have become more
radical over time, who refuse to compromise and who will not engage

with an unethical system, even if it means going without the millions needed for a navy of colourful boats and the perks of the trade.

The generators grunted into action, immediately establishing a comfortable two-stroke rhythm you could feel underfoot. Denise and I had heard Athel down in the engine room, a torch in his mouth, his tools clanging on the deck, as he coaxed the machines into action, talking to them gently. We had been pacing nervously up and down the narrow walkway, calling out now and then to make sure he was all right, for it was very dark down there. Suddenly the place lit up — the lights were on, there was life, there was energy. We wandered around without saying a word, not wanting to disturb old ghosts or provoke the ire of Sir William, whoever he was. The mess looked as if it had been abandoned halfway through breakfast: plates encrusted with dried egg yolk, a layer of mould floating on what must have been a cup of tea, pieces of toast that had turned into lino.

Denise broke the silence. 'Blimey, they were in a hurry to leave.'

We saw lots more wood and brass, and found a walk-in fridge, cabins down below, even a laboratory. There was a wide, comfortable feel to the ship's hull, like childbearing hips on a woman. She felt totally safe.

We returned to the office and told the others we'd found the boat we were looking for. 'Of course, she needs a bit of work,' we told Charles and Allan. 'She's covered in rust, and we'll have to get rid of the trawl gear on the deck.'

Someone had recommended a Mr Eastwick to Denise, a man from Great Yarmouth who'd had a lifelong involvement with trawlers. He was the person who had first told Denise about a likely vessel sitting in the London Graving Dock, telling her to send him a few snaps of the boat and a brief report on her condition. He then decided to come to London with his engineer to check the trawler in person, and told us she was indeed worth bidding for, and that when bidding for a trawler it was best to do so in multiples of seven.

Denise and I sat in the pub below the office and decided on the arbitrary amount of £42,725 as our offer for the boat. It was a total stab in the dark, which took into account the superstition regarding sevens.

'If our tender is accepted, we'll have to come up with ten per cent of that for a deposit,' Denise said, busily writing figures on the back of an envelope.

I trusted her financial nous implicitly. But we only had £2000 in the bank from fund raising — we'd have to find the rest somehow. Yet sitting round the table in the office with Shandy the Labrador as our collective foot rest, we could hardly contain our excitement when we heard our tender had been accepted.

'Stone the crows, Den,' I said, ' I only have twenty quid to my name. Where are we going to find that kind of money?'

Charles suggested we see the manager at Lloyds Pall Mall branch — our local bank. He said he'd talked with him on the phone and he sounded quite a reasonable fellow. David had gone to Canada to try to sell his marina at Secret Cove — there was plenty of time to tell him about the boat later. Compared to us he was rolling in it, having made a lot of money over the years. He was also supporting a family, so we never asked him for a contribution from his personal savings, nor did he offer. He'd dropped out of the picture as far as we were concerned — all his comings and goings had given him a very transitory feel. Secretly I was relieved he was overseas. Not that I didn't love the salty bastard. And he had his uses — he could certainly pull off a deal.

I noticed Charles' toe poking through his boot as we stood in front of the bank manager. We'd been given an appointment after hours, and had been shown in past the bullet-proof partition. I looked around wondering whether this was where HRH and family banked. I'd suggested we remove our 'Fuck the Whalers' badges and Charles had brushed his hair, quite greasy now owing to the limited washing facilities in our condemned building.

'What did you say you wanted this money for?' the bank manager asked, looking at us over his horn-rimmed spectacles. Charles explained. He had the poshest accent among us so we had elected him our mouthpiece; besides, he had the knack of sounding convincing. I realised I'd bowed my head, as I'd been trained to do at school when in front of my 'superiors'. That's how I noticed Charles' toe.

'I'll give your organisation a £2500 overdraft facility against personal insurance policies belonging to you, Miss Bell, and you, Mr Hutchinson,' the bank manager concluded after a myriad questions. He looked at us with his head cocked sideways, a bemused expression on his face. He paused for a moment, then said: 'You know what? I actually believe in what you're doing. Thousands wouldn't. Sounds quite mad, but I have this feeling you'll pull it off. Good luck.'

We waited until we got outside before hugging each other in delight. Brilliant! We had enough for the deposit.

'I'll lend us a thousand pounds, the rest of my savings, for operating costs for the office,' Denise said as we hurried back there, an autumn chill in the evening air. 'Oh, and we'll need to come up with a new name for the boat. It's a condition of sale, apparently. Board of Trade regulations. We can register her as a yacht — she's under five hundred foot — and that way we can bypass the class survey.'

Charles was lagging behind as we raced across a pedestrian crossing at an intersection. The sole had come unstuck from his shoe, the one with the hole at the toe, and was flapping as he walked. 'Do you think we can buy Charles a new pair of shoes?' I asked as we waited for him to catch up.

We linked arms as we walked up the street, a scruffy band of gypsies about to take the world by storm — Denise in the same old suede coat, only with many more stickers now, and her much-loved dog by her side; Charles a tall, shuffling man in ill-fitting pants and a flapping shoe; and me, a small, dark woman with patched jeans and high-heeled boots. We each had a mischievous glint in our eye, and great hope in our heart.

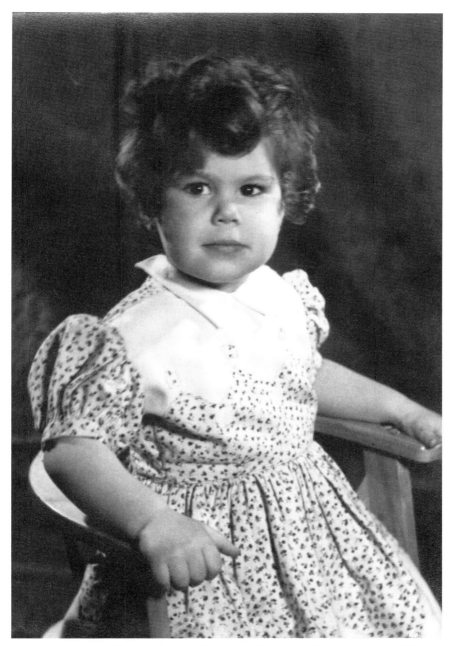

Posing for the Chelsea photographer in my handmade dress at the age of 2.

My first memories are of Tite Street, Chelsea, in the early 1950s.

*Hair oiled to keep it in place, the spotless mohair cardigan —
this is me around the time of my first protest action.*

My mother in her early thirties.

This is my favourite photo of my father, Don Pedro.

The library at Don Torcuato with its hanging candelabras.

Hardly poor and certainly quite pretty — this is my brother enjoying life as a West End actor.

My mother took this photo of an asado during a ride with the gauchos from Rincón de Luna.

Some of my friends at Northwood College the year I was expelled. I am in the middle of the second row, proudly wearing a CND badge on my jumper.

Allan in the office at 47 Whitehall.

Remi on one of his many visits to 47 Whitehall.

David striking a typical pose during our first directors' meeting at 47 Whitehall.

Pete helps me scoop up rice after the pressure cooker exploded in the galley.

A toilet roll separates me from the most beautiful woman in the world. Brigette Bardot shelters in my tent on Belle Isle during the 1977 seal campaign.

Chris keeps a watchful eye on the whaling boat from his Zodiac during a whaling campaign.

Clockwise from top left: *Denise in the mess doing some paperwork.*

Charles on board the Rainbow Warrior.

Chris and Hilari on board the Rainbow Warrior *during the first Spanish whaling campaign in 1978.*

Us gals in the mess of the Rainbow Warrior.

The Sir William Hardy *being moved from the London Graving to the West India dock. Denise, Chris, Athel, Charles and I stand on the foredeck and marvel that she can actually move.*

The first crew of the Rainbow Warrior, *1978. Back row (right to left): Stefan, Simon, Eric, Pete, Nick, Allan, Charles, Hilari, Alaistair, a unknown journalist. Middle row (right to left): Tony, Denise, Remi, Sally, Tim, Athel. Front row (right to left): Pieter, David, me, Steve (who had joined us in Hamburg), Fred, Jean-Paul.*

Pete holds his first press conference in 1978, after cutting his hair.

Jean-Paul's famous photo of the Rainbow Warrior, *taken between the Faroe Islands and Iceland during Zodiac training.*

The bridge of the Rainbow Warrior *in 1979, with Bruce at the wheel and Jon on lookout.*

I fell in love with the s/v Fri *from the moment I saw her in 1979. She oozed adventures on the high seas, and smelt of linseed oil, tar and sprouting potatoes.*

Martini shows off his warrant and his political inclination while under arrest in El Ferrol.

Athel and Jon share a quiet beer while under arrest in El Ferrol.

Chris and a crew member come to Athel's aid after his boat is destroyed by a barrel of radioactive waste he had managed to catch as it was dropped into the sea from the Gem.

Bruce and I in front of the Pacific Fisher *as we make our way into Barrow.*

An old warrior is farewelled and buried off the coast of New Zealand on 12 December 1987.

Luc and I on our wedding day in New Caledonia, 1991.

My beautiful daughter, Brenna, at the age of 17.

Happiness is contagious around Naawie (left) and Woody (right).

8

I stared at the wall opposite my desk. I'd pinned up a note: 'You're only blue if you're a whale and have a harpoon sticking out of you.' I'd put it up to stop me feeling dejected every time we had yet another phone conversation with a marine mortgage broker. We had two weeks to come up with £39,352.50 — don't ask me what the pence were for — and we had nothing in the bank. A freezing office didn't help; we just couldn't afford to heat the place properly. Charles and Allan walked around in blankets at night to keep themselves warm, Denise wore gloves with the fingers cut short to sort through the merchandise during the day, and I lived in my djellaba. We were all run down, neglecting our health and not eating properly. We also suspected we were under surveillance of some sort — we weren't quite sure what, we just had a feeling. A couple of men from Scotland Yard had come over to ask us if we knew we had a body slumped over a typewriter in the back office. Allan had put his head down for a moment's shut-eye and had fallen asleep for several hours on top of the Olivetti. The policemen said they'd received a call from the Central Intelligence Service, so their offices must have been nearby as well. Someone — they had obviously been quite observant — hadn't seen Allan move for a while, had become concerned and had asked the police to check out the situation. I escorted the two officers through to the back and a rather startled Allan.

'Oh good, sir, you're alive!' said one of them, before going on to explain their concern. 'Someone has been keeping an eye on you, just in case. Thought you'd been murdered, sir. Shot.'

'You would have had to use binoculars to see anything,' I said to Allan after the policeman had left.

'Wonder if it was them who changed the locks downstairs,' Denise added, after Allan had recounted the story over a cup of comfrey tea.

We'd arrived at work one day and discovered the office had been broken into. No one had slept there that night and Allan's briefcase was missing. Several days later I noticed a file containing my correspondence with Native American activists at Akwesasne, whose territory straddles the Canadian–US border, and with the Aurukun Council in Queensland, Australia, had also been taken. One of the activists from Akwesasne was planning a visit to the United Nations in Geneva early the following year and wanted to come to London to discuss how we could assist in his people's struggle for self-determination. I had initiated contact with them, wanting to maintain that sense of solidarity with indigenous peoples already established by Greenpeace members in North America. I felt that pressing issues of colonial injustice and human rights should be embraced by the environmental movement, and was keen to see us similarly involved in the campaign against uranium mining in Australia.

'Their fellas were in here the other day,' I'd said while showing out the police officers, referring to the CIS. 'Any chance of asking them for my file back?'

I listened as Charles did his very best to convince whatever bureaucrat was on the other end of the line to cough up nearly 40,000 quid for us to buy a trawler and go save some whales. He used his posh accent to the max. Nonviolent confrontation, direct action — he repeated the words over and over again like a mantra. I didn't like them, to be honest. *Confrontation* and *direct* — one was too bellicose, the other not subtle enough, but we didn't have time to think up catchy little phrases.

'You wha'?' You could hear the sniggering in the background. 'Cop a load of this lot. They want to go out and chase Icelandic whalers. Say they've found an old trawler and want some money to buy 'er! Ha bloody ha!' Others were less polite.

By now we knew our focus would be Icelandic whaling in the North Atlantic. Allan's research had revealed four catcher boats in the Icelandic whaling fleet, each with 150 pounds of exploding harpoon. The whales — mainly finbacks (nearly as big as blues), some sperm, some sei — were towed back to the processing station at Hvalfjordar. The operation was owned by a Mr Loeftsson, who was also the Icelandic delegate to the IWC, the body established to regulate whaling. Remember that in 1972, at the Stockholm Conference on the Human Environment, a motion had been passed — unanimously — calling for a 10-year moratorium on commercial whaling. Icelandic people ate whale meat, but it was not a vital source of protein. They exported about one third of what they took. Scientific evidence showed the populations of both finback and sperm whales were shrinking to critical levels, yet still the hunting continued. Ascertaining the exact size of any stock was extremely difficult, and calculations of hunting quotas were based on inexact science, sheer guesswork and industrial bloody-mindedness. Finback whales were already protected in the southern hemisphere, but sperm whales were still being hunted for their spermaceti oil, needed by a cosmetics industry which had not yet cottoned on to jojoba as a substitute. Charles did his best to present the evidence. It was a race against time. Didn't these mortgage brokers understand?

'Go and tell them you just don't have the money!' David was irritated to say the least. 'For fuck's sake get down there and tell them you don't have a cent!'

Charles and Denise disappeared down to the other end of Whitehall, to the Board of Trade, to tell them we were broke, while David carried on berating us. He'd returned from Canada after we'd phoned to say we'd made an offer on a boat, and his attitude certainly wasn't doing anything to improve our mood.

'They asked us what we could afford!' Denise said incredulously when she and Charles returned, having walked back up Whitehall with a bit more of a spring in their step. 'I think they felt sorry for us.'

'Tell them we'll give them £25,000,' David said. His nose had been put out of joint. In his absence, Allan and Charles had secured a deal with the World Wildlife Fund (WWF) in the Netherlands. They'd taken the Greenpeace film of the Russian whaling campaign over to Holland in the hope of getting it on television and soliciting donations for our campaign. The WWF there agreed to set up a specific account for the donations, as Greenpeace didn't officially exist in Holland at that stage. Anything over and above £45,000 would revert to the WWF.

We advised the Board of Trade of our revised offer for the *Sir William Hardy* — we'd grown quite fond of the old bastard — and it was accepted, with the proviso that an additional £12,000 would be paid for bunkers, an extra engine and propeller, and spare parts, bringing the total to £37,000 — we made sure there was a 7 in there somewhere. Now all we could do was wait, in the hope that the generosity of the Dutch public would enable us to raise the cash. Luckily for us, no other bids had been made on the boat and our offer had been officially accepted.

There was a diffused pink glow in the office and out on the street. People smiled at you, and of course you beamed back. This was amazing. Everything was coming together effortlessly, actions flowing one into the other, everyone doing their bit. David's negativity had been hard to handle but we were used to it. We'd given up pacing round and round the office waiting to hear back from the WWF, pretending we were busy, staying nonchalant, chitchatting away. Whenever the phone rang, people stopped, in midsentence, in midstride, to listen.

'We've got the fucking money! We've got the dosh, guys!' someone yelled. The donations had come pouring in. We could buy the boat. Finally.

'Bet you've never signed such a whopping big cheque in your life,' Denise said as I sat, pen in hand, staring at the thing.

'I certainly haven't.'

I held back for a few seconds, just to savour the moment. We would sign in pen and ink, of course, with blotting paper alongside to make sure it didn't smudge. Denise had written the words out very neatly. 'Thirty-two thousand, two hundred and seventy-five pounds' — we'd dropped the pence. I signed with a flurry of swirls and loops, more expansive than my usual signature. The boat was ours.

There are many stories about the *Rainbow Warrior*, for even in her lifetime she became legendary. Among them are many myths, some good yarns, a lot of half-truths, and a plethora of tales that are just plain nonsense. But historical accounts should aim to be as accurate as possible; they don't need to be turned into fiction — the truth is magical by itself. Over the years, I've read — and heard — many accounts of how I came to give our ship the name *Rainbow Warrior*. Each account is a version of the truth. What follows is my contribution.

I'm not sure if any of us were paying attention at the time — some details remain fuzzy — but a book was being passed around among us. It was called *Warriors of the Rainbow* and had been put together by William Willoya, an Inuit, and Vinson Brown, an American biologist and anthropologist who was also a Baha'i. The two men had written and published many books about native Americans, ecology and peace. This particular book had been published in 1962 and was a collection of prophetic dreams, some collected from native Americans by Willoya in his travels around North America, others from the Aztec people and the peoples of India and the East Indies. The message of the prophecies, still relevant decades later, is simple: 'That men should love one another and understand one another . . . nothing of selfishness nor vanity, nothing of narrowness nor pride.' The collection opened with the story of a wise old woman, Eyes of the Fire, instilling the Indian spirit in her great grandson, Jim, who is on a quest to find out why their people have allowed the white men to take their lands. Eyes of the Fire says that one day their people will 'teach the white men how to really love one another and how to love all mankind'. As she sends Jim on a vision quest, a rainbow appears and she tells her great grandson it is 'a sign of the union of all peoples like one big family'. She then counsels him to 'learn to be a Warrior of the Rainbow, for it is by spreading love and joy to others that hate in this world can be changed to understanding and kindness, and war and destruction shall end!'

An account then follows by Vinson Brown of a dream he had every week for four years until he turned nine. His father, who was the doctor on the Pine Ridge Reservation in the late 1800s, showed him a beautifully beaded doe-skin bag he'd been given by a Sioux chief, whose son's life he had saved. The chief had been told to give the prized Oglala pipe bag, rescued from white soldiers, to the first white man who did something good for them. In Brown's dream, a beautiful dove appears, circling down from the sky. A group of Indians watching the dove from a hilltop suddenly spring up, their rags replaced by headdresses and buckskin clothing covered in beads and shells, and begin to march up into the sky after the dove. Others join them, following the white bird, and a rainbow forms in the sky: 'a rainbow of unity and vision so marvellous . . . the promise of a wonderful change coming'. These warriors of peace — the Warriors of the Rainbow — appear throughout the book's collection of prophecies, and Willoya concludes that they will mix love with understanding in their medicine to heal the world, and 'the youth shall once more do great deeds of selflessness and heroism'. I thought the basic message of the prophecies offered great hope and found it touching in its simplicity; it also seemed to fit with what we were trying to do.

We were sitting in the office strategizing one afternoon — Charles, Denise, Allan and I. We had a campaign to plan and David was insisting we do a publicity tour of Europe before heading north to the Icelandic whaling grounds. It all sounded boring to us — we were champing at the bit to get to Iceland to try to stop the whaling. We were expecting

Remi to visit from Paris to help nut out how we'd get the show on the road. I can't remember exactly how it came out, but I suggested we call the boat *Rainbow Warrior* — after all, we were taking up the warriors' mantle by trying to stop the whale slaughter. Charles suggested we ask *Blue Peter* — the popular kids' television programme — to ask their audience for suggestions. I resisted, saying something about that programme being only for namby-pamby middle-class kids, but then said he should go ahead as long as, at the end of the day, we still called her *Rainbow Warrior*.

When Remi arrived, we showed him the modest paperback by Willoya and Brown. 'Let's name the boat *Le Combattant de l'Arc en Ciel*,' he said — an almost direct translation of the book's title — explaining that it fitted in with something he'd been reading about dolphins.

'Too long,' I replied. 'She's called the *Rainbow Warrior*.'

And that was that.

I picked up the book and looked at the illustration of native Americans in their traditional clothes walking up through the sky, being led by a dove. It was painted by a Navajo artist and was also called *Warriors of the Rainbow*.

'Let's paint a rainbow on the ship, and a dove like this,' I added, pointing to the picture in the book. Someone else suggested a green hull and the Kwakiutl totem. We were fizzing — it was so right.

We decided we'd move the boat to a more accessible place within the West India Dock. There her rust was hand-chipped by an endless stream of volunteers, and the painting had commenced by the time David returned from yet another jaunt overseas. He stood beside me at the edge of the dock, looking at the rainbow-decorated hull in front of him, and the white dove on green under the name *Rainbow Warrior*.

'Why the hell are you painting her up like this? Goddamn rainbows, waste of time!' He was angry we were holding things up with aesthetic details.

A young artist, Michael Taylor, had contacted us after he'd seen one of our T-shirts in the music press. He told us he'd sketched the *Sir William Hardy* as an art student and would be happy to supply us with the artwork, which we could use for publicity. He submitted a design for the overall look of the ship, incorporating the rainbow, dove, Kwakiutl totem and green hull and various other features we'd agreed, and added his own touch here and there, in particular a beautiful painting of finback whales on the stern. He also produced a meticulous schematic diagram of the ship, which, sadly, may have led to her sinking in Auckland all those years' later.

In New Zealand, antinuclear activism had been part of the nation's consciousness since the explosion of a giant thermonuclear bomb above Johnston Island in July 1962. Thousands of miles to the south, New Zealanders had witnessed a man-made sun — an artificial aurora in the upper atmosphere. Many of those who saw this cataclysmic event subsequently became antinuclear activists. Among them was a nurse from Auckland, Elaine Shaw, who became a founding member of Greenpeace New Zealand, formed around the same time as the Greenpeace Foundation in Vancouver. Both organisations represented groups of people coming together to protest against nuclear testing.

Elaine had heard about the *Rainbow Warrior*, and she'd written asking whether we'd consider bringing the boat to the South Pacific to assist in a protest against French nuclear testing at Mururoa. We all agreed this was a likely direction for the boat in the not too distant future, but we needed to take care of business closer to home first — there were endangered whales to save.

I sent Elaine a copy of Michael's schematic drawing of the vessel, interior and exterior, which I was later told was copied by Christine Cabon — the French spy who infiltrated the Greenpeace New Zealand office in 1985 — and sent to the Direction Générale de la Sécurité Extérieure (DGSE, the French intelligence service) in Paris so saboteurs would know where to place explosives to sink her. When I finally met Elaine in 1986, I was devastated to hear that it could have been the very copy of the drawing I had sent years before that had facilitated the destruction of our precious boat. We were immensely proud of her, and naturally sent pictures and diagrams of her to everyone, wanting to show her off — the people's boat. We wanted to honour the commitment of all the volunteers who'd come to help, little old ladies among them, chipping away at the rust with their handbags on their arms as the rainbow butterfly emerged from its cocoon.

People were begging for a chance to crew on the *Rainbow Warrior*, and an opportunity to put their lives on the line to express their outrage at commercial whaling. 'Put me in front of the harpoon! I'm 40 and dispensable. Use me!' urged one supporter. But the process of gathering a crew started slowly. We needed to hire a few professionals first to run the boat — a captain, an engineer, etc. — although the rest would comprise volunteers with a variety of skills.

'A couple of our guys would like to volunteer to go in those high-speed dinghies you people use,' a Cockney voice across the table said. We were sitting in an exclusive Italian restaurant in the centre of town, and the guy sitting opposite had picked us up in a huge white Rolls, almost as wide as some of the streets we had driven down to get to the place. 'They watched the film of your whaling campaign on TV — nice soundtrack,' he continued. 'Your geezers opening the throttle in slow-motion, like vroom, vroom — nice touch that, nice.' He made a motion with his hands, as if accelerating a motorbike.

My problem was I already resented this large, rich, red-faced music impresario, and I certainly hadn't heard of his band — the Electric Light Orchestra (ELO) — when we received a phone call requesting our presence at the launch of their new double album, *Out of the Blue*. A promise was made of a donation to our campaign. We'd receive the royalties from one of the tracks on the album — an instrumental entitled *The Whale* — and *Out of the Blue* went on to become the fastest-selling LP of the time.

'You go, Susi,' Denise had suggested. 'You're so much better at that kind of thing than I am. I wouldn't know what to say to half of them poncy music people. The musicians are good guys, it's their management that sucks.'

I was intrigued. I'd never heard of the band, yet apparently they were international superstars.

The plane was a medium-sized jet, hired for the day by the ELO's management. It was crowded with journalists and people who worked in the music industry. I sat next to a journalist from one of the music papers.

'You don't look like you're in the music business,' he said by way of an opener. I looked at my Tibetan cloth boots and my drawstring pants, both worn and patched. No, I thought, I don't. I glanced quickly at the trendy crowd I was trapped with on the plane and felt very alone. Everyone seemed to know what they were talking about except me.

'Who's Jeff Lynne?' I replied when someone asked me whether or not he'd be mentioning the track at the launch. An orange-haired man in glasses squeezed past the people blocking the gangway. Bottles of Southern Comfort were being passed around, and some of those present were already quite pissed. He leaned over and whispered in my ear: 'It's just not done to say, "Who's Jeff Lynne?" in present company.'

I felt as if I'd committed a mortal sin and wanted to get off the plane immediately — I was surrounded by tsk-tsking freaks. I felt safer with the journalist. He'd turned the situation to his advantage and was making it the focus of his story, scribbling away and firing endless questions at me. I hadn't the heart to ask him about this Jeff Lynne character — I didn't want to show my ignorance any further.

We landed in Munich and were driven to a recording studio for the launch. Champagne and a sumptuous meal had been prepared several storeys up, and, after eating, we took the lift down to the studio itself. More bottles of champagne were opened — these people could certainly drink — and an older man called Don Arden arrived. I was told he was a rock manager, and he certainly looked as if he was in charge. The next thing I knew I was being escorted into a soundproof chamber, where I was left on my own. Peering through a glass partition I could see almost all my travelling companions on the other side, champagne in hand, with this Mr Arden at the front. Everyone was looking at me. 'What the fuck . . . ?' I thought. I looked around for a way out. It was difficult to see where the door was. The place reminded me of a padded cell I'd been shown when visiting a mental home in London as a teenager. I felt like a trapped animal. Someone must have seen the look on my face, for they came in to explain what was going to happen.

'They're going to play you the track first and then there'll be a presentation.'

I made a note of where the door was when the person left. It wouldn't be that hard to get out if I needed to.

Suddenly the music started. It was like being in the music room of my old school, with brilliant acoustics — a containment of sound. I listened, curious to see how these musicians would describe the whale's magnificence with music. Would they mimic its natural sounds, incorporating them in the melody?

I was startled by the explosive glare of repeatedly popping flashbulbs. A line of cameras was being pointed at me as I stood dejectedly off-centre, my back half turned to them, head slumped. Oh God, I thought, I'm in the middle of a fucking PR exercise. How was I supposed to behave? Should I burst into tears at the appropriate moment to show how moved I was? I was extremely angry. It was fine for them to give us their money

— of course it would help — but I hadn't agreed to be part of the showbiz. I shut my eyes and stood rooted to the spot. If anyone asked me how I felt when the track finished I would slap them.

The room on the other side of the glass lit up. There was a microphone. The very London voice of the man everyone was paying attention to said, contemplatively, 'Ah, the whale — nice fish.'

In retrospect I'm very thankful we were separated by a plane of glass. That comment was the straw that broke my camel's back. I stormed out of the studio and collapsed onto a sofa in the foyer as the rock impresario droned on in the distance. There was a mention again, from the older guy, about some money for us from the track. There was something on the record cover, too.

People had been flown around the world just to be told that? How ridiculous. I knew I was making a bad job of showing how grateful we were, but the whole occasion seemed like nothing more than a marketing exercise on their part and I didn't believe a word of what they were saying. If the guy really cared about whales, he'd know they weren't fish.

Sinking into the huge cushions on the sofa, I noticed a young man with long hair and a friendly face sitting on a chair opposite. He said he was waiting for someone from the launch to leave the studio, and we got chatting. He told me about his home and family, and I told him how out of place I felt there. I said I much preferred to meet musicians alone, without the crazy circus surrounding them. 'People should get their facts right,' I said, repeating the comment about the whale being a fish. I'd actually quite liked the track, I told him, it wasn't that. I rambled on a bit. A door opened and the orange-haired bloke who'd dressed me down earlier with his remark on the plane came out.

'Gotta go.' The young man with the long hair stood up. 'Nice to meet you.' He shook my hand. 'Hey, man,' he said to Carrot-top, and disappeared into the studio.

'That's Jeff Lynne,' the orange-head whispered, stooping towards me as I recoiled into the cushions from his boozy breath. 'He's the one who wrote *The Whale*. Get it?'

I felt reassured sitting next to the same journo on the way back. The roadies were falling over themselves in the gangway, slugging Southern Comfort and pinching the hostesses' bottoms. The pilot's voice came over the intercom asking for less revelry and more chivalry. Someone tried to fly the plane — it made for an exciting story later. The cops were waiting for us when we landed. It was a case of pop stars behaving badly. I slipped unnoticed from the chaos, glad to be away from all the hype. It had been exhausting.

Sitting in the restaurant several weeks' later, I sensed the quid pro quo expected of us as the red-faced businessman leaned forward. 'Thought of a name for her yet, ducky? You know, your boat? What about *ELO*? Whaddya reckon? Look good down the side.'

'Shit,' I thought, madly trying to think up a reply. I didn't want to compromise the promised money by being rude or revealing my fundamental distrust of the man. 'You mean Environmental Liberators' Outfit? That's a possibility,' I fired back quickly. There was no way they were going to get what they wanted — band members as Zodiac drivers, 'vroom vroom' and a boat called the *ELO*.

No one could buy a place on our ship or take over her image for financial gain. We were extremely protective of her, and of our own vulnerabilities. Life was going to get very public if David had his way. 'Would you guys let the Aga Khan on as crew?' he asked tentatively one day, several months after our maiden voyage. He should have known better. No one cared if the guy was stinking rich. 'Not even if the ship is just going back to port?' he pleaded. 'For a few day's only? P-l-e-a-s-e?' There was mention of a tennis star as well, and an offer from someone high up in the Rothmans tobacco company. Our European tour had given David a lot of contacts and, a businessman at heart, he was really trying to help. I needed to accept that. But sponsorship flags flying alongside our own? This isn't what it's about, old man, I thought, looking at David with the compassion I often felt for him. Get with the programme. By then we'd shown we could get the show on the road without anything but donations from the public and the sale of our merchandise — we'd had a turnover of £100,000 in our first year as Greenpeace Ltd, over half of which we'd raised ourselves in the UK.

After berating me for wasting time with aesthetics, David went on board the boat and sidled up to a volunteer sitting on the deck at the stern, chipping away in silence. He squatted down beside him and started to chat, asking him questions — why was he here?, what did he do?, and so on. It was one of David's appealing qualities, this desire to communicate with everyone and anyone, which invariably led to his ending up in the pub later on to continue the discussion. He had a depth of humanity that was often marred by his desire to control what was happening around him. He didn't believe in democracy and insisted decisions be made by a small group of people. This command structure would ultimately prove very difficult for me, as I felt everyone involved should be consulted. People were risking their lives. They needed to have a say.

It's him!' Joni and I shouted in unison.

A young man had been shown into my bedroom, a prospective flatmate for our latest communal house, this time on the main road through Stratford, in northeast London. Joni and I had been sitting talking on the floor in front of the fire. Joni was Australian and had been helping get the *Rainbow Warrior* ready for 1 May, the official departure date.

The main body of the house was above two shops, one selling reggae music, the other unusual instruments from around the world. I'd spend my evenings in the latter, lying on the cushions on the floor, listening to an eclectic collection of sounds from countries near and far, drinking dandelion coffee. My bedroom was directly above the other shop, a Rastafarian hang-out, and on Saturday mornings I'd be woken by the beat of loud music. Clouds of marijuana smoke would drift out onto the street, people sucking on milk bottles that had been turned into chillums. This was a religious gathering. The worshippers had dreadlocks down to their waists, and they read from the Bible as they moved in time to the music. I loved the way they spoke — their use of language had a rhythm and a spiritual depth.

The odd punk-rock muso would enter the shop, their lard-coloured face making them look like a ghost among all the West Indians, their skinny, pasty arms sticking out of ripped clothing held together with nappy pins, the occasional pin fastened through bare flesh. There seemed to be an allegiance between the two groups — the smooth-muscled, mocha-skinned, clear-eyed rasta men and the angry kids from 'White City' — one that was based on a recognition of struggle, of solidarity. I admired the anarchic spirit of the new music I was hearing. Its lack of texture didn't interest me at all, but that didn't detract from its truth. The revolution everyone had sung about in the late 1960s and early 1970s had been very middle-class and fuelled by recreational drugs. Who else could really afford to trippy-dippy in their paisleys as a lifestyle choice, or at weekends? Sure, there had been a contribution to art, fashion and music, and certainly to literature, from all that flower power. It had also been a lot of fun, but politically nothing had really changed. The poor were getting poorer, US-sponsored terrorism overseas was increasing, and a woman with a room full of handbags had been given carte blanche to destroy Britain.

I'd felt a sense of moment when Hendrix had played *Star Spangled Banner* in front of thousands at Woodstock, burning the Stars and Stripes in front of thousands, incinerating it musically, metaphorically, spiritually. His 'sky-church music' had become the anthem of a generation, his legacy rebellion, representing the outlaw mainstream society still struggles to absorb. Youth had put up with boring old men and women waffling on for far too long. I'd heard them in the House of Lords, above the snoring of the most honourable member in the corner, making sure the ruling classes never lost out. I'd expected to hear more lofty considerations of governance in that historic chamber from the noblest of men, but their real game plan soon became clear.

Outside, in the city of London, nothing worked. Phone boxes were vandalised, their handsets left dangling out of smashed windows and 'Fuck the Lotta Yer' carved in the paintwork. Clocks — if they weren't smashed or broken — invariably told the wrong time. I cycled daily to the newly opened Greenpeace office in Whitehall as the trains never arrived on time. I enjoyed the exercise, although the streets stank of rubbish, bins and bags piled high spilling their contents across the pavement and onto the road. No one gave a damn. Bomb craters had become monuments to despair where the homeless — drunks, junkies, the insane — sought respite from the cold. I'd buy a jam doughnut at a bakery just before I reached the Thames, stuffing it into my mouth as I continued on my way through the City.

Joni had been telling me about an Australian surfer she'd seen in the post office in Trafalgar Square.

'How can you tell he's a surfer?' I'd asked.

'By the way he dresses,' she'd replied, 'but mainly by his long blond hair. It's bleached by the sun.'

I reflected on whether or not I'd ever met a surfer. The summer months I regularly spent on the Aegean island of Samos, off the southern coast of Turkey, brought me into contact with a few overseas travellers, among them antipodeans journeying overland back home to Australia or New Zealand. An American photographer friend, Steve Pearson, was living on Samos with his Irish wife in a small village on the coast. He'd been a photographer during the Vietnam War and had had no inclination to return to the US. He had decided to make Samos his home, and he and his wife invited me to stay with them one summer. Over the years the island had become a precious hideaway, my sanctuary and place of retreat. It was my firm belief that if I were to become an effective activist, I needed to get away, sometimes for several months at a time, and do something entirely different — live among other cultures, learn a new language. That was the best way, I figured, of not becoming stale, jaded or burned out. It was important to strive for a holistic, multidimensional approach to campaigning.

I was fascinated by Joni's surfer, how she'd managed to spot him and single him out from what must have been a crowd of travellers all clambering for their poste restante.

'Australian surfies stand out, Susi. They just do.'

I told her about a dream I'd had, years before. I was looking at the tanned back of a man sitting cross-legged on a sandy beach gazing out at the sea. The man had long fair hair. I couldn't see his face, but I knew he was connecting with the ocean. He exuded a great feeling of love. My young mind had interpreted the man as Christ, possibly because of the long hair, as most men wore theirs short at that time.

'Maybe Jesus was a surfer,' I quipped.

We were preparing to go down to the local bathhouse for a much-needed wash. The house only had one small sink upstairs, while the toilet was in an outhouse at the bottom of a small garden.

'Hang on,' said Joni. 'I'll just go and make sure someone's downstairs to let this guy in. It'd be terrible if he got stuck outside in the rain.'

As she spoke, a faint memory of someone I'd seen a couple of days before surfaced like a great whale rising from the ocean depth of consciousness. I hadn't cycled to work that day and had been walking home from the train station, shuffling along the road in my thick djellaba, the hood hanging loosely around my head. As I approached the house, I noticed a blur of something vital, animal and alert out of the corner of my eye. I couldn't see properly past the silk border of the hood, and caught only a fleeting glimpse of a handsome, tanned male, with long blond hair, moving catlike through the flow of local pensioners. It was one of those all-knowing moments, an instance, a flooding of cognition.

On another occasion recently I'd had the feeling I was being watched as I walked into the little alleyway along the side of the house. I had been

126
≡

distracted by someone trying out a sitar in the instrument shop and had promptly forgotten the experience. Only now, when Joni mentioned rain, did my mind travel back to that moment.

'It's him!' I yelled as the man came in, poking his head timidly round the corner.

'It's him!' Joni yelled back, recognising her surfie from the post office. Our flatmate, who'd answered the door and shown the prospect in, looked at both of us as if to say, 'What the fuck?'

'It's him!' we yelled again, in unison. 'It's him!'

'Do you think we should explain?' Joni asked as we walked to the bathhouse. 'We were a bit loud. Did you see the look on the poor guy's face? I think I heard him say his name was Chris. How about inviting him to dinner?'

Two days later, after we'd given our new flatmate time to settle in, I found myself knocking timidly on his door.

'Come in,' a voice said gruffly.

I was extremely nervous. I fancied him like crazy, and could feel his attraction for me, but I needed to be careful. He was like a wild animal, scared and magnificent at the same time. I didn't want to frighten him off, so I tiptoed in. He laughed when he saw me. He was lying in his sleeping bag in the centre of the room, on the floor. The contents of his pack were neatly displayed around the room. It must have taken him all of 5 minutes to unpack and we'd given him two days.

'I was wondering when you'd show up,' he said.

I wasn't accustomed to such a broad Australian accent and it took me by surprise. My voice sounded so 'frightfully frightfully' as we started to talk, hesitantly at first, then more animatedly. He was naked, and I could see the outline of his muscled body beneath the thin covering as he lay back on his arms. His fair hair reached his armpits and curled around the shorter hairs there. I had to restrain an overwhelming desire to get into the bag and lie up against him. I wanted to be reached, intensely, 'like the maelstrom-tip' in my wild she-whale clutch. I'd read him D.H. Lawrence's whale poem by the fire in my room when he'd come for dinner, and he'd stroked my face by the dying coals after Joni had gone. The two of them had described the Australian outback to me, and its unique spirituality, as we gazed into the hearth. I had been entranced. I knew a lot about uranium mining in Australia but very little about the place itself.

'We won't make love here,' he said, kissing me gently, his tongue feeling its way around my lips. 'We'll wait until you take me to the boat.'

I'd told him about our whale campaign, the *Rainbow Warrior* and the office in Whitehall. He'd just returned from several months in Iceland. After winning an Australian surfing competition he'd decided to go to the place furthest away from Melbourne, and Reykjavik was where he'd landed. I could see he was shocked about the whaling when I told him, but he said he wasn't sure whether he wanted to get involved. He was supposed to be on his way home, where he had a girlfriend waiting. My heart sank. I wanted him all to myself.

Round his neck was a chain with a small Buddha attached. 'I noticed you have one too,' he said, touching the small jade figure at my throat.

This time we were lying together on my mattress, half naked, and I ran my fingers through his long hair. We desperately wanted each other, but he was holding out for some reason, yielding, then suddenly pulling back, then yielding again — it was driving me nuts. I could feel his engorged penis between my legs, pressing against me. I was throbbing, moist with desire.

'No,' he said finally, dragging himself away from under me, my legs loosely curled around his waist. 'Let's save ourselves until we get down to the boat. It'll be amazing that way. It'll be special.'

'Do you believe in serendipity?' I asked, rolling us both a cigarette.

'Bugger serendipity. I followed you to the front door to see where you lived.' He looked at me out of the corner of his eye, zipping up his jeans, half-smiling as he spoke. 'I spotted you a few days before, on the other side of the street. The guy in the shop below was most helpful. Told me you lived upstairs and there was a room for rent. I had to find out who you were, wild-looking woman in a baggy wool coat. You got me hooked.'

'Den gave me the key to the boat,' I said, grabbing Chris by the hand. 'Come on, we're off for a night of passion. We'll pick up some cider and veg curry on the way.'

Chris had finally decided he'd give us a hand getting the boat ready and then assess how he felt about joining us for the trip to Iceland. I had this vision of him in a wet suit, soaked to the skin, hand on the throttle of a Zodiac, long hair and beard covered in blood. He was looking up at a harpoon gun, eyeballing the harpooner, while off to one side a finback mother was too tired to sound, her calf keeping watch.

I'd been irritated by David's comment that we needed 'a blonde' to ride in the Zodiacs to 'turn it on' for the whalers. The sexist bastard, I'd thought. 'I've got a blond,' I'd said, just to rub it in, hoping it might shut him up, as we all crowded into the captain's cabin for yet another secret meeting. 'He's got shoulder-length hair and would look good in a wet suit.'

I couldn't help thinking Chris would make an excellent Zodiac driver. He'd been a surfer, he knew how to ride the ocean underfoot and he'd go with the flow. We needed people like him. I still fancied him like crazy.

We opened the door of the captain's cabin and tiptoed in. It was the first cabin after the stairs on the port side, and a small brass plate with 'Captain' had been screwed above the wooden door. It was a comfortable-looking place, with rounded edges to the fittings, and had a small sink, a bunk and a day bed. It felt warm. We lit a few candles and sat on the carpeted floor to eat our dinner.

I was amazed that we'd managed to hold off having sex for so long — Chris always went back to his room at night, leaving me in a perpetual state of arousal. Perhaps he did it on purpose, as some form of extended foreplay. Wasn't that what Tantric yoga was all about? I remembered some of the stuff Dad had told me.

Chris lay down on the layered pile of sleeping bags and blankets. He'd taken his T-shirt off in one fell swoop, and his tousled hair fell onto his brown chest. 'Come here,' he said, pulling me down.

I was extremely nervous, and overwhelmed by the intensity of feeling I had for him. He rubbed my nipple under the woollen vest I had on, moaning slightly as his tongue probed and lapped deep within my mouth. I felt his hand between my legs, pulling at my underwear, thrusting his fingers inside me, his thumb on my clitoris, pressing — a gentle frottage. Wave after wave after wave, I pulsated and shook, and screamed as I tore his hand away.

'Thought you'd like that.' He grinned. 'Come here, get on top of me.' He lay down, removing his drawstring pants. I lifted my long skirt and straddled him, the tip of his aroused penis pressing against me. I leaned down so he could lick my stiffened nipple and then swung around and went down on him gently as he tried to control himself. He lifted me up towards him until he had positioned me over his mouth, his hands pushing my buttocks down as he sucked me dry. 'Fair dinkum, you smell delicious,' he said.

And so it went on for hours, until we were both covered in sweat, exhausted, scratched, and bruised from pushing against the bulkheads in our ecstasy, a burning sensation in every membrane. Finally, he pulled me down on his erect penis. He'd come several times already, but this was the first time I'd had him inside me. I moved carefully, lowering myself slowly, feeling myself open further as I took in all of him. He thrust gently as I leaned back in pleasure, feeling stretched to the limit. In contrast to the sexual fury of the last hours, this was hypnotically slow. I felt him up against my cervix as I clasped him to me, tightening and relaxing the muscles of my vagina. He liked that, clenching his jaw as he tried to control himself. Slowly we brought it on, summoned the serpent, trembled with love and rolled 'with massive, strong desire, like gods'.

We awoke in the morning, sprawled out across the cabin, damp hair plastered to our bodies and the smell of sexual juices everywhere. We could hear people on the deck outside, banging around.

Charles came in with a cup of tea and a cheeky look. 'Well, did the earth move?' he couldn't resist asking, as Chris and I quickly tried to straighten up.

'Yes, even on water.' I said, winking.

'Hurry up you lot,' Denise's voice teased us from by the laboratory bulkhead. 'We've got a show to get on the road here.'

'Have you seen my Buddha?' I asked Chris as we folded up the bed linen. By now we were feeling quite coy about how abandoned we'd been with each other during the night.

'No,' he said, checking his own was round his neck. We searched for a while but couldn't find anything, the chain or the jade figure.

'Maybe it was flung through some opening in the bulkhead and is somewhere in the ballast, floating around, to be found a hundred years from now,' I said. It'll bless the boat and keep her safe, I thought. It'll become part of the legend.

Charles opened his bag in the mess. He'd plonked it down on one of the tables, lifting it up with both hands it was so heavy. It was full of hammers and wire brushes. 'Well, we have to get the rust off somehow,' he said. 'There's only a few months until the whaling season starts.' We looked at each other in silence, the enormity of the task ahead sinking in. We bent our heads momentarily, considering our likelihood of success.

'Shit! We'll do it. I know we will.' Denise's face shone with hope, tears in her eyes.

'No one can work without a good feed.' It was Allan's voice; he had been waiting by the door for a chance to surprise us with a bag of goodies.

This was the first time we had all been together on the boat, sitting in the mess, around the tables, as if we were old hands. There was a dartboard to the left of the serving hatch through to the galley, and a notice board to the right, where we'd pinned up a work schedule for chipping duty, a list of parts we needing to purchase and receipts for takeaways we'd bought.

I was fascinated by the galley deck with its red tiles and narrow slotted channels — to facilitate drainage, I speculated. These features became an immense source of frustration for the galley crew, who gave up trying to sweep the place spotless, hampered as they were by the muddled placement of the tiles, the grooves of one running in the opposite direction of those of its neighbour.

'Ergonomics must have been a dirty word to the engineer who thought this one out,' I said to Hilari Anderson, a New Zealander we'd chosen as ship's cook. It made no sense at all. Once, I spent literally hours sweeping up rice for 30 people after a pressure cooker exploded, the lid ricocheting around the galley several hundred times faster than the speed of the boat herself. I had to chase individual grains down the grooves with a small hand brush, an exercise in extreme patience that I performed stoically, listening to some good music on high volume as I moved methodically across the deck, one tile at a time.

9

Denise wore a Viking helmet she'd made out of tinfoil. Standing on the foredeck of the *Rainbow Warrior* we cracked open a bottle of cheap champagne. It was 2 May 1978, and Tower Bridge was slowly opening up in front of us, giving us passage to the North Sea. It had been an absolutely crazy year, one that had passed in a haze of rust and paint, of welding and metal-cutting, as we removed the trawl gear and installed a hydraulic crane on the top deck for launching inflatable craft. Charles had scoured the country, if not the world, for second-hand parts for everything. We were all absolutely buggered. The chipping gun had been going day and night, Chris working his way around the boat, hours at a time without a break. He would collapse into his bunk at night, still in his overalls, covered in small flakes of rust.

A man called Nick Hill had replied to an advertisement Denise had placed in a maritime-union newspaper asking for professional crew. He was a certified foreign-going ship's master and had experience of Antarctic waters. Our first mate was another professional seaman — Alaistair Hamilton. I had an uneasy feeling about him — he seemed to like things very structured. Four other professional seamen also volunteered their services: Pete Bouquet, second mate; Dutchman Simon Hollander, chief engineer; Tim Mark, second engineer; and Terry Tandler, electrical engineer. Simon clashed with Charles, who had assumed the role of third engineer, over his endless shopping around for second-hand parts. Simon couldn't understand our penny-pinching ways and was easily frustrated. At sea, Terry was replaced by a young Swiss — Stefan Akermann. Athel joined as outboards engineer and Chris as leading hand, while David, Allan, Remi and a South African cameraman called Tony Marriner ranked as deckhands.

Hilari's 17-page letter outlining her reasons for wanting to join the campaign had touched everyone in the office, but it was her skill and experience cooking vegetarian meals at Food for Thought, a well-known London restaurant, that secured her position. She was also minister of cultural affairs in the newly declared Republic of Frestonia, between Shepherd's Bush and Latimer Road, in west London. The republic's territory comprised row of squats on Freston Road. At the time, it was council policy to rehouse families, not individuals, so all the inhabitants of Frestonia shared the surname Bramley, their motto being *Nos summus una familia* — 'We are all one family.' International media had swamped the republic, the story captivating the imagination of people around the world. Visitors would present their passports on entering Frestonia and have them stamped as at any other country's border.

Hilari lived in some old tearooms — the Champion Dining Rooms. Visiting her there was one of my treats. I immediately warmed to this expansive woman with hennaed hair. She spoke poetically, in metaphors, and surrounded herself with art, and I sensed she would bring a touch of earth mother to the boat — the wise one, the seer.

Denise and I joined the crew as stewardess and cook respectively. Our official photographer was Frenchman Jean-Paul Ferrero, and along the way we were to pick up two more Dutchmen — marine biologist Pieter Lagendijk and an Icelandic-speaker called Eric Mehtenbroek — Greenpeace cameraman Fred Easton, a nurse — Sally Austin — and various members of the press for good measure. For the time being, for our maiden voyage out of the London docks, we were 17 people, representing eight nationalities.

Bob Hunter jumped onto the foredeck of the slow-moving vessel as we made our way past a small bridge. He'd flown into Heathrow, wanting to congratulate us and wish us bon voyage, and had raced across London from the airport. Unable to wait because of the tide, we'd left without him, but he'd caught up with us further down the river. I was glad to see him. After all, this was the first boat Greenpeace actually owned and we wouldn't have been able to get as far as we had without the dramatic film footage of inflatables confronting the Russian whaling fleet. He came below to the small cabin Chris and I were sharing. We'd moved into the 'cook and boy' berth to make room for Hilari in the cabin opposite the galley, and no longer had the luxury of a sink or porthole. I was distressed at spending so little time with Chris. The romance of our first night together was still there, but had been well stowed for the time being while we got the show on the road — or, should I say, the high seas.

'Make a note of everything that happens, Susi,' Bob advised. 'This is history in the making, and it needs to be recorded as accurately as possible. Your job is that of chronicler.'

I felt a sense of pride that this founding member of Greenpeace had given me such an important job. In hindsight, I can see he was far more astute about human nature than I was at the time, recognising the potential in some to reinvent history for the purpose of self-aggrandisement. Call it stupidity or naivety, but I believed in the good intention of everyone — I think most of us did. Why else would people have given up their time and energies to be part of such a crazy plan? We had absolutely no idea how we'd find the whalers; we didn't even know if the boat would leave the basin, let alone reach the North Atlantic.

'We did it! We fucking did it! We told those fuckers we'd do it, and we did,' I said. We raised our plastic mugs of champagne in celebration; we were going to let it all hang out.

I gazed up at Tower Bridge as we motored through, marvelling at the ingenuity of its construction, the operation of its moving parts. People lined the embankment and bridges, standing on benches and railings, cheering us on.

'I bet the pilot thinks we're a bunch of loonies,' Charles said, as he and Allan climbed up the metal steps to join us. I turned around, leaning against the bulkhead, and looked back at the ship's bridge. I waved. The official-looking man at the wheel didn't react. Oh well. Everything had been newly painted, even the fo'c'sle. It was nice to have fresh air blowing through us, clearing all the metallic dust out of our lungs. Chris was back on the lower deck, tidying up the lines.

We'd been next to a warship for a couple of days, and a press conference had been held on board the *Rainbow Warrior* to announce our Icelandic whale campaign. It had been fun chatting to the uniformed crew. We were so proud of what we'd achieved, and had worn tired grins from ear to ear as we showed the naval officers around. We were amazed we'd pulled it off in such a limited amount of time, and that the professional seamen with us hadn't abandoned ship. They were doing this without pay. Everyone was a volunteer.

After we'd spent more time on board, I would bitch about Simon's sloppy Dutch custard. It came in cartons, and he'd always leave one open on the mess table. On his way to and from the engine room, he'd pick it

134

up in his greasy hands, have a slurp and put it down again. Then, the moment there was a bit of Atlantic swell, it would fall off the table, spilling its contents onto the deck — sticky rivers of dark-yellow liquid that weren't easy to mop up. Finding his carton gone, Simon would fetch another, open it and leave it on the table again. I ask you. There were boxes and boxes of this stuff in the pantry — what was a girl to do? It was a study in anthropology, really. Our individual cultures would come to the fore in times of stress, and familiar food proved a great comforter.

Down below, some of us would smoke hash and throw the I Ching for guidance, cramming into one of the small cabins to sit on the bunks with our legs dangling over the side. We'd get metaphysical and make predictions about how we'd find the whalers. One day, Nick came looking for us to sign some official papers. We were sitting around debating the meaning of the latest hexagram we'd thrown when he knocked at the cabin door. I could see he looked surprised, maybe even shocked. The pungent smell of hash, mixed with incense, was everywhere. We tried to explain what we were doing — analysing our actions from an alternative perspective, talking with our guardian angels, finding out the best way of moving forward. Here was a man who was used to being guided through the ocean by radar, charts, sextant, maybe even satellite. And we'd be directing him using a Chinese oracle thousands of years old. I made sure I had a couple of moments alone with him later, just to chat and sound him out — to make sure he was really 'on board' and not having second thoughts about being our captain. He certainly seemed to care a lot about declining whale populations, like many in the merchant navy we'd met, or who'd written to us or phoned to say they were seeing fewer and fewer whales at sea.

I hoped I'd be able to prove myself a reliable crew member. I wanted to contribute on board and be an able-bodied seawoman, not a cook or a stewardess, but was having problems convincing Chris. 'Sheilas belong in the galley,' he'd said one day, not realising how far out he was sticking his neck with such a sexist statement. I'd done some work on deck in port, chipped a bit of rust and done some painting. I wanted to learn everything there was to know about being at sea — the terminology, how to work the lines, how to make things fast, how to belay and weigh the anchor. The names of things had an ancient ring; they belonged to generations of seafaring people and were spoken with great respect, as if their use automatically incurred a sense of honour on the speaker. I liked to work with Charles, who knew more than I did about things nautical and was very patient. Chris was such a perfectionist. He didn't want anyone messing up his beautiful boat; she was the product of his sweat and tears, his raw lungs, his lacerated hands, his destroyed sinuses. Allan and Charles were feminists and behaved like sensitive new age guys, years before their time. They both cringed in solidarity when Chris came out with his role-defining statements.

'She doesn't seem to be having too much trouble getting some life back in her,' Charles said, referring to the smooth motoring we were enjoying as we moved slowly out of London towards the Thames estuary. All those second-hand parts had been taken to pieces, cleaned and put back together nicely lubricated, many of them by Charles and Athel. There had been something quite handsome about the individual bits of machinery littering the decks, on carpets of newspaper, as they were routinely overhauled. Now they had come to life, working in unison, the whole mysteriously greater than the sum of its parts. There was a sense of confidence about the boat as she parted the water with her prow, anxious to get out to the swell she'd been built to accommodate, to contain it within her thighs like a lover.

Finding us barefoot on deck, first mate Alaistair yelled at us. He insisted we wear proper footwear at all times — steel-capped boots, like his. He showed me one night, when we were on watch together, how far forward he could lean, holding onto his mug of tea, taking advantage of the swell. He was like a limbo dancer in reverse. He held his breath and went very red, trying to get as close to the deck as possible without spilling a drop. He'd been dining out on that stunt for a while, I imagined, and would have some stories to tell after this campaign. I felt sorry for the man, though. By then he'd given up trying to instil any form of discipline in us — we just ignored his barking. Perhaps he would have felt happier if we'd worn uniforms, saluted and shot back a crisp 'Aye aye, sir!'

The pilot had disembarked — relieved, no doubt. We were now entirely under our own steam, the sun was setting and we'd had far too much champagne. 'Bugger! I forgot I'm on watch early. Better get some shut-eye,' I said, and left the party.

'Grub-bottom. Wake up.' It was Chris's voice. He'd taken to calling me Grub-bottom after I'd sat on a patch of wet paint. I heard him repeat something about hands and cocks and socks — an Australian ditty — as I spiralled back into consciousness. I'd been given the 4.00–8.00 a.m.

watch, just after his. My heart had sunk when I'd seen the roster. The timetabling would mean the death of our relationship — we'd never be together. Just grin and bear it, I'd told myself, we'll make up for lost time somewhere down the line. I clambered up to the bridge, nervously clutching a mug of coffee and rubbing the sleep from my eyes. I sensed something special as I opened the door quietly.

'Morning everyone,' I said, trying to sound confident and professional. It was dark on the bridge, only the green glow from the radar and the small lights blinking in the distance visible at first glance, with the sound of the ship's radio cutting in every now and then. I could make out the outline of figures leaning against the bulkheads, looking through binoculars. An instruction would be given to the person holding the large wheel, who'd make a slight change of course, then steady as she goes. As I stood by the wheel, waiting to take it, I looked at the compass in front, watching as it veered slightly off course with the ebb and flow of the swell. I couldn't wait to grab the wheel and hold our ship to her course as I watched the sun rise, to keep my hands on the warm wood for hours at a time. Everyone spoke in subdued tones. We were the eyes of the boat, we needed to be vigilant; this wasn't a place for animated chitchat. It would be from here that we would sight our first whale — hopefully, before we came across our first whaler.

We made our way from one north European port to the next — for press conferences, for David to strut his stuff, for the crew to have a break. The sense of camaraderie grew daily as routines were established and the boat was thoroughly shaken down. We dropped in on an antinuclear demonstration in Scotland, where David was stoned and made a stupid speech. 'Wish he'd shut his gob,' I said to no one in particular as we listened to him over the PA system. He was trying to be cool, to be hip — we knew that — but I thought it undermined the dignity of what we were trying to achieve when he got too loose. And we were all fed up with his 'Can anybody lend me some money so I can buy you a drink?' — it had done its dash.

When we arrived in Hamburg, a huge team of people was waiting. A concert had been organised — by whom I'm not sure — and a famous German jazz pianist played on deck, with an audience of several hundred seated around the boat and on the wharf. The piano had been lowered on deck by crane, and spotlights put up among the rigging. At the party afterwards, the 'in' crowd gathered onboard to socialise, drink expensive champagne and mingle with the crew and musicians. It was our first taste of what would become a way of life, juggling public space with private.

We felt very out of place in our ripped and diesel-scented clothing and — a few of us — our wooden clogs, or *klompen*, purchased in Amsterdam. On the metal deck, *klompen* drove those below to distraction. We'd also bought ourselves some blue padded jackets with a fleecy lining, some wet-weather gear and some dry suits. Those of us selected as crew for the inflatables had custom-made suits. We practised getting in and out of them against the clock at a moment's notice, flinging our clogs to one side and catching our pubic hairs in the thick zips when we moved too fast. It was pretty obvious who the *Rainbow Warrior* crew were when you looked around the elite gathered in Hamburg — if you could spot them, that was, hiding behind some bulkhead or other. Some of the hired crew went ashore to visit the clubs for which the city is famous, scrubbed up and in their Sunday best. They had a look of excited anticipation on their faces, bordering on the lecherous, as they psyched themselves up.

Things had become very confusing in the final weeks in London as word of our proposed voyage had spread. I was still spending most of my days in the office, tidying up loose ends and moving my stuff out of the house in Stratford into storage at home in Northwood. A young woman called Susie Brandes had joined us in Whitehall. She was researching the use of jojoba, and promoting it as a substitute for whale products used in the cosmetics industry. She, Joni and Pete Wilkinson were to staff the office while we were at sea, holding the fort until our return.

A benefit concert had been planned in a small town just south of London. A local band called Dire Straits was playing, and we were going to be given the concert takings. 'I can't understand people who steal from the poor,' I said to Charles later, fuming, when it was discovered impostors had claimed the money the week after the gig. 'But you came and collected it,' the guy said to me when I phoned several weeks later, wondering when the cheque would arrive. When I asked him to describe the people, he said there had been about five in all. 'The men had beards, the chicks long hair — everyone in overhauls.'

A year later I was walking along Portobello Road with Hilari. We passed a young man pontificating from a soapbox and I caught the words 'Athel' and '*Rainbow Warrior*'. I was keen to hear what was being said about us. A small group of people had surrounded the speaker, and some had thrown money into a hat he'd put on the ground in front of him. 'And I says to fellow engineer Athel, I says open up the throttle, mate, give her your best. And as we zoom up towards the whaler . . .' He was working the audience with his body language and expressive tone. He was good! 'Just as we're putting ourselves in the firing line of the harpoon, I see the whale, and she's covered in blood . . .'

'Have you ever seen this guy on the boat?' I asked Hilari as we stood in the crowd listening to his stories of our recent exploits in Iceland.

'Never seen him in my life,' she replied.

'He was raking it in,' I told Denise later. It was bizarre. I felt hurt that people would rip us off by pretending to be us, or to have been with us at sea. They were stealing a part of our history for personal gain.

Most of us were very glad when the European tour ended in Norway and we could finally head for Iceland. It felt as if we'd been on the road forever, never at sea for long before the next port, the next media crowd, more parties.

David had already moaned about the women on board; we numbered four after Sally joined. We stood accused of being bouncers, of censuring the women of the night who tried to sneak on board in the early hours of the morning to tiptoe from cabin to cabin, plying their wares. We were told we were preventing the male crew from getting their rocks off. A different port, a different chick — they were in demand. This was David's take, of course, and he did tend to exaggerate. It wasn't only sex workers or groupies who found their way into the berths, journalists would also do the rounds — musical bunks we called it. 'Oh, but they're all so sweet!' one woman reporter exclaimed when sharing stories with the women crew of her on-board trysts.

I sat in a pub in Lerwick wearing my poncho from Jujuy. We were watching Argentina play England for the World Cup on the telly, and of course I was rooting for Argentina. In hindsight I realise this was a bit cheeky. Even though ownership of the Falkland Islands at that time was more of an issue for ordinary Argentinians than for their British counterparts, and the Falklands War still lay in the future, passions ran high on such occasions. Like my mother, I always made a point of calling the islands Las Malvinas, adding — as she did — 'They're ours, you know.'

'I'm surprised you didn't get lynched and cause a right argy-bargy wearing that get-up,' Athel said when we had returned to the ship.

We headed for the Faroe Islands the next day, with a full tank of fuel and a larder stocked with fresh produce. One of the tasks before us was to register David as the master of the *Rainbow Warrior* in the Shetlands. Nick was feeling somewhat antsy that he might lose his licence for endangering the boat and crew should we be taken to court. I think it had finally dawned on him that we were serious about our intentions to disrupt the whalers' activities and would be risking our lives. Those of us assigned to the Zodiacs had begun some rigorous training while at sea — a welcome respite from the seasickness many of us were now suffering. Remi and I were already competing for space on the seats in the mess; they were a good place to curl up when you were feeling frightful but didn't want to miss a minute of the excitement.

One evening, the Zodiac I was in became lost in heavy fog when the engine broke down. Our walky-talkies didn't seem to work when we were out of sight of the *Warrior*. All we could do was float, bobbing around like a rubber ducky, waiting, listening. We set off a couple of flares as David became increasingly paranoid, whether as a result our collective mechanical incompetence or because the fog made him feel claustrophobic I don't know. I knew we'd be found. It was just a matter of not losing faith. He seemed relieved when a familiar bow appeared out of the mist, almost running us down.

Alaistair had taken to his cabin and we hadn't seen him in days. 'Do you think he's all right?' I asked Denise. 'He was acting pretty strange last we saw him. Did you see him sprinkle salt on that daisy in the mess vase before he popped it in his mouth?' I was trying hard not to laugh. The poor guy was probably having a nervous breakdown, our antics having finally driven him over the edge. I banged on the bulkhead adjoining his cabin.

'Are you all right in there?' I asked. A muffled voice answered. Something about the Cod War and a score he had to settle with Iceland on behalf of the Royal Navy. Sounded complicated.

He didn't turn to wave goodbye as the Zodiac sped off towards the coast. He'd left his cabin quietly, carrying his bags, when told his services were no longer needed and that we would drop him off as near to an airport as possible. He could fly home and get some professional help, talk with someone about it all. I can't say I blamed him.

A coastguard plane had been sent out each day to report our position, but we hadn't managed to crack the code the four whaling vessels we were hunting used to report back to the whaling station, and had very little idea where they were. Our radar needed some spare parts, so we anchored half a mile out of Reykjavik in the diffused light of a midsummer's night, the stony landscape stark against an indigo sky. Hilari and I were dropped ashore to buy supplies, and I noticed how beautiful the local women were, with their wild and passionate eyes. I passed this on to Athel when we returned to the *Warrior*, a dozen limp lettuces in our baskets. They won't go far, I reflected; it'll be tinned food for the next few weeks.

By now it was early June and we had only three weeks before the IWC was due to meet in London. We needed to find the whalers. We spent the night singing sea shanties from county Cork with the crew of a classy yacht — the *Spirit of Labrador* — but soon had to resume our watches, scanning the horizon for a whaler's crow's-nest.

We headed north, to the west of Iceland, with the majestic Atlantic Ocean breaking over us, mountains of icy water crashing on the foredeck. I stood in wonder on the bridge, watching as the *Warrior* skilfully cut her way through, working with — not agin — the swell. Steering her in the tough weather of those quasi-Arctic latitudes was both exhilarating and challenging. I'd found my sea legs at last and was revelling in the adrenaline-pumping, on-the-edge-of-your-seat stuff that was going on.

We knew the catcher boats were much faster and far more manoeuvrable than the *Warrior*. We'd tried following one after we'd spotted it carrying dead finbacks to the whaling station, and it had disappeared in front of our eyes. The sight of dead whales being dragged through the water and up a ramp to be flensed affected us immensely. I spent days trying to scrub the stench from the ship, from myself, from my mind. It was awful.

What we had managed to do by now, however, as we were being shown round the whaling station by Thordur Asgiersson, the manager, was photograph the whalers' secret code in the radio room. As Eric analysed it, he remained glued to our set, finally managing to get a direct fix on all four whalers' communications with the station, at two-hourly intervals, with details of whales caught and expected arrival times. He called it 'The Catcher Show'. We had another plan up our sleeve as well, a way of tracking the whalers down by marking off a grid, from south to north, as we methodically patrolled a couple of hundred thousand square miles of ocean.

♥

Pete squatted on the deck of the cabin, untangling the long red hair beneath his navy-blue beanie. 'It's just not working, folks,' he said with a hint of desperation. 'We're not going to find them in time. Nick thinks we should consult the I Ching before we change course again.'

For days, perhaps weeks, we'd been on patrol in a perpetual twilight zone of grey sky and grey ocean. I'd spent much time on the top deck, bundled up in a sleeping bag, straining my eyes, staring at the horizon, looking for the whale killers. Here at the top of the world, in the curved space of the aurora borealis, it was hard to tell where ocean ended and sky began.

I'd been feeling immensely melancholic since seeing the huge limp carcasses being torn apart at the whaling station. Their innards had been blown apart a day or so before, and the bay had become filled with blood as their lacerated skins had released the pent-up destruction inside with a hiss and the pervading stench of death. We'd all been very quiet for several days afterwards, keeping to ourselves, trying to process what we'd seen in our individual ways.

Following Alaistair's departure, Channel Islander Jon Castle had flown in to Reykjavik to take over as first mate, and his easy-going manner made for a much smoother running of the boat. Jon was also a professional seaman, with a skipper's ticket like Nick. David found it quite strange that Jon insisted on being rostered for galley work when he wasn't required on the bridge, and was a bit suspicious of his egalitarian ways.

Pete looked at us. 'We'll run out of diesel soon if we're not careful. We've already covered nearly three thousand miles of ocean.'

Hilari's voice cut in. She sounded hopeful. 'Let's see what the I Ching says.'

Somewhere, on a scrap of paper, there is a written record of the hexagram thrown that mid-June evening near the Arctic Circle. First there was: 'Hsu/Waiting. Strength in the face of danger does not plunge ahead but bides its time, whereas weakness in the face of danger grows agitated and has not the patience to wait. If you are sincere, you have light and success. Perseverance brings good fortune. It furthers one to cross the great water.' The moving lines — nine in the first place — 'the danger is not yet close . . . yet there is a feeling of something impending' — six in the fourth place — 'bloodshed seems imminent' — and six at the top — 'the waiting is over; the danger can no longer be averted' — changed the hexagram to 'Kou/Coming to Meet'.

The media on board noticed there hadn't been an alteration in the ship's course as expected — we'd been proceeding in long straight lines for ages, the sun's position always predictable — and they were getting impatient for their footage.

'Found the whalers, have you?' a soundman asked sarcastically as I passed the mess.

'It furthers one to cross the great water,' I answered cryptically. 'We aren't changing course as planned.'

They looked fed up. I couldn't bring myself to tell them we weren't altering course on the advice of a hexagram, but hey, crossing the great water was as good a direction as any. We had little to lose.

Hvalur 9 appeared on the horizon, her angled body cutting into the backdrop of sky like the steel killing machine she was. She was dragging one dead finback and chasing another, which had slowed down and was now swimming in circles, sounding frequently. You could sense the animal's anguish. The whaling boat seemed to be toying with it. We could see the harpooner waiting for the signal to climb the steps to the gun. He was chewing gum. It was all very macho, very testosterone. We'd arrived at the killing fields; slaughter was in the air. The funny thing was that no sooner had we decided not to alter course, as we'd previously planned to do before consulting the I Ching, than we found the whaler. Just like that. Some say a few dolphins and a rainbow appeared just beforehand. Be that as it may, there was no time to contemplate the mystical — focused action was needed. It was into the eye of the storm. David didn't want to discuss it with the crew — he wanted an executive decision. 'This ain't no time for democracy,' I heard him shouting as we charged to the changing room and scrabbled around for our gear.

I'd become quite good at jumping into our little rubber boats and was feeling fairly confident about being part of an inflatable crew. However, although we all knew the dangers of what we were doing, nothing — but nothing — could have prepared us for the real thing. It was our first taste of driving the small craft at speed in such rough conditions. To give you an idea of what it was like — the force from the impact of a rigid-hull inflatable travelling at high speed against a 5-metre swell cracked the metal casing of the gearbox in the centre of the boat. Imagine the effect on soft tissue, over and over again. You wouldn't wish it on your worst enemy, believe me.

We knew the catcher boat would have to return to the whaling station within 30 hours of having caught the whale lashed to its bulkhead, otherwise the meat would spoil, and that the trip would take around 12 hours. We calculated that if we could keep the harpooner from taking aim for 18 hours or so, the boat would then have to leave to make it back in time.

Pete was driving the Zodiac I'd been assigned to, and I tried to take a photo of him, water collapsing all over us, as we churned through the sea at ridiculous speeds. I caught the eye of a *Hvalur 9* deckhand. He was yelling something in Icelandic, spitting and throwing his lit cigarette at us. Someone else chucked some tomatoes — what a waste, I thought, we'd seen few fresh vegetables in weeks.

We took it in turns, careering back and forth between the *Warrior* and the whaler, an inflatable always in front of the harpoon, the whale to one side. No matter how hard he tried, the harpooner couldn't get the aim he needed. Once I saw him throw his hat on the deck out of sheer frustration before giving us the fingers as he retreated down the narrow catwalk. To and fro we went, all night and all the next day. Chris was out there the whole time, positioned in front of the harpoon like a pilot fish on a shark; his was the constant presence, he never gave up. We'd bring him fuel and food at four-hourly intervals. David was fussing about him like a mother hen; he wanted me to go and persuade him to return to the *Warrior*, to tell him someone else would take his place.

I was feeling slightly concussed as I wandered around the boat trying to get myself back into an inflatable. Earlier, Jon had helped lift me out of the Zodiac; my brain hadn't been connecting with my body at the time so I hadn't been able to give him a hand. I'd become this limp, wet doll flopping over the gunwales, landing in a heap on the deck. I'd been taken to a cabin and plied with Jon's famous medicinal whisky, an excellent aged drop. 'I remember smashing into the deck of the Zodiac with my head,' I'd said, trying to lift myself onto my forearms, feeling the mellow warmth of the nip caress the inside of my stomach. I could remember people helping me out of my wet-weather gear, as if in a dream, and helping me into my yellow overalls. I had been given one of the cabins with portholes — just until I recovered. Then it was back to the front line again.

At one stage I was watching Chris from the bridge, with David. I saw him lunge out with his knife when the chain attached to the harpoon came crashing down onto the Zodiac. David was livid. How could Chris have a knife? We were supposed to be nonviolent.

It's not much fun being in the water near a whale fighting for its life, an explosive harpoon ripping open its guts. Instead of that life-affirming spout of water from the blowhole, a fountain of blood and gore rains down like hail, the whale whips the water with its tail, rising and sinking, and everything moves in a whirlpool of frenzy. When the *Warrior* visited Icelandic waters the following year, the second time round, the crew witnessed the most violent killing of a finback. A Welshman who had joined the crew — Welsh John, we called him — described it to me when they had returned to port. Chris' long hair had been dripping with whale gobbets. A journalist desperate for the story was banging on our cabin door. Welsh Jon and I were sharing the berth opposite the galley at the time, as Chris had left to do some undercover work in Spain. Welsh John refused to come out and meet the journalist — he was still shell-shocked and didn't want to talk. No one did. How do you describe something like that? The whale had taken 15 minutes to die.

'We need to find a place where our veterans can go and recover from their experiences on the front line,' David said to me afterwards. 'A small farm in Tuscany or somewhere in Greece. What's Samos like?'

I'd been dreaming of returning to Samos with Chris, of incredible sex under the Aegean sky — anything to keep my mind off the endless bashing and jarring in the inflatables.

Hvalur 9 had returned to the station, its hunting endeavours fruitless as long as we were around. The whale we had been protecting had slowly gained enough energy to slip off quietly into the distance. We had returned to Reykjavik for a press conference amidst grumbles from a few of the crew, who would have preferred to continue patrolling the ocean in case another whaler appeared. A public debate was organised between the owner of the whaling station, Mr Loeftsson, who was due to represent Iceland at the IWC, and ourselves, with Remi and Allan putting our case. Allan — the debate had been his idea — was cool, calm and brilliant. There can be no quotas, he argued in front of a huge gathering of Icelandic people, because the IWC admits it has no idea how many whales are out there.

'It is a question of moral responsibility.' An Icelandic man in the audience had stood up, and in an impassioned voice he made a very moving speech about protecting the finbacks for generations to come. Mr Loeftsson remained unconvinced, reiterating that our actions against his whaling operation inside Iceland's Exclusive Economic Zone (EEZ) had been illegal. I wondered if he'd conveniently forgotten Iceland had voted for a 10-year moratorium on pelagic whaling at the Stockholm Conference in 1972.

I'd been impressed by a story I'd heard about a road being built through the centre of Iceland. A pile of sacred boulders had been moved to make way for it, and all the chickens in the country had immediately stopped laying eggs. When the stones had been returned to their original site, the chickens had started laying again. The innate spirituality of the land was reflected in the generosity of the debate that day. Remi and Allan were on one side of the stage, Mr Loeftsson, nervously stroking his beard, sat at a table on the other side, while David, in the middle of the front row, kept his beady eye on everyone.

'Head for the sun,' Jon Castle said when I asked him for a course as we pulled out of Reykjavik Harbour. I was at the wheel and this was his first watch as master since taking over from Nick. My last glimpse of Nick had been in Reykjavik as he was being driven ashore to catch a plane; he needed to return to paid employment. His hair had grown shaggy and he hadn't shaved in days. Someone had given him a string of beads, which he was wearing doubled up around his neck. He'd become one of us, had given us unconditional loyalty, and I loved him for it. He seemed quite weary — he probably hadn't slept in weeks. Pete was now first mate. Another friend, Ken Ballard, was due to join us soon, but for the time being we'd run the ship with minimal crew, taking her back home slowly, down the west coast of Scotland to Dublin and then to Falmouth. Alaistair had shown us how to spell 'Fuck whalers' with our signal flags, and we flew them brazenly as we returned to the trees and stars of the lower latitudes.

The *Warrior* had taken on a poetic, Celtic feel under Jon's warm guidance. He was the archetypal gentleman outlaw with exquisite ocean-going manners, as behove a master mariner. He'd followed the sun himself throughout his life, walking the path of light; he had that look in his eyes. Hilari and he became especially close, seeking out each other's company when they weren't on watch or in the galley. We all shared a love of literature, music and poetry — the ship was developing a courtly air.

'Here,' Jon said, taking the wheel from my hand, 'let's do a little dance of departure. It'll fuck with their heads down below but who cares.'

The *Warrior* pirouetted a few times as he guided her in ever-increasing circles out of the Reykjavik harbour. I popped my head into the captain's cabin, now doubling as an office, to reassure David, Denise, Allan and Charles that things were fine up on the bridge, it was just something Jon needed to do.

'Sure we can trust this guy?' David asked, looking over his glasses at me like a concerned father.

'Absolutely,' I replied.

10

The Galicians had been killing whales off the coast of northwest Spain since the eighth century so it might have been somewhat presumptuous of us to bowl on up to the Masso Company's two processing stations south of La Coruña and tell them to stop. Masso's four whaling boats were killing up to 200 finbacks every year. The owner of the company — Juan Masso — admitted killing protected species such as the humpback and the blue, and couldn't see any reason why he shouldn't. In the mid-1970s, however, his company had been forced to cut back its operation, close two of its four stations and withdraw four whaling boats. The whale stocks were rapidly becoming depleted and now business wasn't so good. As Spain didn't have a seat on the IWC, few people were aware of what was happening off its coast. We wanted to find out, so we sent Chris to keep a watch on both whaling stations and track the number and species of whales being brought in.

Both Denise and I had decided to leave the *Rainbow Warrior* once we got to Falmouth, in Cornwall. Denise was needed back in the office and things had become increasingly strained between Chris and me. There just wasn't time for a relationship and we were both exhausted. We'd endured months of round-the-clock activity with no more than a few seconds of intimacy before I'd have to go on watch or he'd be summoned to attend to some problem. I confided in Hilari and Jon when we were in Dublin.

'Best to get off the boat and go and have a think,' Jon suggested. He was very practical about these things. 'One small step at a time,' he counselled. 'Arrange to meet up on Samos.'

'He'll never come,' I said. 'He's far too involved now. He's become a radical.'

Hilari promised to keep an eye on Chris, saying she'd keep him company in the 'cook and boy' cabin even though it meant losing a porthole on the world. I'd miss listening to them teasing each other.

The original plan, the one formulated in the Whitehall office, had been that we'd go to France after Iceland and announce a campaign against the dumping of heavy metals and chemicals in the Mediterranean. But Pete Wilkinson had been sniffing around Sharpness, on the upper Severn estuary, in Gloucestershire, and discovered a boat being loaded with barrels of radioactive waste to be dumped in international waters off the coast of Land's End, the southwest tip of England. We'd puzzled at the 'dumping grounds' marked on our marine chart as we'd rounded this extremity, and now we knew what was being dumped there — 5000 barrels filled with radioactive waste. We also knew what the prognosis was likely to be once the barrels rusted — radioactive pollution of the ocean with stuff that could have a half-life of 25,000 years. Even worse, no one knew; it was being done in secret.

Allan, with Fred and Tony, our two cameramen, left immediately for Sharpness. Posing as a television crew they managed to film the waste being loaded onto the ship — the *Gem* — and interviewed a few of the young crew as well. The Scottish captain had been to the dumping ground 36 times. Multiply that by 5000 barrels and you get the picture.

It didn't take much to persuade the crew of the *Rainbow Warrior*, now under the alternating captaincies of Pete Bouquet, affectionately known as Cap'n Bogey, and Jon Castle, to return to the high seas and intercept the *Gem*. The plan was to try to catch a barrel of waste and show the world what was going on behind everyone's backs. Hilari and Chris were the first to arrive at the dumping ground after a bumpy seven-mile ride in their Zodiac, which destroyed Hilari's camera. The crew of the *Gem*, too young to know better, perhaps even oblivious to the fact that they had blue radiation detector buttons pinned to their clothing, were dumping two barrels of waste at a time from four derricks. One barrel had lost its lid but no attempt was made to fit it back on. This was scary stuff. The other three Zodiacs caught up and, after several attempts, Athel managed to catch a barrel in his boat. The inflatable snapped in two and Athel was rudely tossed into the air — it made for great television. The Atomic Energy Authority had a lot of explaining to do — everyone wanted to know what was in those barrels.

'I've met the man I want to marry,' I announced to my mother as she opened the front door. I hadn't told her I was coming; it was all very last minute.

'I'm so glad to see you are all right,' she said, giving me a hug. 'I heard the woman on television say someone had been knocked out in Iceland. I knew it would be you.'

I'd slipped off the boat without saying goodbye to everyone and taken a train. Chris and I had made a vague plan to meet on Samos. 'Tell me where, tell me when, and I'll be there,' he'd said. I didn't believe him. I'd given him the name of a tiny mountain village in the middle of the island and three consecutive dates on which to meet at noon in the main square, then left. I'd booked a bus ticket to Samos in London before going home, and dropped in to the new Greenpeace office, near Blackfriars Bridge.

Perhaps I was being oversensitive, but I was starting to feel extremely uneasy about the direction the organisation was taking, with all the marketing, merchandise and trademarking. I remember seeing a large moneybox shaped like a native American's head on someone's desk — someone I'd never met before. Was this for donations for the *Rainbow Warrior* or a prototype *Rainbow Warrior* moneybox, I wondered? Either way, the vulgarity and inappropriateness of it shocked me; whoever these new people were, I thought, they were into the money side of things — big time.

I slept all the way to Samos, opening my eyes every now and then on buses and boats to make sure I was still following the right road and crossing the right sea. I knew the route well by now, and where to catch the ferry in Piraeus. When I saw the proud outline of Kerkis — the highest mountain in the Aegean — rising out of the early-morning mist, I knew I was on the home straight. The journey had given me time to reflect. I'd left England with a gut feeling that the original vision of the *Rainbow Warrior* was being irrevocably changed, that our 'box-office' appeal was dictating how we behaved, and that we were being marketed commercially to solicit major financial investment.

We'd survived Iceland but we hadn't stopped the whaling. That would take a few years. As well as all the high-powered action stuff, which was expensive, we needed to come up with a scientific model to determine the size of the whale stocks being hunted. Of this I had no doubt. This would prove the industry's point about quotas was totally invalid. It was obvious its figures were based on guesswork, random sightings of whales and the assumption that each whale sighted was a different animal.

Whales are migratory creatures, I reasoned; they move great distances. What if the same whales were being counted over and over again? No wonder some of the rarer species were having problems finding mates — there weren't many of them left. There must be some way of recognising individual animals in the ocean, I thought, drifting back to sleep as the old ferry to Samos belched black smoke and someone wiped up the goat shit on the deck. I had no idea at the time that on the other side of the Atlantic researchers at a small university had just started trying to distinguish humpback whales using their flukes as ID.

'What do you do, you know, in the real world?' We were coming into Karlovasi, Samos' small western port. An Englishman had been chatting to me for a while. He had the most beautifully sculpted face, and said he was a writer and part Yugoslavian.

'I'm a gardener,' I said, quickly, surprising myself. I'd had enough of being in the public eye; I was still raw from the whaling grounds. I wanted to go somewhere and just be me, to nourish myself with natural beauty. The most fertile island in Greece, Samos overflows with springs and forests and extraordinary people. Pythagoras was born there, and I'd spent many days and nights in the canyon at the foot of Kerkis, near Megalo Seitani, a magnificent beach several hours' hike from the nearest road, where he once sought refuge. Pythagorus was an eclectic to say the least: a Zoro-astrian sage guided by Apollo, a mathematician, a vegetarian, founder of numerology and the harmonic scale. He was chased all over Samos by the tyrant Policrates.

Mountain passes, in places cut out of the stone, zigzagged across the island's rugged backbone. I'd already walked most of them, sleeping in olive groves at night. At the foot of Kerkis, I could hear the hum in the reflection of sound in the enclosed stone canyon, and wondered if that was how Pythagoras had been inspired. It vibrated in perfect harmony. At night, the phosphorescence in the water would rise up like a ghostly veil above the bay. This was also the habitat of the most endangered seal in the world — the Aegean monk seal — a very shy creature and rarely seen.

Steve was still living on Samos with his wife. He'd joined the *Warrior* for part of the Icelandic campaign and then returned to the island. I slept on the ground in front of their one-room *kalivi*, much to the temptation of the local priest, who chased me around the whitewashed stone barn at every opportunity, trying to grab me from behind. The young English writer, Billy Johnson, had rented a place nearby, as had a Swiss woman, Rita Emch, who spoke fluent Samian. I explained to the locals I was waiting for my husband to arrive.

'Let's hope he's strong,' one of the village women said, trying to shift a heavy millstone. Most of the young people had left the island to find work or to study, or, in the case of many young men, because they had been conscripted. Turkey was less than a kilometre away and Greek soldiers were everywhere, driving their vehicles up and down the coastal road between Karlovasi and the town of Samos, trying to look important. There always seemed to be something going on between the two countries, even though a lot of the older people on the island had originally come across from Anatolia.

I showed the woman a photo of Chris. 'Get rid of the beard,' she told me, and then pointed to a small *kalivi* on the hill she said I could rent. It was right in the middle of a vineyard, overlooking the sea. An old peach tree shaded the front of the small building, which had been built into the side of the hill. I could pick the large yellow fruit from one of its branches while lying in bed. Fresh goat's-milk yoghurt was dropped off at dawn, in earthenware pots covered with muslin. For breakfast I sliced peaches and arranged them neatly over the yoghurt, then cracked open some walnuts a passer-by had left me. I sprinkled these on top of the peaches, then dribbled village honey over the whole lot. Bliss. There was a toilet — the long-drop variety — above a steep rise, a goat's-hair mat hanging in front of it to provide some privacy. Rita advised me to make sure there were no scorpions on the seat before I pulled my pants down.

I spent the days waiting for Chris walking along the coastal road to Aghios Konstantinos to buy bread, pick up the mail and chat with Billy and Rita in the central café as we watched the villagers ride their mules lazily past. The eccentricities of the individual characters in the village appealed to me; it was like being in the middle of a Marquez novel, in an archetypal village of the kind I'd seen in northern Jujuy. There was the man who dyed the ears of his giant white poodle a different colour every day, ambling in his old patched suit with his walking stick up and down the dusty road, going nowhere with such gentleness of purpose. There were the women who carried trays of baking to the central oven and swept the cobbled walkways, later covering them in whitewashed patterns, giggling as they gossiped. The older women would harangue Steve for washing his wife's underwear in the outside basin and hanging it on the line, screeching their disapproval. We tried to fit in by working with the locals in the fields. Rita's fluency in the language was invaluable. She was a trained nurse and used her car to transport the elderly to the doctor or the hospital. The old people would sit in the main square at night, under the plane trees. They were philosophers, debating the origin of life under a canopy of stars. Some wore turbans, and on cooler nights would rub their hands over copper braziers ablaze with coals.

I walked up the road to Vourliotes on the first appointed Saturday of Chris's and my reunion. I hadn't heard from Chris in weeks, not since I'd left the *Warrior*, and had no idea if he would show up or not at our designated meeting spot. I sat outside the small café on a brightly painted wooden seat. A couple of old men were swinging their worry beads back and forth, discussing what had happened when a bag of Parathion, an organophosphate, had accidentally been spilled into the village stream. A dog and a donkey had died from drinking the water, and a small child had been rushed to hospital after eating Parathion-sprayed cherries. I knew many of the farmers on Samos couldn't read and had no idea how dangerous the pesticide was — numerous deaths worldwide had already been attributed to it, and its use posed a grave threat to wildlife. In Sweden, 3000 black-headed gulls had been killed in one incident, while in the United States, over 65,000 red-winged blackbirds had died after one aerial spraying. News of the spill had travelled to our village as well and had been the topic of an impassioned debate in the *platia* the previous night. Everything had been growing perfectly for thousands of years, someone argued; why did they now need to use chemicals?

I waited until sunset for Chris, and returned home alone.

'Do you think he'll come?' I asked Billy and Rita.

'He'd be an idiot not to,' Billy replied. 'What better place to replenish his inspiration and strength?'

I'd gone to Vourliotes twice now, and had come back alone on both occasions. On the last of our three dates, I set out once again. Halfway to the village I stopped and sat down at the side of the road, feeling totally dejected. I knew he wasn't coming. I'd already decided I'd work on a project Allan had mentioned — a protection programme for the Aegean monk seal run by the International Union for Conservation of Nature and Natural Resources (IUCN). He'd asked me if I'd heard of a place called Megalo Seitani on Samos, a major breeding area for the seal. The

IUCN wanted to make it a marine reserve. How wonderful, I thought, that this most favourite place of mine was also home to this shy creature. Of course I knew Megalo Seitani, I told him.

I walked along the coastal road to the turn-off to Vourliotes with tears in my eyes. I'd been having problems organising my thoughts and the ping-ponging of ideas and feelings was driving me crazy. 'That's it,' I said to myself as I flopped down outside a café near the junction of the two roads, 'I give up.' I was hoping that if I surrendered to defeat my mind would settle and I'd be able to focus more clearly. I hated the way my emotions got the better of me.

'Meeting someone special?' the café owner asked, bringing me an ouzo on the house. I'd been repeatedly asking him the time, waiting for love's death knell to strike at noon as I chain-smoked.

'I don't know,' I replied, the words trailing off, my eyes following a scooter driving past. Something long and golden seemed to trail behind it. 'No,' I said absent-mindedly, trying to make sense of the passing blur, 'I'm not waiting for anyone.' A split-second image of the person riding pillion was wreaking havoc with my brain. Brown baggy shorts with a splattering of green paint, strong thighs gripping the seat — it was Chris. And now he'd gone. 'That's him!' I yelled, trying to figure out what to do. There was no way I'd be able to get to Vourliotes in time. He'd arrive there in about 10 minutes, on the dot of noon. I was miles away. He'd be gone by the time I got there. I stopped the first car that came past and asked the driver if he could drop me off as close to Vourliotes as possible. 'Emergency!' I panted. He was only going as far as the turn-off, but that was OK with me — I had to try everything to get there in time.

I raced up the road, running as fast as I could in my flimsy sandals, the cicadas, full throated, cheering me on, the grimacing trunks of the old olive trees wishing me well. I imagined the queen of the Olympian gods, Hera, whose monumental temple lay on the other side of the island, whispering in the wind as she created a magical back door I could use to get me to Vourliotes in time, some ancient underground passageway. I slowed down, lungs heaving from the effort of running, wheezing as I gasped for breath, hating myself for smoking. 'Come back!' I yelled as I staggered round a corner.

He was standing in the centre of the road, chewing on a long tuft of grass, his sweat-stained T-shirt tied around his waist. 'Grub-bottom. You know better than to yell in public,' he said softly. 'Sorry I'm a bit late.' He looked at his watch. 'It's five past twelve.'

We stayed in the café at Vourliotes until it closed. Chris wanted to see the place where we were meant to have met so we walked all the way up, stopping every now and then to indulge ourselves in some close bodily contact — it had been so long. 'Love is in the air tonight,' a village woman intoned musically as she walked past, grinning. When the café finally closed we ran down the stone steps, all the way to the coast. It would take a few hours to get back to my *kalivi* in the hills.

As we skimmed each step, our bodies moving in unison down the ancient pathway, I told Chris the story of one of the women who had been working in the surrounding vineyard and had seen my Victorian-lace petticoat hanging out to dry. She asked me if it was my wedding dress. 'I hope it'll be dry for our wedding night tonight, Grub-bottom,' he said, pinching my buttock. I felt a twinge of sadness. I knew he'd be gone soon, off again on another adventure. His outstanding skills as a Zodiac driver and *Warrior* crew member wouldn't be something Greenpeace would let go lightly. Would he be able to withstand the pressure of the lifestyle, I wondered?

'It's all your fault, Grub-bottom,' he mumbled as we lay beside each other on the four-poster bed in the early-morning light, the Victorian petticoat quickly abandoned after the first self-conscious moments of lovemaking. 'You got me with that poem by D.H. Lawrence, you sneak.' His eyes were closing, he was falling asleep.

'Aphrodite is the wife of whales most happy, happy she,' I recited, sotto voce, breathing the words into his ear, 'and Venus among the fishes skips and is a she-dolphin . . . dense with happy blood, dark rainbow bliss in the sea.'

I could hear the women in the fields starting their daily routine, and knew they would come and spy on us. I made sure our naked bodies were covered with a cotton sheet before falling asleep. Their children would climb the tree and arrange themselves like ripening fruit along the branches, looking in on us as we lay in deepest slumber.

After the successful interception of the *Gem* offloading its radioactive waste in international waters, the *Rainbow Warrior* had gone south to La Coruña and the Spanish whaling grounds. Joni had gone as Zodiac crew, and they'd successfully prevented one of Juan Masso's boats, the *Carrumeiro*, from killing a whale.

The *Warrior* circled the whaling boat for hour after hour in the hot sun. Sounds of humpback whales were played to the Spanish crew over loudspeakers on deck, attracting hundreds of dolphins to the area. During the night the Spanish navy sent out a frigate and a patrol boat to inform the *Warrior* of Spain's 200-mile EEZ and asked her to leave. *Por favor.* Hilari, favoured I Ching consultant, threw a hexagram showing retreat to be 'humiliating, youthful folly', so a unanimous decision was made to stay put. The following day the crew watched the whaler and the frigate pointlessly changing position, trying to figure out what to do. Cap'n Bogey amused himself with tapes of *The Goon Show*, and Hilari baked potato bread.

Two enormous finbacks surfaced, and the *Carrumeiro* took off, Zodiacs and navy ships in hot pursuit. The frigate cut across the *Warrior*'s bow, dangerously close. The harpooner — it was Spanish tradition that the captain fired the shot — was unable to take aim; several Zodiacs were in the way, and eventually he gave up. As we followed the whaler back to La Coruña, our signal flags read 'Thanks for your cooperation.'

An admiralty official, the harbourmaster and an interpreter boarded the *Warrior* just inside the breakwater, demanding that she'd be tied up alongside the *Carrumeiro*. 'Give us an hour to sort out our engine problems, *por favor*,' Pete said. 'And no, you can't use our radio to ask for further instructions.'

'Bugger this!' Cap'n Bogey retorted when the deputation had left to make its phone call. 'Weigh anchor!'

A spontaneous decision was made to leave and head for Portugal under cover of darkness. Hilari and Jon blacked out the ship, Simon cranked up the engines and the *Rainbow Warrior* clocked a maximum speed of 12 knots pulling out of the harbour — something of a record.

David flew in to the charming port of Viano de Castelo in Portugal to tell the crew the Mediterranean campaign was most definitely off — we were in debt to the tune of £18,000. We were also needed in Jersey, in the Channel Islands, where a small group of very wealthy Greenpeace supporters had organised a float for a flower carnival called the Battle of the Flowers. Hundreds of fresh blooms had been flown in from Covent Garden to make a replica whale and Kwakiutl totem.

Charles had finally left the *Rainbow Warrior*, heading to the United States to study human ecology at a small university in the Acadia National Park on Mount Desert Island, off the coast of Maine.

None of the crew felt particularly comfortable at the carnival, where they were photographed with tax-evading millionaires and a headline in the local paper read 'Crew of Greenpeace Ship Unpaid'. From Jersey the *Warrior* sailed to the Isle of Wight, then on to Calais, where Chris left to join me in Greece, and from Calais to Amsterdam, to David's baby — the Greenpeace Europe Conference.

True to the Jersey headline, some of the crew were absolutely broke by now. Instead of attending the conference's campaign-planning and budget-preparation meetings, Hilari and five other *Warrior* crew members left the ship at 3.00 a.m. every day to work in a gherkin factory in Ede, 60 miles from Amsterdam. Hilari's job was to stuff dill into jars of pickled gherkins as they rolled past her on the production line. Three days later she left the job 250 guilders richer. After the conference, the *Warrior* returned to the Isle of Wight and then visited the Southampton Boat Show, to strut her stuff as a private yacht. It was now mid-September 1978.

In early October, the British government announced its decision to cull half the grey seal population of the Orkney Islands, caving in to pressure from local fishermen, who said the seals were eating their fish. The usual story. The fact that the grey seal had been a protected species for over 60 years didn't seem to deter the government, and Norwegian seal hunters were called in to kill the mothers and their pups. The storm of protest following the *Warrior*'s campaign in the Orkneys was so huge it forced the government to call off the cull, and *Rainbow Warrior* became a household name overnight.

I returned from Samos, back to the 'cook and boy', replacing Hilari as cook, who in actual fact was irreplaceable — who else would have attempted lemon soufflé in a force 11 winter gale in the North Atlantic? Chris had started his overland journey back to Australia. One late summer's morning I'd waved goodbye as he left on the weekly ferry to Turkey. 'Keep your backside to the wall over there,' a young Greek friend had advised, pointing across the straits to Kusadasi. The women in the village had put Chris to good use, using him to move heavy stones and pick olives, and couldn't understand why he was leaving after only a few weeks. 'Are you getting divorced?' they asked.

Walking back onto the *Warrior*, to join a skeleton crew of old-timers, I felt I'd arrived home, as if I was slipping on a pair of old, comfortable slippers. The office kept details of our whereabouts totally secret from the general public, including our supporters, while we went into a much-needed winter hibernation.

The following year's work started with the first sortie of a lengthy campaign against the transport of spent nuclear-fuel rods to France and the UK for reprocessing. A ship with its lethal cargo was due to sail into Cherbourg, but we called the action off at the last moment because of the death on board of an engineer. The *Warrior* then sailed to Norway to prevent Norwegian sealing boats leaving for the slaughter of harp seals off the Canadian coast, and then back to London for an intensive refit to prepare her for a return to Iceland in May.

I'd been making bridle paths through the woods near Mum's Northwood home for the Hillingdon council. Athel had been working with me, having fun driving a quad over the rough terrain. It was soothing to be back among the trees of our childhood. Greenpeace internal politics had started to become unbearable. Everyone wanted a slice of the pie and people with huge egos had started to get involved. A song about the exploits of the *Rainbow Warrior* had even made it to no.1 in the Dutch hit parade.

'I don't want to be part of the organisation any more,' I said to Athel during a break. We were sitting on some exposed tree roots at the bottom of the wooded valley. 'All they do is fight over who was first, and who owns the name Greenpeace. This isn't what the *Warrior* is about, suing and countersuing each other, and power trips.'

It was already apparent that the *Rainbow Warrior* and Greenpeace represented two entirely different paradigms. One was based on a sacred yet radical belief system honouring Creation and universal understanding, in support of which people joined forces to protect the planet; the other was nourished by commercial enterprise and a desire for power while espousing a pseudosolidarity with the first, which seemed to me a very superficial perspective. The eager careerists didn't understand that the most significant changes to humanity were effected first within the individual, at the profoundest level. The *Rainbow Warrior* wasn't about empire-building, it was pure expression, a *cri de coeur*, a moment of catharsis, an exclamation of the people: we have had enough! I couldn't figure it out — where was the right to a livelihood in all of this, in all the bickering and squabbling over money? Someone had told me there was a plan to copyright the word 'rainbow'. Money can drive you crazy.

I'd decided to resign as a director of Greenpeace. I could sense a certain discomfort in Allan and Denise as well; things had been so much simpler when it had been just us. I would remain a volunteer crew member; after all, the *Warrior* was my home, had been since the day I'd first set foot on her. She was the place where I felt the most comfortable, where I could live with like-minded people. The tensions within the organisation were absent on the boat, where we seemed to operate on another wavelength, one of love and consideration. We grew telepathic — there was no need for endless discussion; we were a harmonious combination. The alternating skippers — Jon and Pete — didn't compete for territorial rights to the bridge or indulge in petty gossip about each other. Internal politics didn't exist on board the *Rainbow Warrior*.

I returned to Samos in the spring of 1979 with Chris. I was going to spend some time working on the monk seal campaign and hoped he would join our small team. I'd met him at Heathrow; we hadn't seen each other for several months, and had only spoken on the phone after he had finally arrived back home in Australia. I was terrified he would reject me. I knew he wanted to return to Iceland to continue the job we'd started there, and I knew he was needed. It was easier for me to trust in the legitimacy of what the *Warrior* was doing if I knew certain people were on board, and Chris was one of them. I'd become fiercely protective of the boat, its name and its image, and I was desperate to protect her from the hegemonic activities of Greenpeace the organisation, as opposed to Greenpeace the movement.

Before taking the bus to Samos we had stayed for a few days in Northwood. I had never shared my bed with a lover at my parent's home. My mother had always shooed my boyfriends off to the spare bedroom, and I felt coy about bringing Chris home and making love, with my mother in the next room. We'd have to choose our moments, I thought.

'He runs every morning,' Mum said at breakfast the first day. Chris had got up early, jet-lagged from his long-haul flight, donned some shorts and gone out for a jog. I knew she was eyeing him up. Having declared I'd met the man I wanted to marry, I knew she'd check him out good and proper. She'd often told me she was partial to dark-haired men, with curly hair, so Chris's blond Nordic looks wouldn't twang her thong. 'He's very tanned, isn't he?' she continued. 'Nice legs.'

Chris and I argued for most of the bus trip to Samos. I'd been in contact with Aboriginal activists in Australia and had been telling him about the distortion of history that had been going on there, and how white Australians ignored what was happening. Chris told me he'd never really spoken with an Aboriginal person, and I harangued him all the way to Athens with strident speeches about 'white guilt'. It was astounding to me that someone could grow up alongside another race of people, whose land they were in, and not even have a conversation with them. Perhaps it was because I'd come from a home where many nationalities, skin colours and religions had come through the front door. I was only beginning to appreciate that not everyone was brought up that way.

I'd decided long before that I'd never question Chris about fidelity — I refused to go there. If he'd had affairs when we were apart, they were his own business, but what I longed for, secretly, was the rock beneath the flower.

In May the Rainbow Warrior left for Iceland, via Great Yarmouth and the Orkneys, and Chris was back on board. We had parted — once again — at the port in Samos, in the early morning, after making love all night in a nearby pension, shutters open, our voices drifting across Vathi Bay. I walked around in circles for a while, processing the separation in my mind, until the sounds of Van Morrison drifting out of our newly acquired seal-project office, the old cafenion on the Aghios Konstantinos water-front, lifted me gently out of my melancholic state.

I immersed myself in the work with Billy and Rita, organising public meetings, touring the island, talking with officials. My photos of the *Rainbow Warrior* and the Spanish navy raised suspicions in a few people — the dangerous, poorly informed kind. I was hauled up in front of yet another overweight uniformed official to explain what we were doing there, with this so-called monk seal project. He made threatening gestures with his hand, showing me how I would have my throat cut if I didn't cooperate, as he sucked through his side teeth to dislodge a piece of meat, one foot up on a chair.

'It's part of the United Nations,' I tried to explain.

'The United who?' he had replied sarcastically. 'Who are they? Never heard of this *United Nations*.'

The monk seal was suspected of migrating between Samos and Turkey, but attempts to ascertain the migration route had fallen foul of the suspicious Greek authorities. When Billy and Rita had agreed to help, they hadn't realised how personally dangerous the project would become. The Intelligence Service for National Security in Athens was convinced our work was part of a CIA plot to help Turkey gain access to the eastern Aegean. Various attempts were made to sabotage the project. Billy and Rita's home was ransacked, camera film was destroyed, and Rita's car crashed on a steep and winding mountain road, nearly killing the project volunteers, when the steering 'failed'.

Little did we know as we innocently dived along the Megalo Seitani coastline photographing the underwater entrances to the monk seal habitat that large caches of weapons were hidden in the area. We had a powerful ally in Melina Mercouri, the Greek minister for culture and sciences: with her help we managed to put an end to the hunting of dolphins in Greek waters for a government bounty, yet she seemed powerless to stop the threats and bullying on a more local level.

Visitors had been dropping by and my spirits were picking up. We were getting reports about the Icelandic campaign via the only phone in the village. Elpeda, the tiny woman who ran the biggest café in the village with her husband, Costas, was in charge of the phone. If she couldn't be bothered working the switchboard with its maze of cables and jacks, she would tell us the phone had a stomachache and was indisposed. This mysterious ailment miraculously came right as soon as the army appeared on its daily rounds, and we used this window of telephonic good health to make a quick call.

We learned from muffled conversations that the *Rainbow Warrior* had twice been apprehended by the Icelandic coastguard for interfering with whaling activities before leaving, again in July, to intercept the *Gem*. This time the crew of the *Gem* aimed high-pressure water hoses at the activists' heads. Glimpses of the Plimsoll line through the heavy curtain of water helped keep the Zodiacs alongside. The dramatic film footage and photographs of the confrontation between the Zodiacs and the *Gem* won television documentary awards and international press photography prizes. The *Warrior* had become a place to make a name for oneself in tele- and photo-journalism.

The front patio of my *kalivi* afforded me an uninterrupted view of the ocean and the coastal road, where a pod of dolphins greeted me every morning, their skin glowing salmon-pink in the early light. I would do some yoga before breakfast, Saluting the Sun, and turning and bowing to the four corners of the wind. It was the only time I allowed myself the freedom to be naked. I knew what the village people thought of Nordic tourists and their obsession with an all-over suntan. Those of us who lived on Samos were always careful not to offend by displaying ourselves in ways that would upset the locals. The main body of tourists congregated further along the coastal road, and we kept well away, especially in the summer months. There was something vulgar about the influx of northern Europeans, having sex openly on the beach and wiping out their brain cells on binges of ouzo. They had no interest in the locals and harassed the local storekeepers for not stocking food they were accustomed to.

The sound of a Vespa penetrated the still morning air. It was way off in the distance, a monotonous drone, cutting through the dreams of the sleeping children, niggling the animals. I imagined a gigantic fly swat flattening it on the asphalt. Art van Remundt, from the Greenpeace office in Amsterdam, had been given a mission. Go to Samos, find Susi and bring her back to talk some sense into Chris: mutiny is in the air.

I didn't know it at the time, but the crew of the *Warrior* had promised to return to Iceland if the IWC didn't vote for a moratorium that year, which of course it didn't. A man of his word, Chris thought it essential to head north again, especially as they'd made a declaration to do so on national television. Denise agreed. She was about to resign anyway, and, still in control of the purse strings, had decided she would withdraw enough money to refuel and restock the boat. There had been a clash. David, by now the self-appointed monarch of the Greenpeace empire in Europe, had other plans for the vessel. So, go fetch Susi!

Art had arrived on the early-morning boat and hired a scooter, heading for Aghios Konstantinos and our plaster-peeling office by the water. We'd rented the dilapidated café shortly after the old man I'd given Brigitte Bardot's phone number to had died. We provided Hondro, the village policeman, with a lot of extra work — collecting intelligence on the supposed CIA operations within. We'd see him lurking in the shadows outside, peering through the windows. There was no time for explanations. I'd been given my orders: fly to Lerwick and stop the boat from leaving for Iceland.

Chris was busy on deck when I arrived. 'Grub-bottom,' he said, looking extremely surprised, 'what are you doing here?'

It didn't take me long to understand what was happening, and I fully supported the crew — returning north and continuing what we had started was the honourable thing to do. I tried to explain it to David later, in

Amsterdam. We all felt the Icelandic people would respect us more if we went back; we needed to keep our word. The *Rainbow Warrior* was detained in Reykjavik, and then released minus our new 8.5-metre rigid-hull inflatable, which had been seized by the coastguard. We'd used this in some of the high-speed chases in the whaling grounds when the *Warrior* hadn't been able to keep up. Denise handed in her resignation when the boat returned to London in August, and joined the Hillingdon council's parks department, as Athel and I had done.

One of the founding members of Greenpeace New Zealand — another Michael Taylor, an astute intellectual and a pioneer of the antinuclear movement in New Zealand — had flown in to Heathrow to put pressure on New Zealand's pro-whaling stance at that year's IWC meeting. He'd dressed up as an orca, complete with rubber flippers, and joined Spike Milligan, Bob Geldof and other celebrities at a huge 'Save the Whales' rally in Trafalgar Square organised by FoE. Thanks to Michael, this was something of a triumph for Greenpeace New Zealand, with the New Zealand delegation to the IWC reversing its traditional pro-whaling position.

After a couple of press conferences in London and Amsterdam, the *Rainbow Warrior* sailed to Falmouth for a month's repair work. At the same time, an old Baltic trader — the *Fri* — sailed into port after six years of activism under the captaincy of her American owner, David Moodie. Built of oak in 1912 in Denmark, the 24-metre schooner had become famous in New Zealand for her protest voyage to Mururoa in 1973, after which she had undertaken a 40,000-kilometre voyage, the Pacific Peace Odyssey, across the Pacific and Indian Oceans, carrying a message of peace to all the nuclear-armed states.

When she finally sailed into Falmouth, her crew hadn't touched land in months, and were lean from the rigours of sailing and a meagre diet of beans and rice. They wore their hair long and knotted, their clothing hand-stitched out of sail cloth; some were clad in no more than a hand-tooled codpiece. They frolicked among the rigging of the old sailing ship like marmosets, with large knives strapped to their waists. I fell in love with the boat the moment I saw her. She smelled of curry, linseed oil, tar and sprouting potatoes, her dark wood oozing adventure on the high seas. Bending so as not to hit my head, I climbed down the fo'c'sle ladder to enter the galley and a world of childhood fantasy, of pirates and explorers. I felt safe and nourished. A small range churned out fresh bread daily, and water was carried in wooden crates bearing Chinese pictographs. There was a wood locker in the main hold, and a sail locker in the mizzen hold. The bilge pump, an old Lister motor, a bicycle generator and a Singer sewing-machine in the master's cabin were all well maintained and cherished. There wasn't a single piece of plastic on the boat — captain's orders.

Greenpeace held its first council meeting on 16 November 1979 at 99 Damrakstrasse, in the centre of Amsterdam. In attendance were Greenpeace representatives from France, the Netherlands, the United Kingdom, Australia, Canada, Denmark, Greece, New Zealand and the United States. Greenpeace Europe was represented by David McTaggart, and the *Rainbow Warrior* by Jon Castle. The bickering and squabbling had stopped for the moment, and the organisation came together over several days to discuss budgets, objectives and strategies and the working definition of 'campaign'. Remi and Allan were still involved, as were a couple of North American activists I'd met during the 1977 seal campaign. Billy represented our office in Aghios Konstantinos, where we'd been given the official title 'Greenpeace Greece'.

Over and over again, the difference in values between the *Rainbow Warrior* and the Greenpeace organisation was highlighted. Jon spoke eloquently with that strength of inner conviction that makes people sit up and take notice. He spoke of first meeting us in London, of finding a wonderfully inspiring movement, visionary yet practical, and of how different it was from other groups; of how even journalists, 'those most toughened individuals', couldn't resist the innocence and bare-faced rightness of what we were about. Years later he wrote in a paper:

> It is an impossibility to analyse this difference in purely intellectual terms, as it is most definitely not an intellectual experience. It's the difference between ancient woodland and a conifer plantation: between the wild salmon and her fish farm kin: between your mother's cooking and a microwave airline dinner. It's the kind of difference you perceive by your heart, or maybe the right lobe of your neo cortex — immediate, startling, final, true. A qualitative difference, a spiritual difference . . . radical, intuitive, sharp, courageous, mould breaking, honest, egalitarian, fresh and lots of fun.

Jon summed us up nicely. But all that was to be thrown on the rubbish heap in the years to come, subsumed by the corporatization of the organisation, with its hierarchies and spineless complacency. They would use the image of the *Rainbow Warrior* to rake in the dosh, and shut out her very spirit and soul, profiting from the myth without ever being part of it. 'Whoever fights monsters should see to it that in the process he does not become a monster,' Jon said, quoting Nietzsche, as we left the meeting.

I returned to the *Warrior* that winter to take care of her in the Amsterdam docks while some of the crew went home for Christmas.

Melina Mercouri had offered us the use of an amphitheatre in the Acropolis, in Athens, for a benefit concert we were thinking of organising for World Environment Day the following year under the banner 'Save our Seas!'.

'I don't think anyone has played the Acropolis before,' I said to the beautiful ringleted woman stuffing envelopes in the Greenpeace office. I'd collided with her earlier as she was leaving. Between filling envelopes and delivering press releases on the whale-stickered Greenpeace bike, dropping one off at every single newspaper office along Fleet Street, she ran a keyboard design company with her brother. I was totally in awe of this gorgeous woman, who, I later discovered, was already an accomplished sound engineer, the first woman in Europe to run a 40-track recording studio. I didn't know all this at the time, having only just bumped into her — literally. I was sitting at the large mail-out table chatting to her when Billy walked in, wearing a hat. He was trying to look smart for all the meetings he was having with conservation executives, trying to find funding to continue the monk seal campaign.

'I can just imagine Van Morrison singing with Theodorakis among those ancient stones,' I continued whimsically. Word had spread among the rock'n'roll community about the venue we'd been offered, and some big-name bands had been phoning in to express their interest.

'If you manage to get Van Morrison, I'll eat my hat,' Billy said, pretending to stuff his hat in his mouth.

'Actually, my friend plays violin in his band,' the young woman said, looking up. 'I'll get her to arrange a meeting for you.'

Some days later, several of us were sitting in a nondescript café in north London with a chain-smoking Irish musician. Not everyone knew who Van Morrison was.

'What do you do for a living, then?' asked a Canadian friend of Allan's, a writer who'd just flown in from North America.

'I'm a poet,' Van Morrison answered her softly, his accent quite American. I smiled to myself; I knew what it was like to seek anonymity and the pleasure of having people relate to you with everyday simplicity that doesn't set you apart. Van Morrison was interested in playing music with the old guys in villages, of jamming with the Samians, and Billy left to try to persuade Greenpeace International to give him the deposit to book the amphitheatre.

A comment by an old fisherman on Samos had intrigued me. He'd said Turks ate dolphins, and called the meat 'pig flesh'. Dismissing this as just another dig at an old enemy I had thought nothing more of it until one day I came across a paper written by an assistant professor of environmental studies at Brock University, Ontario, entitled *Turkish Dolphin Fisheries*. I had stumbled across the huge, unregulated hunting of cetaceans. The only way to expose it was to travel to Turkey, posing as a marine-ecology student, and collect as much information as possible from the eastern Black Sea, where most of the hunting took place. An Australian Greenpeace volunteer offered to accompany me.

It was the worst possible time to travel to Turkey. The day we arrived the dean of Istanbul University had been assassinated, several other professors murdered, students machine-gunned in class, and others shot dead as they staged a small protest on the Bosphorus. The country was under martial law, while the university was cordoned off by the military, with staff members hiding inside. On the night we arrived, an oil tanker that had been slowly burning on the Bosphorous since a collision, blew up, and terrified people ran screaming through the streets. We were told travelling east overland would be very dangerous, so we boarded a plane and flew direct to Trabzon, a Black Sea coastal town near the Soviet border.

In the past, oil from the three species of dolphin being hunted had been used for lighting, but now it was used in soap and margarine, as a leather softener and in paint. Once deodorised, we were told, it couldn't be matched for quality. Young, pregnant and lactating animals had dominated the catch in recent years, because of their greater oil content. Tens of thousands of dolphins were shot every winter, when their fat content was at its highest, with the government supplying the hunters with guns and bullets. Up to half of the animals shot sank before they could be retrieved and taken to the processing station.

'The dolphin is sacred in the Muslim religion,' a young student of ecology called Ergii told us in Istanbul. 'One of our prophets, Yunus, is named after the dolphin.'

Our feet were wet. As our eyes grew accustomed to the dim light of the flensing room we realised we were standing in several inches of blood; it covered the entire floor like a carpet. I had recognised the smell at the wrought-iron entrance to the processing station — the smell of dead marine mammals. We had been allowed in, smiling prettily, when we had explained we were students from the University of Amsterdam. Having produced our fake documentation we were shown around the station by the director himself. We counted several hundred young and baby dolphins, including a lactating female with milk still oozing from her teat. It had been a bad day, according to the director. One of the workers, his hands and overalls drenched in blood, told us that the dolphins were like humans and cried tears when they suffered pain. We shot several rolls of photos, and at the end of our tour the entire work-force at the station lined up for a group shot.

Following a series of bizarre and frightening incidents we were forced to leave Trabzon extremely quickly. We had befriended Lau, a young Danish engineer working at another processing station — this one for anchovy — assembling equipment supplied by his company for half-price, as a goodwill gesture to a developing nation. Westerners were rarely seen in Trabzon, let alone women travelling on their own. No woman ventured out after dark and all the men carried weapons. Lau told us we weren't safe and insisted we leave as soon as possible. He said we were being closely watched and something was being planned — he couldn't tell us what without compromising his own safety. We arranged to meet him in Istanbul, where he'd tell us what was going on.

We reached Istanbul on 15 December, the feast day of the prophet Noah. Our student friend, Ergii, had prepared a traditional pudding for us. He had been shocked to learn his country was killing thousands of dolphins for the export of their oil. We met Lau in the relatively safe surroundings of our hotel. He told us he'd been offered vast sums of money to procure Western women for the white slave trade, and that many police and high-ranking officials were part of a syndicate that controlled trade in heroin, made from the opium poppies that flourished in the hills behind Trabzon. He asked us to withhold information on our trip to Trabzon until he'd left the country in March the following year. He was convinced that if the dolphin hunt became a public issue outside Turkey, his life would be in danger. He was certain he was being followed, and had received no mail from home. He was also prevented from phoning out of the country, and his Danish predecessor at the factory had mysteriously disappeared before completing his contract.

The trip to Turkey seemed unreal. I wrote a report for Allan but spoke with no one about what had happened in Trabzon, deciding to wait until Lau had left.

In mid-January 1980, the *Rainbow Warrior* left for Guernsey to await the arrival of the *Pacific Swan*, which was due to offload barrels of spent nuclear-fuel rods at Cherbourg for reprocessing at Cap de la Hague. One evening we drank far too much French cognac with some British naval officers. The next morning I heard someone banging on the hull with a metal object — it sounded as if the person was attacking rusty paintwork. I bowled up on deck and, my hangover talking, yelled at a young man bent over the side, chipping at the bulkhead. He was a young volunteer from America, Steve Sawyer, who'd just arrived to join the crew. 'I'm ready and willing,' he said. 'Put me to work.'

The *Pacific Swan* had been diverted because of the presence of the *Rainbow Warrior*. There had been a vigil and demonstration in the harbour at Cherbourg, and we'd been escorted by three French warships, rather unceremoniously, out of French territorial waters and outlawed from entering them again. We returned to Guernsey to put on our thinking caps and decided we'd get ourselves arrested in order to try to stop the *Pacific Swan* from docking in Cherbourg. One of the crew left for France to organise support action in the harbour with local antinuclear activists, using a few Zodiacs. The *Warrior* returned to lie in wait on the edge of French territorial waters, and when we located the *Pacific Swan*, in thick winter fog, we followed her into Cherbourg. 'Women are best at steering,' Jon said to me after calling me up to the bridge to take the wheel.

Riot police were lined up along the quay, overdressed for the occasion with an array of weapons. The bow of the *Warrior* hit the side of the wharf gently; there was a painful squealing of rubber on rubber. We'd crashed, having come up a narrow channel in hot pursuit of our quarry in terrible visibility. Boof! Another crash. The boat rocked violently. The impact had come from the side — we'd been rammed by a navy vessel. Waves of militia boarded the *Warrior*, looking like giant spiders in their black uniforms as they clambered over and around things, yelling commands in French. '*Où est votre capitaine, madame?*' a young Frenchman asked, dressed in zips and pockets stuffed with gadgets. He'd leapfrogged over the gunwale and entered the bridge from the deck. When we'd hit the wharf Jon had murmured, 'Shit. Sorry, boat,' and gone to put a dab of red lead on his scratched bow. From the bridge window I'd seen him in his overalls coming out of the fo'c'sle, paint pot in hand; the flood of military personnel had passed him by. We bounced to a standstill right next to the *Pacific Swan*, were immediately arrested and then released even more quickly when local unions threatened to go on strike.

We returned to Falmouth to recuperate. It was now obvious to the nuclear industry that the *Rainbow Warrior* meant business.

11

Now let me set the record straight, once and for all. I had absolutely no idea I'd be the only woman on a boat with 19 men, in the middle of the Irish Sea, in winter, and that we'd remain at anchor not days but weeks. Show me a woman in her right mind who would want to be. Most of the male crew I knew and I felt comfortable around them; others I'd met only recently, and some had fallen prey to the seduction of being on such a famous boat and the female attention it tended to attract. I'd seen husbands show their wives and children round while a newly acquired girlfriend, a port bimbo picked up in the local bar, waited patiently at the aft entrance for the family tour to end. I despised these men for their infidelities; at the same time I was somewhat envious of their ability to 'pull chicks' solely by dint of being on the boat. No men paid the same attention to the women crew. Should a male punter come on board he would invariably remain tongue-tied in our presence. I wondered what it was about us that prevented them from having a relaxed conversation.

At times I felt incredibly lonely, almost as if I were a second-class citizen. It was difficult to meet people on the boat and make real friends among the visitors. It was hard to socialise in a place that was both home and, at the same time, a public venue, without it becoming a crazy 24-hour revel. Individual crew members entertained family and friends in port, cramming people into the mess, while most of the others disappeared ashore for some peace and quiet. For those of us who'd been together for a while, for whom the ship was home, with respect for one another's space and a little silence, these invasions were intrusive and at times intensely upsetting.

We didn't want to have to tell people the same stories over and over again, but that was the reason many came on board. We needed them to be the public face of the vessel, whose job it was to be our mouthpiece.

We couldn't do the job properly ourselves. As visitors crowded into our small cabins while touring the boat, they'd stare at items on the bulkhead by our bunks — intimate mementoes, poems, a photo of a dog. They'd stare at these things as if they'd never seen anything like it before — a stare of vacant bewilderment. Invariably, their gaze would turn on you, and they always looked so stunned, as if asking 'Why you?' I felt extremely vulnerable. If only those probing stares had been accompanied by normal conversation I probably wouldn't have felt so exposed, and so ambivalent about our public face.

There's no better conversation stopper than to say you were the only woman on a boat with 19 men in the Irish Sea. Unfailingly a curious male voice pipes up: 'What was it like?' Women already know what it must have been like — they share their knowledge with a couple of knowing glances and a wry chuckle or two. Men, however, probe — they want to know more. 'Bet you had sex with loads of them' — the assumption is inevitably made, followed by questions: 'How many?', 'How did they compare?' and so on. I never answered. Instead, I liked to tell the story of the *Playboy* calendar.

The purpose of our long wait in the Irish Sea was to be ready when the *Pacific Fisher* arrived with a shipment of nuclear-fuel rods. After we'd been at anchor for a short while, Athel, who was back in his beloved engine room, decided he'd pin his *Playboy* calendar to the dartboard in the mess. In his white, grease-covered overalls, his long hair tied back in one of his colourful hair nets, he tacked it in place in a confident gesture of male camaraderie. He knew his fellow crew would appreciate the new model each month; after all, there were only men on board at the moment — except for Susi, of course, but she didn't count. He smudged the face of Miss March with his greasy fingers and tried to wipe it off, affectionately. I caught a flash of his signet ring on his filthy hand, his family's heraldic crest engraved in the middle. He was the only person I knew who sent letters sealed with wax bearing the imprint of his crest, and I chuckled at the contrast between the noble aristocrat and the grimy mechanic. He didn't see me watching from the door of my cabin, directly opposite the mess. He stood back and admired the pin-up with a grin of appreciation, making sure the calendar was straight.

When he had left the mess, I went in and had a quick look myself. I'd already seen the calendar in the engine room, where someone had made a gruff comment about the bowels of the ship being the men's domain and that no one — in particular Denise, Hilari or myself — had the right to object to what was chosen as decoration there.

Little did Athel know, but I'd been given a *Playgirl* calendar for Christmas by Gert, one of the Dutch engineers. Gert was a huge pit bull of a man, squat and round, with a shaved head and tattoos. He wore a black leather collar with inch-long metal spikes around his neck. He had massive hands covered in rings and was one of the kindest, most gentle men I'd ever met. He took to accompanying me, almost like a body-guard. Together we checked out the dives around the central station in Amsterdam, where he always greeted a lot of people on the street.

One evening he took me to a small Surinamese restaurant he maintained was by far the best in town. He said it was too dangerous for me to go there alone, and halfway through our meal I understood why. It must have been a botched drug deal; bags of white powder were slammed down on tabletops as people yelled at each other and someone picked up a chair and smashed it on the ground. Someone else came charging in off the street. I watched it all in slow motion, my fork frozen halfway between bowl and open mouth. What on earth . . .? Gert grabbed me, and before I knew it I'd been stuffed behind the counter as the scene continued to play itself out on the other side. I'm sure I saw the flash of a gun as I peered over the top during a long moment of silence. I felt a rush of adrenaline, and if it hadn't been for Gert's reassuring wink and the sheer volume of his body in those creaking leathers next to me, I'm sure I would have made a dive for the pavement. Eventually the door slammed twice, and we heard the commotion trail off down the small canal-side street. The restaurant slowly came back to life, as if nothing had happened. My bowl of food was whisked away to be reheated as more people, looking like tourists, came in to eat. I wondered if they'd have come in if they'd known what had happened only minutes before.

Gert had other uses as well, including procuring the services of a lady of the night who offered discounts for Greenpeace activists. Her workplace — something of a cross between a shop window and a garden shed — had *Rainbow Warrior* stickers all over it. When Ken Ballard turned 30, we arranged to get him drunk, deposit him at her front door and pick him up a couple of hours later. Gert had worked out the logistics and arranged payment. I believe there was a substantial discount, and after a whip-round among the crew we had enough for Ken to celebrate in style.

Christmas 1979 on the *Rainbow Warrior* was a low-key affair involving the consumption of a lot of home-baked food sent by crew members' mothers from around the world. Knowing we were going to be sailing into the chill wind of the Irish Sea had also inspired a few of them to knit jumpers. Jon, proud of his Channel Island heritage, always wore a handmade Guernsey, its dark blue contrasting warmly with his red hair and freckles.

Gert chose a private moment to present me with his gift. The *Playgirl* calendar fell out of the wrapping paper onto the deck and opened to reveal the tanned torso and well-toned buttocks of a man with a pout. 'I thought you'd like that for your cabin,' Gert said with a cheeky smile. I was amused by the calendar, and bemused as well. Did they think I was a sexless being in need of artificial stimulation? I consoled myself that at least he hadn't included a dildo. Did they think I needed a steady boyfriend? How did they see me? Did they even perceive me as female? After all, we wore pretty much the same kind of clothing. I had my standard uniform of white sweatshirt under dark blue dungarees, and tied my long hair in plaits so it didn't blow around when on deck. Quite a few of the male crew had long hair as well. Skinny and flat-chested, in regulation baggy overalls I could easily be mistaken for a young man. The best way for me to meld on board was to conduct myself in a purposefully androgynous way.

I thanked Gert for his sensitive gift, telling him I'd never received a *Playgirl* calendar before. 'Have you seen one though? Have a look!' His smile was growing wider by the second. I told him that as I'd be sharing my cabin with a man, I wouldn't risk offence by displaying it, but would keep it in the drawer under my bunk. 'For medicinal purposes only,' Gert said, with a wink.

At lunch time the crew filed into the mess, helping themselves to food in an anticlockwise rotation that took them past the various breads, spreads and drinks and round the tables to the benches on the far side. There was a knack to eating in rough weather — to positioning your plate and timing the raising of your fork to your mouth. It was always best to work with the rhythm of the ocean. Often, someone's plate or bowl would escape and shoot down the table, to be caught in mid-flight and returned. There were nifty little side flaps with hinges and locks on every side of each table which also did a good job of preventing disaster, though not a perfect one. Occasionally, a loud crash, invariably met with a raucous cheer, announced the end for someone's meal as it hit the deck. Everything in the mess was contained, or secured to a bulkhead or the deck itself — lashed, blocked, locked, nailed down. Only the plants in their macramé sling swayed freely under the skylight, at times furiously.

As the guys shuffled past the *Playboy* calendar, comments were exchanged: 'Have you seen the tits on this one, mate?' and so on. I tried not to show any emotion. I took my place in the queue and bit my tongue. All around me there was a buzz of excitement. I felt like a naturalist observing members of another species in the field. I sat down and ate my food in silence, trying not to be noticed. Later, I tiptoed back to my cabin with a plan. I would pin my Mr March next to their Miss March and await further developments.

The deed done, I didn't have to wait long, and as fate would have it, Athel was the first to notice. Perhaps he'd gone to the mess for a private viewing of Miss March and to congratulate himself on breaking an unspoken *Warrior* taboo. I observed him once more from my cabin, again remaining undetected. But it was to the *Playgirl* calendar he casually strode. He flipped over the pages and I could see he was examining each Mr Month critically, his head tilted to one side as he checked out their credentials. From time to time he frowned slightly, something obviously bothering or unnerving him. I waited until he'd reached late autumn before making my entrance, feigning nonchalance.

'Oh, hello Athel.'

'Do you know who stuck this up, Sooze? Was it you? Where did you get such a disgusting thing?'

'It was a Christmas present,' I said. 'Where did you get yours?'

I started flicking through the glossy coloured photos of naked males, making comments on each.

'Which one turns you on the most, then?' asked Athel with a tinge of irritation.

I studied each specimen for a while before replying, 'Mr August wins hands down.'

'And what exactly does Mr August have that I don't?' he asked, glancing quickly at the blond-haired stud perched on a rock by a forest waterfall. I laughed. I could see my calendar bothered him more than his bothered me.

'Let's make a deal,' I said. 'Let's take both calendars down and put them away.' I remembered Gert's words. 'And let's put them both in the medicine cabinet for use on those occasions when a little perk might facilitate the healing process.'

'Done,' said Athel, and we shook hands.

If anyone noticed the *Playboy* calendar was no longer there, they didn't comment. Fickle creatures.

It was March 1980, and we were in international waters off the west coast of England, opposite one of the most notorious nuclear complexes in the world. Known as Windscale at the time, the site is now called Sellafield, after the place where it was constructed in 1947 to build Britain's first atomic bomb. Earlier that year we'd been served with an injunction to prevent us from interfering with the free navigation of vessels in and out of the docks at Barrow-in-Furness, where the *Pacific Fisher* was due to deliver her cargo of nuclear-fuel rods from Japan for reprocessing at Windscale. Details of her movements were classified, and we remained at anchor several miles out as we couldn't comfortably enter British waters for fear of being seized. The board of directors of Greenpeace Ltd had transferred all assets, namely the *Rainbow Warrior*, into a holding company, Rainbow Warrior Holdings Co. Ltd, so the vessel couldn't be seized if we broke the injunction.

Since 1960 Windscale had been leaking up to 450 litres of contaminated water a day from its 320,000-litre silo. One five-year study, published in the *British Medical Journal*, had recorded the childhood leukaemia rate in neighbouring villages at 10 times the national average. In 1977 the first major enquiry into nuclear reprocessing in the UK had taken place. It lasted 100 days, and heard evidence for and against the building of a new plant, the Thermal Oxid Reprocessing Plant (THORP), intended to reprocess nuclear waste from the UK and abroad. THORP was given the go-ahead the next year, as Margaret Thatcher was promising to order one nuclear reactor for every year she was in office should she be elected.

It's impossible to showcase a nuclear reactor in a flattering way. We'd driven to Cumbria from London a few months before as part of the logistics exercise we carried out before any campaign. We had with us a state-of-the-art Geiger counter. On a remote stretch of coast, just north of the little town of Seascale, we looked out across the Irish Sea, and then north. There, against the horizon, its late 1940s stacks belching steam and a dome with a distinct air of menace about it, stood the birthplace of the first British atomic bomb. Barbed wire separated this chamber of death from the innocent grassy headlands and grazing stock. The two-kilometre pipeline discharging supposedly low-level radioactive effluent into the sea was kept well out of sight.

As I looked across the countryside I shuddered at the thought of Cumbrian families cradling their dying children — sacrificial lambs at the patriarchal altar. It made no sense. Why would a species engage so urgently in its own self-destruction? I strained to comprehend the logic. Radiation may very well be invisible, but when it registers on a Geiger counter it produces an instantly recognisable sound. Once heard, it is never forgotten. As we drove slowly towards one of the gates to the plant (*Lasciate ogni speranza voi qu'entrata* — Abandon hope all ye who enter here), the frenetic clicking started. I was sitting in the back seat of the car, and leaned forward as we stopped to see what levels of radiation were being detected. One of the windows was open.

'Close the window, Stringbean,' I said, instinctively trying to keep the stuff at bay. Stringbean's real name was Mark Long, and he was the *Warrior*'s radio operator. The Geiger counter continued its toxic detection like some virtual woodpecker in a sound loop. If anything, it sounded more defiant with the windows closed. I got out of the car, closely followed by the others. It made no difference. It was everywhere, and you couldn't see it or smell it. We quickly got back in the car and drove in the opposite direction, back out of the shadow of death. I thought of all those people living in such apparently delightful surroundings, on the edge of the Lake District, with this invisible menace all around them, this twilight zone of isotopic madness in their back yard. What antidote had they been offered to protect them from something they neither understood nor desired to have in their lives? Was anyone even listening?

When Jon mentioned we'd be at anchor for a number of weeks, as close to the channel entrance to Barrow as was safe under the terms of the injunction, he said it would be a rough ride. We'd had experience of the North Atlantic in inflatables in summer, off Iceland, and that had been bad enough. This may have been the more enclosed Irish Sea, but during the tale end of winter it was bound to be just as much a challenge. I didn't want to go through all that high-speed chasing and constant pounding against what might well be an even bigger, nastier swell. Jon told me the *Pacific Fisher* wouldn't be operating on normal radio channels, so we'd need to be able to deploy our small craft at a moment's notice once she'd been spotted on the horizon.

A new first mate had joined the ship in Amsterdam. Bruce Crammond was a New Zealander, from Te Puke — a name I had no idea how to pronounce correctly when I first read it, but which, when it came out the way it did, was appropriate for someone who became so seasick. When I was on watch with him on the bridge, he'd frequently excuse himself, walk out on deck and vomit lustily over the side before returning to his post. We got on well; he was always cheerful and never complained.

It was decided two small boats would follow the *Pacific Fisher* into Barrow and try to prevent her docking. Two people would be assigned to each boat, and the driver could choose the other crew member. Bruce, who'd been trained as an inflatable driver on the way up to Barrow, picked me. I had sufficient experience by now to know what was required of the person riding shotgun, and had worked with Bruce before. He said my presence and inane chatter calmed him down as he tried to keep the small craft on course in the hostile seas. I knew that while the minutiae of life often unsettled me and I could panic easily over trivial things, in extremely dangerous situations I remained centred, working through my options methodically and without emotion. When it really mattered, I seemed to be able to cope with uncharacteristic sang-froid.

Launching a small boat from its mother vessel at high speed and in rough weather is not an easy task. Jumping into it from a height, as it buffets against the hull or swings around with a life of its own, is no picnic either. Our boats hadn't been designed for this kind of weather, and although we were able to provide some practical information to the manufacturers about their performance in extreme conditions, it was anything but a joyride to be in one. Most of the manufacturers thought we were mad, but thanked us anyway for test-driving their products.

Imagine, if you will, the embarrassment of jumping into a Zodiac held alongside as it thrashes and jerks like a rodeo yearling, and missing. Television cameras and photojournalists record your every movement as you leap confidently into the void. There's farce even in heroic action, and in the most charged moments there's often comedy, although it may not seem so funny at the time.

We practised jump after jump, the driver opening the throttle as soon as his companion landed and speeding away. Years of horse-riding and t'ai chi came in useful for me, as good balance and strong legs were needed in order not to be bowled over, or thrown out, by this initial thrust of horsepower. My favourite way of riding a Zodiac was to stand right up forward with my feet firmly tucked in under the fold of the air chambers on either side. I'd hold onto the rope, made fast to the bow of the boat, like a rein. With my knees bent slightly and my centre of gravity low, I'd become totally receptive and pliant to the ocean. At times, the jarring from slamming into wave after wave became unbearable and the only way of coping was to disassociate and yet be fully focused at the same time. On those occasions when the experience was more like driving repeatedly into a brick wall than bouncing across water, some of the crew wore kidney braces to prevent internal injury.

In each inflatable there was a fuel tank and a waterproof screw-top container lashed to the deck. The latter held useful items such flares, a torch, a portable two-way radio, a compass, a small first aid kit, and — most importantly — some chocolate. I'd long given up wearing a 'zoot suit' with 'Greenpeace' emblazoned on the back. I felt such garb was of benefit only to the media, and it was difficult to move around in. Those of us who'd spent considerable time in these boats knew loose-fitting thermal clothing was far more comfortable. We'd be drenched within the first minute anyway — no amount of fancy wet-weather gear could prevent that. My only concession to uniform was the dark-blue woollen beanie each of the original crew had been given. It had a rainbow on the front, and I now deeply regret throwing mine away in a fit of pique over the commercialisation of our vision. More often than not, though, I wore a hat from the Andes my father had given me. Knitted from brightly coloured alpaca wool, it was long and pointy, with shoulder-length earflaps. I could stuff things in its cone — a packet of Drum, a lighter, more chocolate — and the flaps kept the biting wind from tunnelling into my ears. This was the hat I'd been wearing when attacked in a train station in Norway by a drunk who thought I was a Laplander and therefore deserved to be insulted. I soon learned a woollen hat is a lifesaver when every item of clothing and every inch of flesh is saturated by cold sea water. A German journalist I spent a long time avoiding made some superficial comment about my hat in his 'serious' magazine, and I was quite hurt. My hat represented so many things to me; it was part of my battledress. But perhaps the most ludicrous question I've ever been asked by a member of the print media was about mascara.

We'd been holding press conferences in Amsterdam and London about the events in Iceland during the *Rainbow Warrior*'s maiden voyage. A well-known women's magazine wanted to write a feature article called 'Women who Risk their Lives to Save the Environment'. Hilari, Denise and I were all highly suspicious of publicity, which concentrated on the person rather than the issue. We finally agreed to co-operate, believing rather naively that if we controlled the process we'd be able to avoid any probing into personal irrelevancies.

A photographer was sent to take endless rolls of what seemed to be the same two photos, posed for at the stern or in the mess. There's a limit to how many times a moment can be captured on film without appearing contrived. I hated my photo being taken and until then had avoided being filmed or photographed on board, even by my closest friends. I wasn't trying to be enigmatic, but my experiences with the Aymaran tribes had contributed to a feeling that having one's image captured on celluloid tainted the spirit. Were we expected to be seduced by the attention as we stood there, chins up high, hands just so? Now . . . hold that position . . . and hold it . . . and hold it. I hoped I looked noble and proud, but I felt self-conscious and sullied.

We were then taken by car to a restaurant on top of a high-rise building somewhere in the centre of London. It was extremely elegant and we were hardly dressed for the occasion. We were met there by the reporter, who showed us to our table and immediately filled our glasses with wine. If this was designed to get us to talk, it certainly worked, and our plan to control the process fell by the wayside in helpless inebriation. One by one we were taken for questioning in a soundproof, windowless booth. I suspect now that the lack of oxygen in the stuffy atmosphere combined with the alcohol to fuel both the bizarre questions and the equally outlandish answers.

'Our readers will be dying to know what type of mascara you use when you're out in a Zodiac defending a hunted whale,' the reporter asked me enthusiastically as she closed the booth door. It sounded as if we were locked in a padded cell, and my head started to swim from the wine and the strain of trying to figure out how to deal with the spin this woman was obviously giving to the interview. 'I'd imagine waterproof, *n'est ce pas?*'

I felt like telling her that, of course, we all carried makeup bags with us when we went out after the whalers, and when there was a lull in the proceedings and the harpooner was taking a break — *carpe diem!* — we'd reach for the pocket mirror and quickly touch up our faces.

I think I burbled something inadequate about not having time for make-up, about having to wear plastic goggles in case the whalers decided

179

to fire bolts from the engine room at our heads with catapults. She seemed most put out. I should have just slapped her and left. I can't remember much about the rest of the interview. I know there was the usual question about sex.

Hilari told me she'd been asked how we had found the whalers off Iceland. 'Well, I threw the I Ching,' she had replied.

'You don't seriously expect me to print that?' the reporter had said.

When the mascara article finally appeared, I was thankful to be out of the country, on Samos, in the remote mountain village of Ambelos. A letter from my mother arrived to say she'd read the piece and couldn't believe what she'd seen: 'Did you honestly speak such drivel?' In my reply, I gave her strict instructions to destroy her copy, and — if possible, please — every other copy she could find. I felt relieved that, looking over the Anatolian plateau , it was highly unlikely the magazine would be on sale anywhere close by.

As we lay at anchor day after endless day, on continual lookout waiting for the *Pacific Fisher*, we got to know each other very well. After all, there wasn't much to do except talk, eat, sleep and keep watch, and as our immediate environment grew ever more insular, we became freer with our personal revelations. There was a constant banging and shaking of metal against metal as we shuddered against the seasonal force of ebb and flood, attached to the seabed only by a robust metal chain that strained to break free. The repeated bracing of our bodies against the next impact, and the swaying, clumsy two-step we all adopted to move around the boat churned up our psyches and wore us out. The strain began to show, flesh being that much weaker than metal, which withstood the challenge with infinitely more resilience.

I was receiving a steady stream of visitors now in my nest opposite the galley. Wanting to capture both the homeliness and the magic with which Hilari had previously invested the small space, I had added a rug and a lantern I'd bought in Istanbul. The lantern peppered the bulkhead with small diamonds of light which moved in time to the ocean. They were mesmerising and enhanced the ethereal quality of the cabin, where Hilari had consulted the oracle and played her violin. Visitors had sought her out for pearls of wisdom or counsel for future action. With her infinite capacity for nurturing, she had made everyone feel special. I could never hope to take her place in that regard, but at anchor on that lonely stretch of sea I often found myself sitting in her old cabin listening to a private tale of despair as it surfaced like flotsam in the ocean of the speaker's mind.

Jon had assigned Martini Gotjé to my cabin. He had generously taken the top bunk, as I found it difficult to keep myself securely wedged in place up there, and had already been flung out of bed a couple of times in rough weather. The first time I'd met him, he'd come on board the *Rainbow Warrior* in Amsterdam when the boat was closed to the general public. Thinking he was some tenacious fan trying to sneak on undetected, I'd stormed up to him and told him to leave. Tall and lanky, with a goatee beard and long, thick brown hair topped with a russet beanie, he looked, rather dauntingly, like a lion.

Someone heard me and came to his rescue. 'This is Martini, Susi. He was on the *Fri*. Jon's asked him to join the ship as first mate.'

I was acutely embarrassed and apologised.

'That's absolutely fine,' said Martini. 'You were just doing your job.'

I should have known who he was, I told myself. I'd seen enough photos of him on the old Danish schooner. He was distinctive looking and something of a legend as a seaman. We exchanged few words after that, as he intimidated me. His knowledge of the nuclear issue was immense and detailed, and I'd marvel at his ability to retrieve facts from the fount of information in his head and analyse them strategically. For the uninitiated who liked to debate any issue simply for the sake of grand-standing or the sound of their own voice, he represented quite a challenge. He didn't forgive fools easily, especially those who should have known better.

I could see he was a master mariner in the truest sense. He had the same wonderful smell I'd encountered on the *Fri* and walked with perfect balance where others were unsteady. He could splice and lash and make lines fast with confident dexterity and knew everything about the stars. He'd been navigator on the *Fri* and purposefully chose the graveyard watch in order to observe the passage of time as recorded in the heavens.

Jon had asked whether I had any objection to sharing my cabin space with Martini. 'I think you'll get on,' he'd said, with a twinkle in his eye. He knew how troubled my relationship with Chris had become. Chris had disappeared again, on further reconnaissance of the Spanish whaling operations. He'd left a cryptic message which didn't offer any clue as to his whereabouts, or when he might be expected to return. I had been left in limbo once again, and I hated how this made me feel.

I had to admit, though, that Chris's stealthy way made him the perfect person to send on scouting trips. He blended into the background and had infinite patience for hanging around and observing. He was also extremely resilient and self-reliant, able to operate entirely on his own, revelling in the intrigue of what he was doing. He wasn't one for writing reports, and passed on vital campaign information by word of mouth. He would often use obtuse allegory to convey something, and this would have to be translated for those who didn't know him well. He was the ultimate loyal friend, but romantically he was awash in a storm of his own, demanding unconditional love but giving little in return. I had finally decided to close this chapter of my life and move on. And it seemed as if Jon was hoping I would do likewise.

I've never been particularly comfortable sleeping in the same room as a stranger. I find it hard even with close friends, so I was naturally wary at first about my new sleeping arrangements. However, as I spent more time around the new first mate I realised why Jon had been so keen to get him on the boat. Martini exuded steadfastness and truth, the ultimate strengths of any warrior. His constancy and methodical approach to problems meant he was an extremely reassuring person to have around. I found myself seeking him out with vague and irrelevant questions, which he'd try to answer as thoroughly as he could. I listened less and less to the actual words, the sound of his voice carrying me to some faraway place where I'd drift contentedly. I loved the way he pronounced certain English words in his thick Dutch accent. Sometimes I'd ask him to repeat them and he would oblige unknowingly, unaware that I was becoming more and more interested in him and had started to scheme.

It was difficult trying to juggle my self-imposed androgynous behaviour with an emerging sexual appetite. I wanted to dress and behave like a woman, a 'cook' with her 'boy', as the small plaque above the old cabin door indicated. Yet I was living and working in a predominantly male world and needed to suppress my femininity in order to survive. I decided I'd wear my womanhood in private, in the confines of the cabin, where I'd brush out my hair, wear skimpy knickers if I could find any, and dab on patchouli. I lived a double life, with infinite satisfaction: outside the confines of the cabin I smoked, drank and farted with the best of them. I crawled through the bilges to give them a good clean, being the smallest person on board at the time, and blew my nose in lube-covered rags. I revelled in the fact that I could do such a filthy job without fear or concern for my appearance, and found I enjoyed getting dirty. Although the showers were piping hot on the *Rainbow Warrior* and the water pressure was excellent, it would still take a while to scrub off all the grime and clean my fingernails. I'd often find small bruises and cuts and never have any idea how I'd got them.

There was nothing quite like the feeling of weary satisfaction after a good day's hard labour, as most of the crew gathered in the mess at dusk for a well-deserved drink. The engineers always walked in carrying old newspapers, on which they obligingly sat in their oil-streaked clothing. They'd invariably be discussing some quirk or other of the mechanical components they'd been dismantling and reassembling. I enjoyed their company, although I lacked any real understanding of things mechanical — to me they were speaking a foreign language. They had a great sense of tribal identity and a look all their own — a pasty complexion from lack of sunlight, overalls, steel-capped boots, tattoos and earrings.

There was always an echo in the engine room. Things clanged and reverberated, or chugged and thonked. There was a pulse to the ship and this was its origin. The sound of the generators was always present, their rhythmic jigga-jigga jigga-jigga reverberating from the depth of the bilge to the top of the radio mast. I admired the patience of our engineers, who, in the most uncomfortable space in the whole boat, would bolt and screw, weld and lubricate, as they found out why things didn't work or how to make them work more efficiently. They were practical, pragmatic sorts who politely ate the healthy mung-bean stews they were served at meal times while secretly harbouring cans of corned beef under their bunks. Athel wasn't really a bird of the same feather, but his mechanical acumen was such that he was easily accepted by the professional marine brotherhood.

The navigators, by contrast, carried the horizon in their eyes. They were the constant lookout, the guardians. Bruce, Jon and Martini patrolled the bridge separately, on different watches, each with his own particular style. Martini liked to walk across the bridge from port to starboard and back again, taking long strides like a musketeer, binoculars in hand as he peered out into the beyond. He'd see things in the night that were visible to no one else, and the radar always confirmed his findings. In the subdued light of the bridge on the graveyard watch he looked like a figure from a painting by Goya. The smell of his dark Van Nelle rolling tobacco permeated the air, and his constant companion was a mug of coffee — black, strong, without sugar. How did he drink so much caffeine and remain so calm, I wondered? I watched as he pored over charts and calculated distances with a set square and compass. Navigation involved mathematics and something called 'shooting the sun'. He'd bring his sextant up to the bridge and patiently explain how it worked. Hearing the words but heeding a conversation inside my head of an altogether different nature, I would move closer to try to feel the warmth of his body. I never learned how to use the sextant. I didn't have a clue. I was utterly hopeless. I was falling in love.

With Jon on watch it was time for inner reflection and long intervals of deep thought. He'd talk quietly, at times inaudibly, with characteristic understatement, tucking his chin into his neck, his words flowing like a mantra. He'd spent time in India and been deeply moved by Buddhist thought. He was a vegetarian, and when not required on the bridge would often cook an excellent curry. His love and concern for humanity were genuine. He often expressed a desire to use the ship for disaster relief, and would respond to Mayday calls on the radio, taking the *Warrior* off course to investigate and offer assistance. He was sceptical about the role of the media in our campaigning work, and the pressure this put us under to accommodate temperamental film crews and their endless deadlines. Ever since the council meeting in Amsterdam he had been growing steadily more cynical about Greenpeace as an organisation. We shared many of the same beliefs, and this strengthened my trust in him.

I longed to ask Jon about the time, in a half-forgotten place, when he'd taken to his cabin with a bottle of rum. He'd emerged later, clearly in an altered state, and asked me to come into his cabin. Laid out on the small table by the day bed, next to the almost empty bottle, was a comb, a pair of scissors, a razor and some shaving cream. He locked the door behind him, drew the curtains and wrapped a towel around his shoulders. He then walked over to the small mirror above the sink. 'Shave my head,' he ordered. I noticed tears in his eyes as we both stared at his reflection in the glass. It was obvious he didn't want to talk. What inner demon was tormenting him? He was too sincere for his own good. A line from the W.B. Yeats poem he had pinned one day under the mess clock came back to haunt me: 'Things falls apart; the centre cannot hold'. Jon was our centre, and we needed him to hold fast. I trembled slightly as I passed the razor over the foamed stubble of the rough haircut I'd just given him.

What if my hand slipped and I drew blood? After completing the deed, Jon's white scalp shone like polished stone. Perhaps this had been the reason for the act — to release an inner light, to free the spirit. He unlocked the door in silence and I left.

One of our concessions to luxury was a tape deck on the bridge. As we lay in wait at anchor, music provided both solace and divertissement. The greatest struggle became not so much with the weather but with ourselves, as ennui set in and people grew irritable. 'I'm fed up at looking at your fucking face the whole time,' Athel said to me one day. 'Can't we find another woman to provide a bit of excitement?' He kept replaying the Pink Floyd song *Is there anybody out there?* Did he think the world had vanished and he was stuck with me, the sole remaining Eve, for perpetuity? I prayed that the *Pacific Fisher* would arrive soon and break the monotony, releasing us from our petty squabbling.

She crept up on us, unannounced, on a day that seemed just like the rest, with nothing to distinguish it. As the early-morning mist was clearing, it was business as usual in the mess, the 'same old same old'. I was clearing the empty coffee cups from the tables, and as I carried them to the galley I saw Denise's crocheted owl through the hatch with its wooden-bead eyes. She'd hung it in the galley hoping it would bring some wisdom to the collective, provide food for thought in times of need. I sighed. I missed Denise — and Hilari as well — and the café atmosphere the mess took on when she was around. She had such style. Her delight in the feel of the beautiful fabrics she wore had taught me much about the sense of touch. I was a mere pleb by comparison in my tatty keffiyeh.

I forget now who saw the *Pacific Fisher* first as she appeared menacingly over the horizon. Uncannily for such an enormous vessel, she glided through the water in almost total silence, like a spectre. Radioactive cooling water from the fuel-rod containers poured constantly from both sides of her hull. I cringed at the thought of getting soaked by the stuff.

Jon quickly gave the order to launch the inflatables. I grabbed my tobacco and an apple, both of which I stuffed into the pockets of my dungarees, and joined the other Zodiac crew lining up along the starboard side. Bruce climbed into the first boat as it swung over the gunwale and steadied it as it was lowered into the water. He looked up at me — he was already drenched. I smiled — he looked like a small marmot in his oversized rain gear and dripping fringe. As the swell brought the small craft up to the deck, I jumped in. I insisted on being barefoot during an action — I found I could move faster in the Zodiac that way, and adjust my balance more easily by feeling the ocean's pulse underfoot. The professional thing to do would have been to wear steel-capped boots, but I'd watched the way Chris moved on board, padding around the deck bare-footed with feline grace, and loved the way we used to greet each other — wriggling our toes together and squeezing them affectionately.

I checked the waterproof container and fuel tank were securely lashed and Bruce nodded that we should be on our way. I caught a brief glimpse of Athel, striding up the deck and leapfrogging into his inflatable. He made it look so easy. He'd apologised for his earlier remark, saying he actually quite liked my face and that I should have concluded he hadn't really meant what he'd said as I'd known him for nearly a quarter of a century. 'We'll position ourselves in the lee of the bow,' Bruce yelled against the roar of the engine as we flew across the crests of the waves. The *Pacific Fisher* had passed us by now and it would take several minutes of exhilarating chase to overtake her.

Martini had given me a little green stone for luck. He'd shown it to me one evening, pointing out an indent across the middle. 'You see,' he said, 'if you put it this way up, it's smiling. This way,' — he turned it around — 'and it's sulking.' We joked about having it on display somewhere in the cabin to let each other know what mood we were in. Several days later he gave it to me when we were on watch together. 'Here, I want you to have this,' he said as he wrapped his hands around mine and slipped the stone into my palm. 'May your life always be sunny-side up, Susi. I hope one day we'll have made a difference.' He looked far too deeply into my eyes for comfort, and I had to look quickly to one side for fear of giving myself away.

I fingered the stone now as we sped towards the mammoth ship, feeling around the crease. I imagined caressing Martini's mouth, and briefly shut my eyes. At times he, too, seemed troubled by unseen wraiths, whose whisperings could easily be mistaken for the whipping wind curling its way around block and tackle. His solace was Irish music — lots of it. He'd compiled tape upon tape of his favourite selections and would sing along at full volume in a strong voice. Like Jon, he'd sailed both sides of the equator and witnessed oppression first-hand — Angola, Mozambique, Pakistan, China, the Soviet Union. He'd been brought up in a staunchly socialist family, proud of his working-class heritage, his mother a tireless member of a close-knit Rotterdam community. His father had been in a prisoner-of-war camp during the Second World War. Martini instinctively avoided Germans, asking them sarcastically, 'Have you seen my bike?' if he ever got into a debate with one — a pointed reference to the invasion of Holland, when the Germans had confiscated all forms of local transport.

I knew Martini would be on the bridge with Jon, the two of them peering through their binoculars, following our every move. The pilot and tugboats, one for the bow and one for the stern, would meet the *Pacific Fisher* at the entrance to the Barrow channel. They would then have to communicate on their radios on Channel 16 for manoeuvring the ship into dock. We knew that when we were out of sight of our bridge crew we would be incommunicado. Our portable radios didn't have a strong enough signal to maintain constant contact over the distance we'd be from the *Warrior*. Jon had told us he'd be monitoring Channel 16 for news of our movements, as he was sure there'd be some communication about us between the tugboat skippers and the captain of the *Pacific Fisher*.

Bruce and I sat under the shadow of the immense bow in our tiny boat. We felt like ants at the foot of a giant as we peered up, but at least it was quite calm and sheltered there, out of the wind. We had no idea whether the crew could see us under the overhang — perhaps we'd managed to sneak in unnoticed. They would certainly have seen the *Rainbow Warrior*, and I wondered how they had reacted. Did our presence unnerve them, or prick their conscience just the littlest bit?

Our vessels moved in unison, with an eerie synchronicity of bow waves as we edged toward the channel, the Zodiac like a flea in the bed of nuclear madness, keeping the industry on its toes. I conjured up a picture of a large, ugly troll, representing British Nuclear Fuels, jumping around fitfully as a tiny rainbow-coloured flea attacked, biting it all over. 'The person who believes they're too small to make a difference has obviously never spent a night with a flea,' I quoted from somewhere, unscrewing the waterproof container and digging out two Mars bars. I offered one to Bruce.

'You think of everything,' he laughed.

As we moved closer to the coast we altered course slightly for the final approach. We knew where the *Pacific Fisher* would dock to off-load the fuel rods for transportation to Windscale. At the designated berth there were two small pontoons at the bottom of a long stone pier. Even at high tide there was a substantial drop from the pier's edge to the water. We'd received vital information on the layout of the wharf and surrounding area from a local protest group — Cumbrians Opposed to a Radioactive Environment (CORE). We knew the tugs would bring the stern in first, before swinging the bow round. Bruce accelerated as we entered the dock, wanting to get into position as soon as possible.

Jon and Martini had been monitoring Channel 16 for a while, Martini pacing nervously up and down the bridge, Jon standing motionless by the wheel peering through his binoculars. Suddenly, the radio crackled and an anxious voice said: '*Pacific Fisher, Pacific Fisher,* do you read me? This is the skipper of your aft tugboat, sir. Do you read me? Over.'

'Roger. This is the *Pacific Fisher*. Reading you loud and clear. Over.'

'There's a small inflatable craft alongside at the aft pontoon, sir, and it's stationery. I think it's a Greenpeace boat, sir. It would be too dangerous to bring in the stern until it is removed.'

Bruce and I had been sitting in the Zodiac alongside the pontoon for some minutes, watching the huge ship turn side-on and the tugboats move her into position. I couldn't imagine what length of rope, what thickness, would be needed to manoeuvre such a monster. She seemed very obliging and appeared to glide gracefully across the water. I could see the skipper of the tugboat nearest us frantically talking on the radio. We were expecting the boat to come to a grinding halt any minute. Athel had arrived and taken up a position by the forward pontoon. We braced ourselves for the approaching drama as we began to hold up an international nuclear operation — or so we thought.

I quickly rolled a smoke. My hands had dried off now we weren't moving and I needed something to steady my nerves. I hated my addiction to tobacco. I was embarrassed to admit that if ever required to abandon ship, I'd make sure I had my rollies before going over the side. I tried to kid myself that by rolling really thin ones, almost the size of toothpicks, I wasn't tainting my image of a warrior woman. It was pathetic, really.

The *Pacific Fisher*'s stern started to move towards our pontoon, rather too quickly for comfort, the propeller churning up the water like egg whites. Surely she should have come to a grinding halt by now? They couldn't seriously dock the boat with us there. I could hear the skipper of the tugboat shouting something; every now and then he'd run out on deck to check our movements. It was pretty obvious we weren't going anywhere and I was hoping he wasn't too angry. Poor bloke, he was only trying to do a day's work.

'Squash the bloody bastards!' came the sudden reply over the *Warrior*'s radio. Jon leapt round. Had he heard correctly? 'Bring the stern in now,' the *Pacific Fisher* ordered the tugboat.

'That's it!' said Jon, racing down to the engine room. 'Bugger the injunction, we're going in. Our people are in danger; we can't just sit around.'

Bruce and I stood up in the Zodiac, preparing ourselves for whatever was about to happen. Although the *Pacific Fisher* appeared to be speeding up as she slid towards us, the actual event seemed to pass in incredibly slow motion. I craned my neck to look up at this sheer wall of steel towering above us and still moving. When would she stop? I looked behind me and saw the stone wall. Would I be squashed between the two? I was strangely fascinated by the prospect. Was this The End? My End? My life hadn't flashed before my eyes yet, so maybe I was being spared.

'Jump Susi, for fuck's sake — jump. Move!'

This was obviously not the time for morbid reverie. It was time to figure out exactly what to do. The inflatable was buckling underfoot, the rubber screeching like a stuck pig as the wooden slats on the deck popped up, then cracked. I jumped onto the pontoon. As I scrambled to my feet, I saw Bruce leap into the churning water by the propeller. I felt sick. He could so easily be sucked under and decapitated. He surfaced, and started gesticulating wildly.

'Get out of there, Susi!' he screamed. 'The fuel tank's going to explode!'

I watched as the tank started to crumple up like tinfoil and fuel spilled out. By now the *Pacific Fisher* was almost completely alongside the pontoon. I was literally stuck between a rock and a hard place. I gauged the height of the stone pier, which comprised large blocks of stone cemented together, and grabbed hold of a weed growing out of a crack to pull myself up. It came away in my hand.

I turned to look at the *Pacific Fisher*, figuring that all I could do now was jump into the water and swim towards Athel's boat. Just as I was readying myself for contact with the freezing sea, streaked with petrol from our destroyed Zodiac, a pair of hands grabbed me under my arms and I felt myself being hoisted up the stone wall. Suddenly, I was standing on a grassy verge, surrounded by several policemen. I could see some barbed wire in the distance and more police — riot police, in fact. It was still quite misty, but I was able to make out the faces of people behind the barbed wire. They were holding placards and chanting. It looked as if there were several hundred. I was impressed.

'Got yourself into a bit of a tight spot down there, dear?' said one of the cops in a typical PC Plod way. I had no idea how I had been lifted. Had they formed a human chain as someone dangled down the wall to grab me? I saw Athel in his boat at the forward pontoon, and it looked as if the tugboat at that end had stopped.

'Would you like a cup of tea?' The policeman thrust a vacuum flask of piping hot tea towards me.

'No thanks,' I said and started to walk off, with a slight stagger. I could feel the wet grass underfoot — the first land in weeks. After being at sea it often took a few minutes for my balance to readjust and I wondered whether the officers would think I was drunk. I could see a way of getting down to the pontoon at the other end of the pier, but it would mean a bit of a swim.

However, as quickly as I had been hauled up the pier wall, I was grabbed, locked in a tight grip and marched by several policemen to the edge of the wharf. The protesters cheered as we approached. I was escorted out of the secured area and told not to try anything stupid. I didn't particularly want to join the demonstration — I was too worried about what had happened to Bruce. Athel would be OK. He and his driver would be arrested — it was probably happening about then — and be escorted off somewhere, and the *Pacific Fisher* would finally come alongside.

There had been no photographers with us in the boats, no one to capture the incident on film. Would anyone believe us when we told them how they had tried to kill us? Perhaps we could sneak back later and take a photo of the mangled Zodiac. But with what? All I had with me was my tobacco and the green stone. The apple had long gone.

I decided to walk to a small cove near the wharf, where we'd planned to rendezvous should we become separated. As I made my way down the headland, the sound of the demonstration fading in the distance, I looked out across the water. I was vaguely hoping I'd be able to catch a glimpse of the *Rainbow Warrior*. I felt alone and was starting to get cold. 'Can I borrow your lighter?' a voice said. I swung round, my heart pounding in my ears. It was Bruce! I rushed up to him and gave him a hug. 'I was wondering how long it would take you to get here!' he joked. 'Let's start a fire. We've got a long night ahead of us.' The plan was that a couple of

190

Zodiacs would be deployed to pick us up at dawn. I was prepared for a miserable night trying to sleep on the shingle in wet clothing.

Bruce told me he'd swum as far away from the ship as possible and then dragged himself ashore. His voluminous wet-weather gear had quickly filled up with water when he leapt overboard and nearly drowned him, so he'd discarded it and was wearing hardly anything at all. We managed to start a small fire of bracken and driftwood and danced around it to keep warm. Now that I was relaxing, I was starting to feel hungry. It would soon be time for afternoon tea on the *Warrior*, and there was still some of Athel's banana cake. What I would have given for a piece then.

Bruce stood up and pointed towards the horizon. 'Can you see anything?' he asked, squinting.

I looked, and barely made out a familiar outline. 'It's the *Warrior*,' I said. 'She's coming towards us.'

Later, in the *Rainbow Warrior*'s mess, as we raced back to the safety of international waters, we sat round telling our stories of the day, sipping the expensive whisky Jon only brought out for special occasions. It had been a close shave all right. Jon said he wished he'd had a tape recorder to capture the *Pacific Fisher*'s order to 'squash the bloody bastards'.

'What a cheek,' he said, in his usual moderate way. 'Did they think I would just leave you there? Not bloody likely.'

Martini had come ashore and picked us up in an inflatable. We hadn't had a chance to talk properly since returning to the ship, as he'd been busy taking over from Jon on the bridge. 'Close call, eh?' he'd said, quietly, as I stood in the head removing my wet clothes.

'Yes,' I replied, 'but I had my stone with me. It's here somewhere.' I rummaged around inside my underwear, where I'd put it for safekeeping, then we stood looking at each other, his gaze filling me with infinite longing. There was really nothing more to say. We knew it would happen. There was time. There was all the time in the world.

'Martini, excuse me, I've just heard on the radio that there's a big storm.' It was Stringbean. He'd been in the radio room and had caught the weather forecast. There was an unusual edge to his voice. 'They're predicting force 11, possibly force 12. All traffic has been warned to look for shelter.'

'Thanks' said Martini, 'I'll be right up.' He turned and looked at me as he left for the bridge. 'See you later, then,' he said. 'Keep warm.'

12

On the night of 13 August 1979, a near hurricane-force storm swept across the North Atlantic, slamming into the Fastnet Race, one of the toughest yachting events in the world, with epic fury. Fifteen people were killed. Of the 303 boats taking part, from 22 countries, five sank, 100 rolled down so their masts hit the water, and a further 75 were flipped upside down. It is now regarded as the deadliest storm in the history of modern sailing.

On the *Rainbow Warrior*, on the same body of water, seven months after that infamous storm, we, too, were about to experience the wrath of the ocean. To complicate matters, we had an injunction hanging over our heads. Keeping to international waters would mean riding out the weather without any form of shelter. It was a tough call.

As the swell increased we cleared the decks, battened down the hatches and stowed everything below. Martini, Jon and Bruce remained on the bridge together, one of them lashed to the wheel at all times. The only thing we could do was point the *Warrior* into the wind at full throttle and try to keep in position until the storm abated or we ran out of diesel.

The storm lasted 15 hours and raged up to hurricane force 13 — the highest recorded wind speeds. I was unable to remain upright because of the ferocious slamming of the boat into the troughs between the gigantic waves. A supernatural force would pick it up as if it were a Dinky Toy, shake it around and then dump it viciously back down. I wedged myself into my bunk, bracing myself for each impact. I could hear stuff flying around in the galley, objects being catapulted from one bulkhead to the other. All that movement and pressure made my head feel pretty weird, as if my brain was being sucked out of my skull. It was too much to bear at times, and I drifted into a state of semiconsciousness.

'Will we survive the storm?' I asked Martini when he stuck his head around the cabin door to see how I was doing.

'I think so,' he replied. 'She's a very sturdy ship.'

During those times of relative calm when the wind abated to a Force 12, 11 or, if we were lucky, 10, I'd try to leave the cabin to see what was happening in the rest of the ship. I encountered a bedraggled Steve in the galley. The place was a mess. A glutinous mixture of aduki beans and molasses was dripping off the bulkheads onto the deck, pots had burst free of their mounts and entire drawers had been flung from their cupboards.

'This is my third attempt at getting the guys on the bridge a cup of tea,' said Steve. I admired his resilience and gave him a hand.

As we struggled with what would normally have been such a simple task, Steve told me there had been a few Mayday calls over the radio. We were powerless to help anyone — we were going backwards very fast ourselves, and trying to get round Land's End. At some point during the storm an oil platform overturned.

By the end, everyone had reached breaking point. We were absolutely exhausted, covered in bruises from being tossed about like rag dolls. I came to lying face down on my bunk in a small patch of dried-up vomit, my hair matted and plastered across my face. Every inch of my body ached. I'm alive, I thought, trying to open my eyes.

Everything was calm and I could hear seagulls. I pulled myself closer to the porthole to take a look. All I could see were a few sunken masts sticking out of the water. Some storm that was, I reflected, before realising we were at anchor outside Falmouth and the masts were casualties of other storms over the years. I was relieved the *Rainbow Warrior* hadn't joined that exclusive cemetery. I could see the outline of Martini's body reflected in the small shaving mirror above the basin; he was curled up on his bunk still in his wet-weather gear.

Jon had pinned a small note to the dartboard in the mess. 'Thanks for all your help during the storm,' it read with his usual understatement.

We returned to Amsterdam to overhaul the engine and have the fish hold transformed into a cinema and library. Meanwhile, the board of British Transport Docks had asked the High Court to seize the assets of Greenpeace Ltd for breaking the injunction at Barrow-in-Furness, or seek a prison term for the organisation's three directors. Our position was that we'd never had any intention of endangering navigation, only of preventing the *Pacific Fisher* from unloading its lethal cargo. British Nuclear

Fuels were the criminals for endangering the lives of thousands of people by transporting a highly dangerous material around the world. It was nothing less than a crime against humanity. However, in imposing fines — a total of £800 — on the organisation and its directors, the judge — Mr Justice Pain — said it would be inappropriate to gaol anyone: 'That they are honourable people, I accept; I do not think prison is the place for people like them'. Sitting in the public gallery of the court, with all its wigs, pomp and circumstance and years of tradition, I felt a renewed faith in the British justice system and extremely proud of our actions. Of course we were honourable people. The judge could see that.

Hilari returned to the *Warrior* during the refit in Holland. I was delighted to have my soul sister back on board, even though her stay would be short-lived because of a reoccuring health problem. Her parting gesture was to organise all the supplies, clean the cupboards and label the buckets of beans and jars of spices. We'd shopped for them together in Amsterdam, Jon making a list and pinning it to the dartboard in the mess. It had read: 'Marmite, tomato sauce, 6 blue biros, 2 pencils — 2B or softer, washing-up liquid, toothpaste', and then in Athel's handwriting: 'Woods Old Navy (medicinal), chocolate biscuits, 180 yaourts [yoghurts], butter, cheese, dancing girls, perch (one, for the use of), feeding trough, beer, fags'.

We sailed to Rotterdam to take part in an unprecedented blockade of boats belonging to Bayer, the pharmaceutical company, to prevent them from carrying toxic chemical waste for dumping in the North Sea. For three days and nights, our Zodiacs, the *Warrior* and an assortment of Dutch barges managed to stop them from leaving port. We had the support of both the mayor of Rotterdam and the water police. The action was called off only when Bayer agreed to have their dumping procedures investigated. I'd been handcuffed to one of their boats, the *Rose-Marie S.*, since the beginning of the protest. The chief engineer had come out on deck and taunted us in German, saying he would start the engines and chop us up like mincemeat with the propeller. I certainly didn't want to die — not like that — especially since Martini and I had fallen into each other's arms one night. We'd become inseparable, best mates as well as lovers. Chris had put in an appearance during the refit, joining us for the upcoming antiwhaling campaign in Spain. He had been a bit taken aback when I'd explained that I'd fallen love with Martini — he'd expected unconditional love, it seemed, in spite of having had an affair himself with a woman from the Greenpeace office in Paris. I told him he couldn't have his cake and eat it too. 'We'll still be friends, eh, Grub-bottom?' he asked. I could see he was upset.

'Of course we will, Rat,' I replied. I knew Chris, Martini and I would have no difficulty becoming firm friends. Chris respected Martini immensely and could see he'd supported me through a very difficult period.

'He's really staunch, that Martini. It's obvious he doesn't give up easily,' he said.

Mother must think I'm nuts, I thought; first Chris, then Martini. In one of our frank chats about men she'd given me a bit of advice. 'Always marry your best friend,' she had said. 'At least that way you know you'll get on.' She was right about friendship outliving sexual attraction. 'Believe you me, darling,' she said, painting her nails as she readied herself for the trip to Rome for her dinner date with Alfredo, the Italian landowner. 'If you wake up years later, after the honeymoon is over, next to someone you can't stand . . .' Alfredo had rented an apartment for her, and she was taking a girlfriend as well — Jean, my mother's constant companion since my father's death. I knew she wouldn't fall for any of it, though — the candlelit dinners, the studio apartment — but would remain true to my father until the day she died. She would never remarry, even if Alfredo were an old friend. There was no harm in my daydreaming, though — the guy was filthy rich.

A Jewish carpenter in his forties, Noah Morris, had joined the crew in late spring, bringing his Northumbrian pipes with him. It was he who converted the *Warrior*'s fish hold into a wonderful space in which we could show slides and films, make presentations and hold press conferences.

We left for Spain at the beginning of June, overflowing with people. There seemed to be cameras everywhere you looked. One film crew had cocktails every afternoon at five, on the dot, the sun well behind the yardarm in their book. I couldn't stand the go-faster anchorwoman, a well-known television journalist who, in my opinion, liked to report from anywhere in the world as long as it was dangerous but was outta there like a flash once she had the story. I'd been on board with her before, when she'd held us up waiting for a helicopter to pick up some footage taken at sea — of her doing something dramatic that would be on the TV news that night. I resented her presence on board; her narcissism annoyed me. It seemed that all she wanted was to report from the front line, she and her TV crew taking up valuable Zodiac space. We had our own film crew, people who were experienced at recording action in inflatables travelling at speed. I also thought she was obsessed with being the star of the show; everything was about her, not about saving the whales.

Somewhere on deck I could hear this woman's voice demanding a place on a Zodiac yet again. We'd followed one of Masso's whaling boats, the *Ibsa Tres*, out to the whaling grounds and had successfully stopped any whales from being killed. The Spanish navy had sent out a corvette, the *Cardaso*, but failed to stop us. A second corvette, the HV *Pinzón*, had appeared, and we'd been ordered to accept a boarding party. I was recovering from a bad blow to the head after being thrown against a bulkhead in bad weather. Jon had forbidden me from going out in the inflatables, and I was on watch instead. From the bridge, I could see the commander boarding the *Warrior* as Stringbean and Jon started removing important electrical fuses without which the ship couldn't operate, in an effort to resist seizure. After all, these were international waters. 'That'll really confuse them,' Stringbean said with a chuckle as he pocketed the fuses in his tie-dyed shirt, leaping down the stairs.

We were towed with great fanfare to the military harbour of El Ferrol, birthplace of Spanish fascism. Two of the navy's most sophisticated warships flanked us, vessel and crew under armed guard as we were escorted down a long, narrow channel dotted with military outposts. 'You won't be able to escape from here,' the commander told us. I knew they were pissed off at our taking off from La Coruña the year before, when we had made them look stupid. A bunch of whale-saving hippies outwitting the Spanish navy was not a good look. This time they'd be doing everything to prevent a repeat performance.

The admiral, his wife and a descending hierarchy of officers, all immaculate in spotless white uniforms, boarded in El Ferrol. Donning white cotton gloves, a handful of officers climbed down into the engine room. I wondered if the rails on the ladder had ever been cleaned — they always seemed to be covered in grease. After a discussion, the huddle of officers removed a vital part of the propeller, the thrust block, and carried it out in not-so-white gloves, presenting it to the admiral as if it were a prized bounty. I imagined their wives up to their elbows in soapsuds, trying to scrub *Rainbow Warrior* grease stains from their uniforms.

Jon offered the admiral and his wife a sherry in his cabin. The woman was beautiful, with dark hair swept into a bun and a hand-embroidered mantilla around her shoulders. She kept on glancing across at Jon and smiling. I could sense he was flattered by the attention; his face was flushed. She turned to speak to him, flashing her dark eyes as she and her husband left the ship, walking slowly behind the thrust block, which was being carried like a baby in the arms of an officer. 'I will come down and have tea with you one afternoon, *Capitán*. Until then, *adiós*.'

Jimi Hendrix was blasting through the speakers on deck, and the young conscripts who were guarding us played air guitar on their machine guns. 'Can we join your rainbow ship when we finish our military service?' one of them asked. Now its whaling activities were no longer a secret, Spain had become a member of the IWC, and we had heard it was exporting whale meat to Japan. As well as British media, we had Spanish, Japanese and Icelandic press people on board. It was very squashed, with all available bunk space taken.

During the action we'd managed to fob off the anchorwoman with the 'too dangerous for your own safety' routine. It seemed to work, and her cameraman looked relieved too. He'd been making himself useful helping in the galley, where I'd got him to sort out our stock of lentils, removing those little stones that chip your teeth.

The TV crews had interesting stories to tell in that hardened-old-sod sort of way. I enjoyed yakking with them and probing their tough exteriors. Jon was concerned I could be haemorrhaging from the blow I'd taken to my head, as I'd been bringing up small amounts of blood. He radioed a ship's doctor, who recommended I be taken to a military hospital immediately on arrival at El Ferrol. I felt strange — not exactly ill, just different. It was hard to explain.

Noah was out on the deck as we arrived in El Ferrol, playing his pipes. We heard the strains of other pipes somewhere in the distance, and were told Galician freedom fighters were welcoming us. In the depth of that simple musical exchange, alliances were formed and struggles acknowledged. A cordon of police and military had formed several metres from where we were to be tied up. Behind the thin blue line hundreds of people waved and cheered their support. Athel and I were on the bridge together, watching the crowd.

'Can you see that stunning woman in the front, the one with dark glasses?' he said to me. 'She fancies me, I can tell!'

'She does not,' another male voice piped up. 'She's looking at me!'

As I descended the stairs from the bridge I heard the anchorwoman's voice screaming at someone in Spanish. Her grandmother was dying, she was yelling; she needed to leave the boat as soon as possible. Surely they won't fall for that one, I thought. We'd been told that none of us could leave, that we were all under arrest. That's the oldest line in the book, I said to myself as the woman repeated her request, laying it on thick. Getting nowhere, she marched up the gangplank with her luggage. We all watched nervously. Videotape of our arrest, shot in the whaling grounds, had been hidden in her underwear. It was our only chance to get it off the boat before they found it. She burst into tears again, pleading to be allowed to leave. No doubt about it, this woman put on a great show. 'Check my bags!' she said dramatically, throwing open her suitcase. The officer tentatively lifted up a couple of items of clothing, stopping abruptly when he reached the lingerie and shutting the suitcase in embarrassment.

'You may go,' he said, and waved her off the boat. Then it was my turn to leave; they were expecting me at the military hospital on the hill. In a shiny black limousine and accompanied by a couple of officers, I was taken off for a barrage of tests and x-rays.

A round-the-clock guard was mounted on the *Warrior*. Two months earlier, someone had planted bombs under two of Masso's whaling boats further down the coast, and we were the prime suspects. We were all being interviewed individually and served our own *papeleta de citación* — a summons to appear in court, in alphabetical order. The military bureaucracy took forever, and we were there for months. We asked for an interpreter and for all documents to be translated into English, and that slowed things down. Martini threatened to go on hunger strike if the *Warrior* wasn't released by the end of June. A letter he wrote to the Spanish authorities stated: 'Since dangerous nuclear wastes are about to be dumped close to the coast of Spain and whales are still being slaughtered, by holding us here you are directly preventing us from protecting not only the Spanish marine environment but the health and safety of generations to come.'

Everything about our arrest had been surreal, like a Bergman movie but with more heart. Jon and the admiral's wife regularly 'took tea' in the captain's room of an afternoon. He would bake biscuits especially. A couple of young women had run away from home, sneaked past guards snoring over *El País* and climbed on board in their tight Levis, seeking out warriors and luring them to the mountains and Galician barns.

We were definitely having the time of our lives as prisoners. We were allowed to go ashore, and had struck up a great friendship with the Galician independence movement. We snuck off to the hills, where the people prepared us a feast of roast pig. 'Please tell her that if I kiss her it doesn't mean I want to marry her,' Tom whispered to me. Along with Gerrit, one of our Dutch engineers, we were sitting round a bonfire looking out over the harbour, drinking the local grog with our Galician friends and listening to stories of their struggle for self-determination. The young women of the town couldn't get enough of the *Warrior* men. They'd turn up on the quay like lovelorn fans, trying to chat up the guards, begging to be allowed on board and following us whenever we went ashore. When it was obvious the ship would be detained for a while, a couple of well-respected local families sent their Warrior-besotted daughters overseas to spend the summer in the Canary Islands.

El Ferrol may well have been the birthplace of General Franco, Spain's fascist dictator for 36 years, but the locals sure could party. A huge music festival was held in our honour — musicians travelled from all over Europe to take part. On board, we passed the time maintaining a routine of slide shows, articles for the local paper and demonstrations. One night a few of us covered the ancient stones of the walled city with flyers, with 'Free the Rainbow Warrior' written in the local dialect.

A few days after our arrest, I was accompanied yet again to the hospital on the hill to receive the results of my tests. I was the only person in the crew who spoke any Spanish and the only person on board to have a direct link with the organisation suspected of planting the underwater bombs, and yet I was the only crew member who wasn't interrogated. I was also the only woman under arrest. Maybe it was precisely that — being *only* a woman — which meant I was irrelevant in Spain's macho military world. When we arrived I was escorted into a large airy room overlooking the harbour, where pastel-coloured frescos of cherubs and angels stared down at me from high ceilings. A crystal decanter of sherry had been placed in the middle of a highly polished desk with an inlaid leather top, three crystal sherry glasses arranged in perfect symmetry around it.

'*Por favor, señorita*, please be seated.' One of the two officers who had entered the room pointed to a large armchair near the desk. He poured me a large glass of sherry, and one for his colleague. 'Cigar?' he offered, reaching into his jacket pocket. I was beginning to kick back and enjoy this bizarre scene.

'¡*Salud!*' The official leaned forward to clink my glass with his. 'Congratulations, *señorita*, you are pregnant. God willing, it will be a male.' The other officer mumbled something in agreement and we all took a sip of sherry together.

It took a couple of liquid mouthfuls for the news to sink in. I was pregnant! How lovely! Then, suddenly, I remembered the x-rays and felt immediate despair. Had I known I was pregnant, I wouldn't have agreed to have them — no way. The officer was burbling on — he seemed quite proud of the fact that he'd made a correct diagnosis of my condition. The blood I'd been bringing up was a hormonal thing, and a simple urine test had confirmed his suspicion. X-rays of my lungs had been necessary to rule out any problems there. 'And remember, do not smoke, do not drink, and eat plenty of lentils.' I looked down at the sherry glass he had refilled, and the cigar he'd given me; I'd already smoked half of it.

'Why lentils?' I asked.

'Because they are full of iron,' he answered, winking, 'and we men need a lot of iron.'

During the night of 3 July, Athel, Chris and Bruce took off in the rigid-hull inflatable, destination the IWC in Brighton, to bring the matter of our illegal arrest in international waters to the commission's attention. The Icelandic coastguard had returned the boat to us eight months after seizing it. It was in a sorry state, and we had to wait for parts to arrive to repair it. Static electricity was interfering with its compass, but the three set off anyway, with Bruce as navigator, using hand-held compasses and detailed charts. They made their way across the Bay of Biscay to the Channel Islands, where they broke down.

Athel and Tim Mark then drove around England trying to locate the blueprints of the engine of the *Sir William Hardy* so they could organise the machining of a new thrust block. The problem was how to get the 100-kilogram part onto the *Rainbow Warrior* in El Ferrol. Driving across the border into Spain in David's old VW campervan, the thrust block hidden in the back, Athel, Tim and Tony Marriner knew they were taking a huge risk, but had plenty of time on the journey to think up a way of smuggling the part on board. It would have to be done in front of the guards — there was no other way.

The guards had grown accustomed to the crew returning late at night somewhat the worse for wear. Tony parked the VW on the quay so they would get used to the sight of it near the boat, and a couple of days were allowed to elapse before an attempt was made to smuggle the thrust block on board. At midnight, a group of drunken revellers returned to the boat from a local bar, Athel among them. He climbed into the back of the van as they staggered towards the boat and pretended to look for something, quickly picking up the heavy thrust block hidden in a laundry basket under some clothing. Stumbling onto the boat under the weight of the engine piece, he appeared drunk to the guards — a little more than usual, perhaps — but nothing to get suspicious about.

In August, the navy went on a two-month vacation, leaving the matter of our detention unresolved. In October, a bail of $142,000 was demanded for the release of the *Warrior*, and, rather than pay the money, which was destined to end up in the hands of the whalers, we planned an escape. American President Jimmy Carter was in Spain on an official visit, and Stringbean, the only US citizen on board, decided to lobby him through the American embassy in Madrid. He was missing his family and was distressed at how long everything was taking. He'd discovered a public telephone nearby which, if you inserted a coin in a particular way — half in, half out, twisting it slightly to the left — gave you a connection. One at a time we'd wander out to the magic phone and make phone calls around the world. Don't ask me how Stringbean figured out the technique — he was a hacker at heart.

'Dear President Carter,' his letter began. He was reading it slowly over the phone to the ambassador's personal assistant.

> I am an American citizen representing Greenpeace USA and I am currently being detained in Spain. Greenpeace has conducted a peaceful protest in international waters 60 miles off the coast of Spain to interrupt the slaughter by Spanish whalers (sic). The environmental ship *Rainbow Warrior* is in the hands of the Spanish Navy and the final fate of our ship and its crew is unknown at this time. I ask that you speak out while you are here on behalf of the whales, and encourage the growing environmental concern of the Spanish people.

Stringbean didn't get a reply, but he did get his passport back and was allowed to leave and return to his family in Tennessee, arriving home as something of a local hero.

I was trying not to worry about the x-rays and the developing being in my uterus. Martini was overjoyed he was going to be a father, but also concerned about radiation damage — he'd seen first-hand the effects of radiation during the Pacific Peace Odyssey when the *Fri* had visited Hiroshima and Nagasaki. My mother phoned our family doctor, who advised I return home as soon as possible and see a genetic specialist. On 8 July, Martini wrote a letter to Naval Superintendent Vadillo, the big cheese in '*Causa 92/30*', as our case was known, requesting he be allowed to accompany me to England. His letter read:

> I believe that I can't let her return to England by herself since important decisions may have to be made. The decision to leave Spain is 100% my own and made independently from the *Rainbow Warrior*. One of the articles of the Convention of Human Rights states that persons have free travel through countries. Since I haven't been officially charged with anything under Spanish military law, I see no reason why I cannot freely return to England. My only crime is that I tell the truth. *Salvad las ballenos* (sic).

Four months later, at 8 o'clock in the evening on Saturday 8 November, under a new moon, the *Rainbow Warrior* left El Ferrol unheeded, motoring gently down the fortified channel in total darkness, her seven crew dressed from head to foot in dark clothing. The guards were due to change shift and had been getting a bit lax with their surveillance, often walking away from their posts. Saturday night was fiesta night and something special was happening in town. As skipper, Jon had to decide when the ship would leave. The guards had been carefully observed and their movements logged. The thrust block had been installed on the propeller shaft, and, with the excuse of having to turn the ship round to do some painting work, the crew had started acclimatising the guards to sounds from within the engine room. The other way round, too, the ship was pointing in the right direction for a hasty exit.

David had flown in at the last minute. He wanted to be on board for the escape, and had dispatched Pete Wilkinson — who in turn had been sent to replace Remi — to the Channel Islands to arrange a press conference. Arriving 12 hours before the appointed time and not wanting to hang around at sea, the *Rainbow Warrior* missed half the press corps travelling there especially to greet her. From the Channel Islands she made for Amsterdam and a special welcome from a huge crowd of jubilant friends and supporters. News had already reached the boat that the Spanish government had sacked the admiral for failing to capture the escapees.

I imagined how the poor guards must have felt, returning to their posts after their clandestine sortie beyond the gates, to find no trace of boat or crew. We were a familiar sight by then — we'd been there almost five months to the day.

13

'So, you're the *Rainbow Warrior* woman everyone has been telling me about.'

The consultant psychiatrist at Rotterdam's main hospital looked like Albert Einstein — small, with shaggy white hair. He seemed warm and friendly, and I noticed his Biro had leaked in his pocket, staining his white coat with red ink — or was it blood? It was hard to tell what was real anymore.

'Passing urine? Bowel movement today? Hallucinations?' The nurse ticked off the various boxes on her chart.

'Hallucinations?' I queried.

'You know, have you seen Micky or Donald anywhere today?' came the reply.

Someone down the corridor started screaming, banging on the door of a seclusion cell. The soundproofing couldn't contain the tortured anguish nor the terrible despair.

We were in the nursery, in a ward several storeys up. I had been rubbing rosemary oil into Brenna's hair when the psychiatrist arrived. Barely a month old, Brenna had been allowed to come with me in the ambulance from Amsterdam. I'd heard her cries from the corridor and begged a nurse to unlock the door of the nursery and let me in so I could comfort her. Several cots had stood empty, and she had been the only baby there. 'Five minutes,' the nurse had said, looking at her watch before locking the door from the outside, only to unlock it a few seconds later to let in the consultant.

We had decided to go ahead with the pregnancy, as it was impossible to tell just what the risks were. I'd thrown the I Ching, and the result — '*Sheng/Pushing Upward*' — had given us hope. 'If you were my wife,' a young Dutch doctor had said on our return to Holland from El Ferrol,

'I'd be encouraging you to have the baby.' And so, on 19 February 1981, at 2.46 a.m., my first daughter, Brenna Jo, came into the world after a 26-hour labour — on an inland-waterway barge called *Orca*, in Spijkerkade, Amsterdam.

Orca was owned by some friends — a couple — who had kindly let us stay on her while they were on holiday. I didn't know it at the time, but the woman, Janie, had become infatuated with Martini and tried to seduce him more than once.

After Brenna's birth, I didn't sleep at all for many days. The moment of her birth had been strange. She wouldn't breathe and an ambulance had been called. In those moments, as the midwife did everything in her power to get Brenna's little lungs to take their first breath, I felt numb, devoid of feeling. The labour had been long, Brenna had been in a strange position, and the midwife had been massaging the neck of the cervix in an effort to push it over Brenna's head. Brenna looked so placid when she came out, lying motionless, her face squashed from all the pushing. I became quite manic, and spent the first day writing dozens of cards to friends telling them about the birth. Within a week, I'd organised a passport for her — we were planning to go to New Zealand — had visited the Greenpeace office, and had shopped and cooked for nearly two dozen friends who had dropped by, some staying the night — in a space the size of a bedroom. The strenuous labour had induced a maddening humming sound in my ears, which was also keeping me awake, and I was breast-feeding every two hours.

The *Rainbow Warrior* was preparing to cross the North Atlantic to the United States, and I had mixed feelings about seeing her leave. She was just across the water from where *Orca* was moored, and 10 days after Brenna's birth I went on board and curled up in the 'cook and boy', praying for some sleep as I was comforted by the familiar sounds. By now, the surface of the earth appeared to be undulating in ripples, to the background hum only I could hear. I was growing more and more agitated, wondering when the noise would lessen or go away.

'There is absolutely nothing wrong with your ears,' the ENT specialist said, pushing away the machine that had been probing my inner ear.

'But I can hear something there,' I insisted. I'd tried everything to get it out, eventually making my ears bleed. How could he tell me there was nothing there?

'I think what you need is a psychiatrist,' was his parting comment. I knew that what I was hearing was real, even though it would take me years to discover I was suffering from tinnitus.

Tom sat cross-legged on the mattress with tears in his eyes. He'd come to say goodbye before the *Warrior* left. He had a box with him. 'We want to give you this,' he said, 'for safekeeping.' Inside I found scraps of paper, crew lists, records of sleeping arrangements, poems we'd written, postcards received, jokes, diagrams — all from the mess bulkhead. 'We've cleaned out the boat, removed her spirit. There's nothing there now. It's the end of the story. You'll look after these, Susi. We trust you.'

I caressed each item lovingly; there were so many stories attached to them, such love, such hope. A chill made its way slowly up my spine, threadlike tentacles of fear creeping across my scalp. Everything looked and tasted metallic, bitter. Something terrible would happen if the ship left Europe, I knew it. I felt it in every atom of my being. All I could think about was stopping her from leaving Amsterdam.

I was eventually taken to the Crisis Centre in Amsterdam and placed under suicide watch. I was allowed out into the park, once a day, as long as I was accompanied by a member of the assessment team.

'Uranus is in conjunction with Saturn at the moment,' the young male staff member said as we strolled around the park. 'Maybe that is why you're having such a bad time.'

I'd been wailing all day long, knees hunched up, rocking back and forth. This was a bit more than Uranus in conjunction with fucking Saturn, I thought to myself. They'd been giving me oral sedation to knock me out, and had told me I'd have to stop breast-feeding Brenna. I was devastated. I adored this little girl with her dark hair and huge eyes. Someone had told us 'Brenna' meant 'to burn' in Icelandic. She had been born to the strains of Irish music and whale sounds, and now this lot wanted to rip my breast out of her mouth and fill me with drugs.

Before prescribing any further medication, the team was waiting until the consultant psychiatrist from the University of Amsterdam had assessed me. I was totally confused, having by now lost the ability to communicate. It was as if reality had moved over one notch, clonk, to the gateway of another realm. In the split second of departure from reality, it felt as if something had grabbed my inner being and devoured it. It was a lobotomy of the soul.

I'd been sitting on the edge of the double bunk we slept in on board *Orca*, staring at nothing, into that realm beyond space, when it appeared through a crack — suddenly — just like the fairies in the legends of old. It was a grotesque mythological beast, an evil-smelling apparition. Cold, damp air enveloped me as I fell to the floor. When it retreated, like a genie into a bottle, it took away whatever part of me it had come to claim.

Try telling a consultant psychiatrist a 'thing' has got your soul. The claim had got me all the way to Rotterdam pretty quickly, with 'Query diagnosis, floridly psychotic' written on the red plastic file beside me in the ambulance. It hadn't helped my case that Janie had also been dragged in to the Crisis Centre, right in the middle of my assessment. She was hysterical, screaming, 'I didn't mean it! I didn't mean it!', and was carried up the stairs by two strong-looking individuals, a jagged piece of broken mirror in her hand, with which she was taking the odd stab at herself.

'Do you know her?' the consultant asked me. We'd both left the room to see what was happening. I explained the connection.

'Have I got schizophrenia?' I asked him. 'Is it something to do with having had a baby?' I wanted answers. Things just don't change like that from one second to the next without some kind of explanation. This was a nightmare, each second more unbearable than the one before, a permanent state of pure terror as I considered the possibility that reality would remain like this for me from now on. It was worse than a bad acid trip I'd had in Fulham back in the early '70s, when I'd tried to phone the police to find out if they had a record of my existence. Athel had literally sat on the phone for several hours to stop me, as I couldn't be trusted not to make the call. The Northwood pavement had pulsated paisley all the way to Cathi's parents' house as a clear-blue Jefferson Airplane sky had grinned down at me. I hated the stuff. Give me peyote any time.

'You've been reading too many women's magazines, Susan,' the consultant said. He looked elegant in a fashionable suit. The Dutch were always so accommodating — everything worked, the trains ran on time. 'We no longer use the term schizophrenia these days, we call it psychosis.'

'How long will it go on for?' I asked, matter-of-factly.

'That is not known,' the doctor replied, 'but it can be controlled with medication, with psychopharmaceuticals and neuroleptics.'

I wondered why they didn't think of a better name. Who in their right mind would want to take something called a psy-cho-phar-ma-ceu-ti-cal or a neuroleptic, let alone be able to pronounce it? There was no way I was going to swallow that shit.

I couldn't figure out what Janie was doing there. She looked so haunted. We communicated a couple of times during our insanity — she was taken to a psychiatric institution in the country, and phoned me to say she was working outside in the gardens. Once, on weekend release, she dropped by to visit. I was extremely unwell at the time, yet there was a sense of solidarity between us, of shared experience through our parallel descents into hell. It was impossible to verbalise much at the time, but I felt she was trying to tell me something. She seemed to blame herself in some way for what had happened to me.

At night, as I lay in bed in the ward, I listened to the night-lights buzzing around the skirting. I still wasn't sleeping, and sedation didn't seem to work. I refused to take any of the antipsychotics that had been recommended. I watched the nurses with their belts of keys and chains unlock the drug cabinet in the hall outside the locked ward and peer in terror through the small window in the heavy door that separated me from reality. Knock-you-out syringes and zombie pills — just as long as none of it was coming my way.

'Why do you want to move to New Zealand?' the registrar had asked me in his office, which was located in the unlocked ward, where I went each day for art therapy. He had a copy of *The Scream* by Edvard Munch on the wall. Talk about subtle, I thought.

'Because it's a great place to bring up kids,' I answered.

'What's wrong with this?' he said, pointing to the grey skyline of industrial Europe. 'This is progress.'

I never spoke to the guy again except to ask if I could see an acupuncturist. What's the point, I thought? What's the fucking point of talking to any of these clinicians? They never validated my experience. I just wanted to figure out a way of leaving the hospital and retrieving my sanity.

There was a particular method of moving patients around the ward. The first room to the left as you came in, after the nursery, was Observation. Here, you were kept for a period of assessment and diagnosis. From there, you moved down the corridor to the main dormitory, from where you graduated to the last dormitory on the ward before being allowed to move through the locked doors, across the main landing, past the drug cabinet and into the unlocked ward on the other side. If you were naughty along the way, it was back to the beginning, a padded cell, or the Department of Neurology, located on the floor above, for The Operation. I'd seen a couple of old men who had come back to the ward after The

Operation, wearing bandages around their heads. They'd been shell-shocked during the war (the centre of Rotterdam had been razed to the ground) or tortured by the Nazis in labour camps. They shuffled around the lounge and corridors, soiling themselves regularly. I never saw them out of pyjamas.

I'd formed a friendship with a beautiful young woman who, in a drug-induced psychosis, had slit open the main arteries in her arms with razors, from wrists to armpits, right down the middle. We'd meet in the nurses' station every night, when everyone else was fast asleep, and share a hot drink. I'd give Brenna her night-time bottle at the same time — the nurses had offered to help, but I didn't want them anywhere near her. I wasn't allowed to spend more than two hours a day with her, and I'd hear her crying behind the locked door and not be allowed to comfort her. I admired my young friend for wearing her raw scars so openly, the long red welts studded with stitch-marks.

Some of us were taken to see a film one evening at a local cinema. Out in public it was a struggle to feel a part of what was going on, and my new friend wore a long-sleeved shirt. We sat together and held hands when the going got rough. People smiled. There was no way they could understand, I thought. How could anybody explain what it was like? We were in another realm, a place where time and space had no meaning, just the constant terror of coping with each passing moment.

'She's looking for her soul,' Martini said in Dutch to a friend on the phone. 'She's behind the couch looking for her fucking soul!' He laughed.

My days in the psychiatric ward had been put to some good use. I'd forced myself to learn Dutch in order to figure out what was being said about me. I can't say I blamed Martini for laughing. I was a pathetic sight, scratching behind the sofa like a cat looking for a place to shit. I was convinced that if I looked hard enough, I'd stumble across my soul, glowing and pulsating with energy; then I'd need to figure out how to get it back inside me. I'd heard that in the Philippines there were people who could plunge their hands into bodies and pull out tumours. There might be a backdoor somewhere, tailor-made for a soul's return.

'Have you thought about exorcism?' My mother was trying to be helpful. 'I mean, maybe you're possessed. I attended the exorcism of a friend once, in Argentina,' she went on. 'The evil spirit presented as a giant slug in her parent's lounge — she was the only one who could see it. The priest came, bell, book and candle and all that — very successful.

Highly recommended.'

I'd discharged myself from the hospital, and was now an outpatient at a community mental-health centre in Rotterdam and getting no better, still refusing to take medication. Martini had found a small flat for us in the centre of town and was working in the docks.

I'd taken to phoning people at random, picking a name out of the directory. I would ask ridiculous questions. I had the idea that if I walked far enough I'd be able to get rid of the foul entity within me, the poison. 'Do you think,' I would ask the innocent person at the other end of the phone, 'that if I walked all the way to New Zealand, it would leave me alone?'

I attempted to kill myself on more than one occasion. First, I tried sleeping pills. I'd been stockpiling my prescription of sleepers, and when I'd collected enough I downed them with some alcohol. I didn't bother writing a note. I didn't know what to say. 'Can't stand it any longer' was all that came to mind; it didn't seem enough. When I opened my eyes again, it was almost a whole day later. What a drag, I thought, I'm still here. I felt terrible and looked even worse. My tongue was yellow and I had parched lips. I thought I'd calculated the correct dose, but something had obviously gone wrong. The stuff was useless.

The next attempt to take my own life was even more unglamorous. I'd been doing a bit of research into what constituted a lethal dose of various household products, and had read that a certain amount of tobacco ingested would give a lethal dose of nicotine. We were now staying with Martini's parents, in a small attic. I felt I was a burden on the ageing couple — they'd been through a terrible war and lived hand to mouth, struggling for years to cope with the aftermath. My little psychosis seemed very insignificant by comparison.

I purchased a bottle of vodka and a 50-gram packet of Drum tobacco and laid them out, ritualistically, in front of me on the dining-room table. I was so fixated, so absorbed by my malaise, that I'd left Brenna outside a supermarket in her pram and walked home alone.

'Where's Brenna?' a neighbour asked as I mounted the stairs to the front door of the apartment. I raced all the way back to the shop, my heart pounding. She was still there, fast asleep, oblivious to the drama playing itself out in my mind. I put her in her cot when we got home, went downstairs and downed the Drum and vodka, stuffing handfuls of tobacco in my mouth and chasing each with a tumbler of spirit. I hadn't factored in the body's own innate sense of self-preservation. No sooner had I got the stuff down than it came up again, unannounced. I was found on my hands and knees, spewing my guts out on the dining-room carpet. Another failure, this one with a capital F.

A gun. I'd buy a gun. That would do the job nicely. I pushed Brenna's pram around the seedier part of town, peering through the dirty windows of weapons' retailers. I was shown a couple of revolvers, produced from under the counter. Did I have a licence? Well, not exactly . . . I left quickly.

My next choice was a jump from the highest building in Europe, which, it just so happened, was only a bus-ride away. Nice one. I'd forgotten, however, that I suffered from vertigo. I'd once fainted on a mountainside on Samos while carrying bricks from a small chapel in a cliff-side cave on the eastern side of Kerkis to a monastery above Megalo Seitani (an errand I was running for an old woman — part abbess, part mother superior, part caretaker. She served Turkish delight on toothpicks to thank me for my trouble. I didn't have the heart to tell her I'd lost a few bricks over the side when I'd keeled over after looking down.) I never saw the magnificent view of Rotterdam harbour, but I'm told it's stunning. I didn't even get as far as the railings on the viewing platform. As I was assisted to my feet by a couple of strong arms I heard a kindly voice say, 'You fainted, dear!' I came to squinting up at a group of faces staring down at me. How embarrassing. How farcical. These failed attempts at suicide were getting beyond a joke.

It's possible to take a couple of slugs of Draino, slit open your wrists with a razor and not feel a thing. It was a spontaneous decision — no planning. I simply got up, went over to the sink and that was that. Martini came into the room, with Brenna, just as I was slicing my left wrist and blood was spurting everywhere. I was hanging over the sink, trying to direct the flow so as not to make a mess, but it was splattering the wallpaper. My heart sank when I saw Brenna. She was screaming. We all were. I sat in the ambulance on the way to hospital waiting to die, and nothing was happening — not the slightest whisper of death, not even the merest hint. I remained in hospital a month, fed through a tube in my nose. Apparently the Draino had burned my insides. Fool me.

This time I was on the neurology ward, where I passed my time reading to a young junkie who had brain damage from some street heroin mixed with dental anaesthesia. She dribbled onto her hospital gown, blowing bubbles with her saliva. Her friends were in the morgue: the same batch had stopped their hearts completely.

After I had been discharged I was taken to Amsterdam to recuperate on the *Fri*, which was now berthed there for a refit, preparing to do some charitable work in Haiti. Martini was keen to return to his old home, and there was another child on board as well, the same age as Brenna. I spent my days hiding under blankets, listening to the trains passing above the canal, planning my next suicide attempt. I would hurl myself in front of one as soon as I had enough energy to get up the bank and onto the rails. I fantasised about oblivion.

The crew of the *Fri* busied themselves around the ship, avoiding me — as one generally does the insane — and largely ignoring me. I felt so alone, incapable and stigmatised. My raw wrists were like Day-Glo in the mess at dinner. I was a freak. Did they understand that it was a full-time effort just hanging in there, in this hurricane-force storm I was in? It had been almost a year now. It wasn't that I was useless — I was trying to get back. Martini had been my anchor and my rudder; he kept pointing me into the wind. 'It'll come right,' he repeated, holding my convulsing body tightly. 'All storms come to an end.'

I hurt my back on deck and was taken to an American chiropractor. One look at me and he knew something was wrong. 'What the hell are you on?' he asked. I told him. I don't know if it was the spinal manipulation he gave me, or the mega-doses of vitamin B he persuaded me to take, or whether or not the storm had just run its natural course, but within three days of my first seeing him, a miracle occurred.

One of the Dutch engineers on the *Rainbow Warrior*, a man called Ton, had come to cook an Indian vegetarian meal on the *Fri*. He brought a copper cooking pot with him, and a mortar and pestle to grind up the curry spices. After the meal, I went to lie down. As I stepped onto the deck — clunk. Reality had shifted back. There are no words to describe the blessedness of that moment. My sentience returned and I felt my wholeness restored. I felt illuminated, as if I'd been reborn. I stepped gingerly onto the footpath — I hadn't been off the ship alone or taken a walk in months. Everything tingled and sparkled. Placing one foot in front of the other with increasing confidence, I walked barefoot through the grass, savouring its cool slipperiness on my skin. I skipped. I danced. I returned to the ship singing. I was back! The storm was over.

A pile of unopened letters awaited me, some several months old.

Among them was one from Allan, who'd finally left Greenpeace and was keen to continue the research on the Turkish dolphin hunt. During my pregnancy I'd passed on information about the hunt to various bodies — the International Union for Conservation of Nature and Natural Resources (IUCN), the Council of Europe (CoE), the Convention on International Trade in Endangered Species of Wild Fauna and Flora (CITES), the World Wildlife Fund (WWF, now the World-Wide Fund for Nature), etc. — and in my absence, during my insanity, it seemed as if all the work I'd done had begun to pay off. The CoE was bringing the matter before the Bonn Convention on Migratory Species (CMS), and in March 1983 I received a letter from the CoE informing me Turkey had banned dolphin hunting. What was possibly the largest cetacean hunt of all time had ended.

Another victory took place on 24 July 1982, when the IWC voted to impose a global moratorium on commercial whaling by a resounding majority of 25 to seven. The practice would be phased out over the next three-and-a-half years, the moratorium coming into effect in 1986. Iceland walked out of the commission in disgust and carried on whaling until 1989, calling it 'scientific whaling'. More recently, it has been readmitted to the commission by a margin of one vote, although it still doesn't recognise the moratorium. Japan and Norway continue to hunt minke whales to this day for 'scientific' purposes, while the commission also sanctions aboriginal hunting in the Arctic and West Indies.

It took me several months to recover fully from the puerperal psychosis a young woman psychiatrist in Amsterdam had finally confirmed, conceding officially what I had long suspected. I knew it wasn't a case of my having read 'too many women's magazines' — I'd never read such things at all.

I'd spoken on the phone with someone who had recovered from the same illness. 'Can you laugh?' I'd asked her. At the time nothing seemed quite so impossible as laughter.

'But of course I can,' she'd replied, offering me the only ray of hope I had in those 11 months of darkness.

I felt like deadwood on board the *Fri*, where people were hammering and sawing, sweating the new deck. I wanted to leave, to lie in the sun, to take one small step at a time. I would get flashbacks and have to retire to my bunk, to hold on and ride it out. While they only lasted a few minutes, they were terrifying: what if I got stuck and couldn't return? 'And if she has a psychotic attack at sea?' someone asked, debating whether or not I should be allowed to make the crossing to the United States. At least I had a certificate to prove my sanity, I thought. I knew it was the fear talking, and the frustration. All they could see was someone lying around and not lifting her game.

In the end I left for the United States by plane, taking Brenna with me. Martini would sail to Florida on the *Fri*. The *Rainbow Warrior* was already making her way along the eastern seaboard. I planned to go to the College of the Atlantic, on Mount Desert Island, in Bar Harbor, Maine, and do its four-year degree programme in human ecology. People will take me more seriously, I thought, if I have some letters after my name.

Martini was very loyal, ever tolerant, but, sadly, we reminded each other of the horrific journey we'd made together and needed to be apart to heal. Not a cross word had passed between us, but that's how it was. He visited us regularly in our snow-covered cottage, and the three of us took long walks on the frozen lakes nearby. I immersed myself totally in my studies, winning both a fellowship and an external scholarship to enable me to study at the college. I also supported myself by working in the library or in the research department of Allied Whale, the college's marine mammal laboratory.

The fellowship gave me the opportunity to catalogue photographs of finback whales in the Gulf of Maine, identifying individuals which returned each year, both long-distance matches and short-term stays. This was to enable us to study finback migrations and home ranges more easily in order to develop a better way of estimating populations. I spent hours at sea peering through binoculars, getting to know certain individual whales quite well, and vice versa. On more than one occasion, whales drew alongside, rolled over and checked me out with their small, intelligent, eyes.

We applied to Greenpeace International for funding to expand the research to cover other areas of the North Atlantic. Although photo-matching promised to deliver far greater knowledge of whales than could ever be obtained by so-called 'scientific whaling', and would have provided sound evidence of the inaccuracy of quota assessments, Greenpeace turned us down. Many more whales could have been saved by investing in our research than continually charging about in high-speed boats in front of harpoon guns for the television news. Yawn. It would certainly have been a lot cheaper.

♥

Steve Sawyer, now one of five Greenpeace International directors, tracked down Martini at my house in Maine to discuss a plan. Rongelap, an atoll in the Marshall Islands, had been contaminated by fallout from Bravo, a 1954 atomic test the Americans had called 'routine', consistently claiming that any fallout on the atoll had been accidental and carried there by an unforeseen change in wind direction. (In 1984, a declassified Defence Nuclear Agency report confirmed the fallout was not accidental.) Three years after the test, the Rongelapese were returned to their irradiated home. More than two decades after the atoll had been declared safe, they were told their choicest food-gathering areas were off limits. Senator Anjain, the island's representative in the Marshall Islands' parliament, appealed to Greenpeace for help. He wanted to move his people to Mejato, an uncontaminated atoll, as quickly as possible.

I hadn't been in contact with the *Rainbow Warrior* since Amsterdam, and had purposefully shut her out of my life. To me, Greenpeace had become a vacuous organisation steeped in internal wrangling and power struggles. Yet when Martini and Steve started planning the 1985 Pacific Peace Voyage of the *Rainbow Warrior* on the floor of my lounge, I felt a sense of renewed hope. 'I'm glad the *Warrior* will be involved in something like this,' I told them. 'It was always our intention that she go to the South Pacific.' They showed me plans to refit the *Warrior* with masts and turn her into a sailing ship, more in keeping with the region she was about to visit. After making landfall in New Zealand, where Elaine Shaw would greet her as she sailed into Auckland, she would head for Mururoa as part of a peace flotilla. It was eight years since Elaine had first requested a visit.

Out of the blue, I received a 14-page letter from Janie. She'd finally got on top of her illness, and wanted to tell me she was the one responsible for what had happened that winter in Amsterdam, she was the one who'd driven me mad. She had been so jealous of me, she wrote, that she had willed a dark power to possess my soul. She asked if I had felt taken over by an evil force, and begged my forgiveness. My response was ambivalent: I felt a degree of undeniable antipathy, yet also enormous empathy. I'd come to view the episode as a valuable life experience. Terrifying though it had been, it was better to reframe it as something positive. I didn't know if I believed Janie's culpability, or indeed if she'd had any role whatsoever in the onset of my insanity. I wrote back reassuringly. I didn't want her to suffer, thinking she'd been responsible.

At College of the Atlantic, I was asked to support a fellow student who was suffering from schizophrenia. She was hearing a multitude of voices commanding her to kill herself. She'd tried to drive her van into a lake and was covered in mud when she came to see me. I cradled her in my arms, whispering to her gently, trying to de-escalate the intensity of the delusions as she tore at her ears when the voices wouldn't let up. Eventually, she returned home and took to phoning me long-distance. She told me I was the only person she trusted, that I would understand because I'd been there.

One day, I was listening to the radio as I cleaned the house of a wealthy scientist who had been conducting research at Mount Desert for several years during the summer. The job was an easy way to supplement my income, and the scientist was rarely there. I didn't pay too much attention when I heard Auckland mentioned in the midmorning radio news. 'Bomb', 'Dutch crew member', 'killed', 'Greenpeace boat' — the words floated past me as I cleaned.

Eventually I looked up, listening more attentively, the slow-moving beast of fear creeping through my body. Had they said Dutch? Which Greenpeace boat was in Auckland? Had the *Warrior* arrived already? The questions raced through my mind. In a panic, I phoned the radio station. They wouldn't give me any information until I told them my connection with the story. I wanted to know which Dutchman had been killed. They asked me where I was and what I was doing in Maine.

Within half an hour of my returning home in Bar Harbor, Channel 5 television news was knocking at my door. A woman in stiletto heels marched in, introducing herself and her crew. The phone rang. It was Martini. He was distraught. After the first bomb blast, he'd gone looking for Fernando, who'd gone to retrieve camera film from his cabin. When the second bomb had gone off, Martini had been forced back up the stairs by the sudden rush of water that poured in, submerging the aft cabins below. I'd always thought of Fernando Pereira, the photographer, as Portuguese.

I tried to hide from the TV crew as I spoke to him on the phone, turning my back, mumbling into the mouthpiece, but the cameraman followed my every movement, sticking his camera right in my face. In the background the reporter was giving a running commentary. I quickly phoned a friend and asked her to come and take Brenna away. I didn't want her to be part of this circus. No sooner had the Channel 5 television van departed than one from Channel 7 pulled up. Same kind of presenter, different outfit.

'Could you stage that phone conversation with your husband again?' they asked. 'When do you expect to be reunited? Will he be flying into Bangor?' They were firing the questions at me one after the other, hoping to get wind of a possible airport reunion before Channel 5. I was still trying to figure out how they'd found me.

'Who do you think did this? There's a rumour it might have been American extremists. Apparently a threatening note was found with a US flag and a skull and crossbones.' A huge fluffy mike, like a stick of black candyfloss, was thrust up to my mouth.

'It's the French,' I answered, live to air on Channel 7.

'How do you know that?' the anchorwoman asked condescendingly.

Did she want it to be the Yanks? Would that make her job any less meaningless, I wondered? I told her about a death threat Remi had received years before. He'd been told to stop researching French nuclear testing if he valued his life. He'd phoned us in Whitehall from a phone box somewhere in the Pyrenees, where he'd gone to stay with his grandmother until the heat came off.

'They want to stop the *Rainbow Warrior* from going to Te Ao Maohi, to French Polynesia,' I told the American people. 'The French don't want the world to know what they're doing at Mururoa and Fangataufa atolls.'

14

The Right Honourable Sir Wallace Rowling thanked me for writing in a 'reasoned and restrained way', but I was fuming. Major Mafart and Captain Prieur, the two DGSE agents arrested for the bombing of the *Rainbow Warrior*, had been released into French custody in return for NZ$7 million compensation. The secretary-general of the United Nations had acted as arbitrator between New Zealand and France, and his decision was final. A couple of months beforehand, David Lange, prime minister of New Zealand, had said: 'We do not have for sale any prisoners . . . if there is to be any form of release, it will be after a substantial period of imprisonment has been served in New Zealand.' Not only were the prisoners for sale, I wrote in my letter to Rowling, they'd been sold *bonne marché* — at a good price.

Brenna and I flew to New Zealand on 27 October 1986 for a three-month visit — Hilari and Mother had clubbed together to pay our fare. I was shocked when I saw the shell of the *Warrior* in Auckland. She'd been stripped, inside and out. Everything was gone, auctioned or siphoned off one way or another. I was upset to see her so empty and devoid of life. I was angry at the people who'd done this to her, removing her dignity.

I set up a meeting with Ngati Whatua, the local iwi. I wanted to hear what they would like Greenpeace to do with the *Warrior*; after all, she'd been bombed in their tribal homeland. They asked if there was any way we could turn her into a museum, or place her on the headland at the entrance to the harbour as a permanent reminder of Aotearoa/New Zealand's antinuclear stance. I was receiving phone calls in the small hours of the morning, and was told of a plan to seize the shell of the *Warrior* and have it shipped back to London and mounted in Trafalgar Square. Prince Charles was being approached — this was a matter of preserving national history. Do something, I was told. But a decision had

218

already been made to scuttle the *Warrior* off the northeast coast of New Zealand. A local Maori entrepreneur wanted her to become an underwater reef. He operated a dive shop and was building a motel near the proposed site, off the Cavalli Islands. It smacked too much of commercial enterprise to me.

I refused to attend the scuttling on 12 December 1987; instead, I went hiking along the Far North coast. Seated on a beach near Cape Reinga, I was reading some notes from a tribal traditions course I'd been attending at Auckland University. I read that spirits of the departed, travelling up Piwhane Bay [Spirits Bay] — the selfsame beach I now found myself on — would leave knotted pieces of flax along the way to show their passing. I looked at my watch. I wanted to observe the moment of the scuttling in my own way.

I shut my eyes as I wished the *Rainbow Warrior* well on her journey to the bottom of the ocean, imagining the water churning around her as she up-ended, pausing to take one final breath before diving down, bow first, heading for her final resting place. Goodbye, Warrior Woman. Ka kite ano. I imagined I saw a glint of jade, a small Buddha pendant, nestling in a metal crevice.

I opened my eyes slowly. It was over now. She had gone. Haere, haere, haere. I looked down, and there, right beside me on the hardened sand, to my right, was a piece of knotted flax, perfect in its symmetry. Perfect.

I returned to Maine in 1988 to graduate and pack up my belongings. The three-month trip to New Zealand had stretched into almost one-and-a-half years. It had been more than just a case of being waylaid. I'd been given permanent residence status, my family were living in Auckland, as were most of my friends, too, and I'd made the decision that New Zealand was where I wanted to live.

I flew to Boston on 7 March 1988 as Cyclone Bola was devastating East Cape. When I arrived in Maine, I phoned Brenna, who had remained behind with Martini, to make sure she was OK. I could hear torrential rain in the background, and she was shouting to make herself heard. I shouted back, waking up everyone in the house where I was staying. 'They're in the middle of a cyclone back home,' I said. It sounded very glam. I realised then that New Zealand — Aotearoa — was where I belonged, that I was no longer in transit, no longer just passing through. I would be returning after graduation, shipping at least a ton of cardboard boxes packed with a lifetime's memories.

In Bar Harbor I flatted with Harriet, a colleague from Allied Whale. She was a brilliant Canadian naturalist who slept in satin sheets with a decanter of whisky on the bedside table and a St Bernard at her feet. She had once attended the opening of an art exhibition at college wearing nothing more than a coat and some heels, and had flashed the quasi-geriatric trustees of the college, — the 'Ivy League' of famous American families. As she left the exhibition she stood at the door and whistled through her fingers. 'Here,' she said, 'cop a load of this.' Everyone turned round, their cocktail chitchat truncated midsentence, as she stood in the doorway, coat open, her tall, red-headed, naked body on gorgeous display.

One evening we went to a concert of zydeco music, played by a band from New Orleans that was touring the east coast. Harriet loaned me a dress with rhinestones for the evening, from her eclectic collection. Wonder if anyone here knows CPR, I thought, just in case an old codger has a turn. Harriet was really fun to flat with. I wore a black, wide-brimmed Navajo hat with her dress and felt Amazonian.

'Say, can I see your brim?' a honey voice asked softly behind me, at the end of the concert. I swung around. The drummer in the band had leapt off stage and followed me to the exit. I had seen he fancied me from the dance floor. His eyes had followed me as he did his drum thing, spinning his sticks up in the air, catching them and pointing them both at me before continuing. 'Now would I be correct in saying that you won't be leaving without your brim?' The southern drawl and muscle-popping black silk body made my molasses run and had my gumbo on the boil.

'Well, of course not,' I replied, sounding very English, and blushing.

Harriet was pacing round the living-room floor. A couple of the band members had come back with us, including the drummer, and I could see she was getting impatient. We had dragged the congas down from the attic — my room — and had been jamming. 'Look,' — she'd finally stopped pacing and taken me aside — 'if you're not going to grab his ass and fuck him stupid, I will.' I didn't need any further prompting.

I didn't want to leave the US and return to Auckland — I was having too much fun. At our class graduation party I got drunk on expensive champagne with a member of the Rothschild family who was a college trustee. We jumped into a Chevvy convertible, bottles of bubbly in hand, and were chauffeur driven very fast through Acadia National Park, our hair streaming in the wind like in an Italian movie. We shrieked with delight, champagne bubbles streaking our cheeks. I stood up in the back and jived to the loud music on the car radio — after all, my hips had been lubricated by the Creole pulse of the South, and there was no stopping me now. Who would want to return to boring old New Zealand after that? And I was due to arrive back in the middle of winter.

It took three sessions, over a cold, rainy weekend, to sit through a 14-and a-half-hour film at the Civic, the picture palace in central Auckland, screened by the New Zealand Foundation for Peace Studies. Called *The Journey*, and made by British film-maker Peter Watkins, it was about the way media distort our perception of the world and the role of the mass media in maintaining structures which militate against disarmament. At the end of the screening there was a public meeting, and somehow I landed a job with the foundation distributing the film in New Zealand. One day, I accompanied the foundation's coordinator, Marion Hancock, to the assessment block at Paremoremo, the country's only maximum-security prison, just outside Auckland, to give a talk. We were told the prisoners in the block were at-risk individuals who were either suicidal or indulged in self-mutilation. They were volatile and disturbed men, some of whom had been segregated for their own safety. My brief was to speak about the early *Rainbow Warrior* days, a motivational talk which was part of a programme designed to counter an epidemic of suicides and self-harm.

The prison complex was shaped like a spider and set deep into the earth. Entry to the cell blocks was through a metal detector and a series of electronically locked doors controlled from a central console, modelled on an Australian design. Maori spoke of it having been built on an old burial ground, of kehua roaming the bleak corridors at night.

'Can you give me some information, please, on the stuff you mentioned, about social justice and the like?' A young man had approached me at the end of the talk. He looked too young to be in prison, and had a large red welt around his neck. He showed me a huge mural of the *Rainbow Warrior* painted on a wall outside the dining room. I tried not to show how taken aback I was to see her image in such a place. 'We're all stuck like a needle in the groove, men still as children,' the young man said. 'All we have to read are 1970s copies of *Woman's Day*.'

My middle-class sensibilities hadn't prepared me for such an acute introduction to society's shadow, to the Kiwi family secret. 'I'll see what I can do,' I promised. I made a point of shaking everyone by the hand. I wanted them to think I was staunch, but I was quaking in my Doc Martens.

It took a year for the Department of Corrections to allow me back into Paremoremo so I could run a course in the assessment block. The hiccup was the word 'peace' in the course title, and a question had been asked about me in Parliament. A rather embarrassed prison officer asked if I was a member of the Communist Party, having been instructed by someone official to find out before letting me continue the programme I'd designed. The motivating force in my insistence on running the course was the suicide of the young inmate I'd spoken with. I was gutted when I heard, and lobbied the minister of justice, using the suicide as a platform to launch the project. He was very supportive and wrote to the prison. Luckily for me he then became prime minister, and the gates of Paremoremo were opened, one year later, as if by magic.

Prison officers sneered: 'You'll never last. They'll chew you up and spit you out. Do you realise who these people are? Multiple rapists and child murderers.'

The first thing I did when I walked in through the gates was stick up a poster: 'Unarmed truth is the most powerful thing in the Universe.' It was my premise — naively, perhaps — that outrage and anger at society could be channelled into something useful. I used excerpts from *The Journey* to launch each session's discussion, and sometimes brought invited guests with me — activists, musicians, film directors, authors, politicians.

I had a group of regulars who attended, Mongrel Mob members mainly, some with faces covered in tattoos. One insisted on sitting with his back to me, sticking his arm up and yelling 'Zieg Heil!' every so often. When he boasted about being tortured by a rival gang, it was the last straw. I invited a Chilean I knew who'd been tortured at the hands of the Pinochet government to come and tell his story to the group, and a couple of them had the humility to admit afterwards how petty their stories were in comparison. I had no problems after that, and we grew to trust each other. I could have left cash on my seat and found it there the following session.

The inmates talked about their lives, sharing intimate details of their horrendous childhoods — the sexual and physical abuse, the drugs and alcohol. They complained that pornographic videos were shown in the early hours of the morning on the in-house channel operated from the central console. One of the inmates had tried to gouge out his eyes after watching one — it had reminded him of his own crime.

What do you say to a man who sticks knitting needles up his penis when he phones you at home from a pub just down the road and tells you he's coming for a visit? I phoned the prison. Yes, he'd been discharged, they said, but don't worry, he'll probably be picked up before closing time for rummaging through ladies' handbags looking for something sharp to hurt himself with. Brenna barricaded the front door and hid under the bed. He never came, having been picked up by the police within an hour of my call. I felt crushed for exposing my family to the risk I was taking in doing such work.

After a year-and-a-half, we came to the end of my course built round *The Journey*, and it was time to leave the assessment block. I ran a couple of further courses in the main blocks before turning my back on prison work permanently. I'd been overwhelmed by stories of the dysfunctional lives of generations of New Zealand families. I was angry at the media for glorifying gang violence, and for being so explicit in detailing crimes against women and children. I needed to stand in the light again.

In 1990 I was part of the New Zealand delegation to the Nuclear Free and Independent Pacific Conference, where I met the man who became my husband — Luc Tutugoro, a representative of the Kanak Socialist National Liberation Front (FLNKS). He was a member of Palika, a progressive left-wing party within the front, and had been minister of economic development under the separatist government of Jean-Marie Tjibaou, the Kanak leader assassinated in 1989. I instantly fell in love with this quietly spoken, handsome man who phoned me several times a day from his office in the territorial congress in Noumea, courtesy of the French colonial system.

New Caledonia is a nonvolcanic Melanesian archipelago less than three hours' flying time from Auckland, with unique flora and fauna and 28 distinct language groups. It was annexed by France in 1853, and 10 years later nickel ore was discovered on the largest island, La Grande Terre. Since then, over 150 million tonnes of ore have been mined, with devastating consequences for the environment and community health. Up to 40 per cent of the world's nickel deposits are in New Caledonia, the planet's only stockpile of a silicate-oxide ore know as garnierite, with reserves predicted to last for another 200 years. Classified as a strategic mineral by the French government, nickel is used for defence purposes and in the nuclear industry. In the early 1990s, a 10-year nickel-export deal was signed with Japan by the Melanesian-owned Société Minière du Pacifique Sud. The exported ore was to be used, among other things, in the construction of Japan's new generation of nuclear reactors. The French had offered the Kanak leaders who signed the agreement an easy development model, which would also guarantee France's own national defence and nuclear industries a steady and uninterrupted flow of the mineral. By 2000, nickel accounted for 90 per cent of New Caledonia's export earnings.

Flying over the beautiful archipelago, I was shocked by the miles of deserted terraces of open-cast mines, and the red-brown blanket of dust covering everything, suffocating coral reefs and poisoning streams and rivers. Nothing, however, could have prepared me for the sight of the nickel smelter a couple of miles from the centre of Noumea — the so-called Paris of the South Pacific — belching out hundreds of thousands of tonnes of nickel dust, a known carcinogen. A Kanak housing estate had been built less than 10 metres from the smelter, two others no more than a kilometre-and-a-half away. Children caught and ate fish from the moat around the smelter. Tailings were dumped in valleys on the outskirts of town and eventually buried under a thin layer of topsoil before housing estates were built on top. An asbestos fibre in the mineral complicated things further. Lung-cancer rates in New Caledonia were the highest in the Central and South Pacific, and asthma-mortality rates the highest in the world. Myeloblastic-leukaemia rates were extremely high among Melanesian children, as were the incidents of brain tumour, thyroid cancer — it went on and on. There was a vested interest, I discovered, in not keeping proper records — the military controlled the medical sector in the territory.

The plane was held up almost an hour at La Tontouta airport as agents for the DGSE rummaged through my papers, photographing and photo-copying everything they found in my bags. 'I'll put you on the mailing list,' I said as they peered at a couple of FoE newsletters. I'd been invited to participate in the yearly FLNKS Congress and made a speech to a field full of colourfully dressed people and Kanak leaders flanked by armed bodyguards. I saw myself on television later, the only white woman in a sea of dark faces. It was unusual for non-Kanaks to be seen in Kanak-dominated areas. A man from the South Pacific Regional Environmental Programme, based in Noumea, told me he'd never spoken with a Kanak in all the years he'd been stationed there.

I had been assisting the FLNKS with some of its press releases in solidarity with the Tahitian people over continued French nuclear testing at Mururoa. The Kanaks had been cut off from the Pacific region during *les événements*, the civil unrest of the 1980s. World attention had been focused on French activities in Tahiti and this had assisted in keeping secret the destructive colonial mining and smelting policies in New Caledonia. A cartoon about me, with the legend 'In bed with Kanak politics', had appeared in the local paper. I didn't feel very welcome. It was time to leave.

Luc joined me in New Zealand several months later, giving up his lucrative job in the territorial congress. He believed his fellow Kanak leaders had sold out to the French and didn't want to be an accomplice in the environmental destruction of his country. I'd seen his old Ford rusting in the middle of his beautiful Tchamba-valley home, riddled with bullet holes. 'This was as far as I got,' he said, with a smile. He felt safe in New Zealand, no longer waking with a start every time a car exhaust popped, thinking it was a bullet, and running for his life, sleeping in a different bed each night to evade capture.

Ironically, a trust — established with the money donated by the French to the New Zealand government for the *Rainbow Warrior* sabotage — awarded us a small grant, under the umbrella of FoE, to study the environmental and health effects of the nickel mining and smelting industries in New Caledonia. During the period of our research we had two visits from DGSE agents, one couple posing as 'peace activists' from Toulouse, in France. Their timing was brilliant. I'd organised a question-and-answer session for a coalition of environmental groups with a visiting right-wing politician from the French territory, and the agents had been sent ahead of his arrival to suss us out. I was immediately suspicious of the guy's haircut, and the brand new 'Peace' T-shirts he and his partner were wearing. They'd picked up some banana cake on the way and phoned from a phone box to say they were in the area. 'Can we come?' they asked, stuffing the bag of cake into my hands at the front door and striding down the hall before I had time to answer.

It just so happened that out in the back garden, in our small sleep-out, Martini and another Greenpeace activist were discussing the Mururoa antinuclear campaign. With them was the American scientist who had found radioactive isotopes in the ocean around the test sites, something the French had referred to as 'a typing error' in the published scientific report of his findings. That same year I received a 17-page letter from Alain Christnacht, the French high commissioner to New Caledonia, about pollution from the nickel smelter, in which he claimed the major source of pollution was the washing-up liquid used in the staff canteen.

Hanging from the outside wall of the sleep-out was a rubber ring with m/v *Rainbow Warrior* painted on its rim. The agents wasted no time in whipping out a little camera and excusing themselves to make their way round the house, inside and outside, taking photos.

When the politician arrived in New Zealand the following week, he quickly cancelled, saying there was no question of his discussing anything which could 'distort the political orientation of France' — whatever that meant. I'd made sure the agents would report back some rather horrifying health and environmental statistics about the industry in which he was involved, information I said I would be making available to the public. We traced their so-called 'peace group' to a fictitious address in Toulouse, where none of the activists we knew had heard of it.

Our home was paid another visit while we were away on holiday, and this time computer files Luc had hidden were stolen when someone broke in through a bedroom window. Luc had been back to New Caledonia a couple of times since becoming a New Zealand resident, and had been followed and photographed everywhere he went. In 1992, however, he and a couple of Kanak friends managed to collect dust and water samples from around Noumea and smuggle them out for analysis at a New Zealand laboratory.

Nickel is so toxic the World Health Organisation has ruled there is no safe level for it in the air. With invaluable help from FoE, we commissioned a health-risk assessment of the smuggled samples. This revealed a nickel concentration in dust from windowsills around Noumea that was three times greater than in the mined ore. It concluded that a 'potentially hazardous health risk' existed in Noumea.

Alain Christnacht loosened his tie as he swung his chair round, sitting astride it as if he were riding a horse. I sat on the edge of mine, heavily pregnant, my small tape recorder balanced precariously in my lap. 'Do you mind if I record our conversation?' I asked. He agreed. I'd received a phone call from him — he would meet me, provided I came alone.

Luc had driven me to the exclusive downtown hotel in a dilapidated Ford we'd bought for a couple of hundred bucks — I still didn't know how to drive. I noticed some men peering at us through the curtains of a room on the third floor. 'Must be them,' I said as Luc turned the car before dropping me off several blocks away. The same men were waiting for me in the foyer. Monsieur Christnacht was in his suite. He told his security guards he wanted to talk with me alone.

'You see, madame, it is like this . . .'

The clever bastard had waited until I'd run out of tape before loosening up. He'd ummed and aahed his way through a discussion about the Japanese nuclear programme, feigning total ignorance. Two weeks later, he would give permission for the transport of radioactive fuel rods through New Caledonian territorial waters, destined for the same programme. 'You see,' he said, repeating himself, 'things are very inflammable at the moment in New Caledonia. If you hand over the results of your research to the Kanak people, they are liable to start a civil war.'

It certainly wasn't simple, the Kanak leaders being implicitly responsible for their own downfall. We'd already given them our findings, and they'd chosen to remain silent. As the FLNKS had a declared antinuclear position in both its charter and constitution, I accused them of double standards. On the one hand they were professing solidarity with the Tahitians in their antinuclear struggle, while on the other they were engaging in a commercial enterprise that supported the very industry the Tahitians were fighting. The Kanak leaders later issued statements condemning the transport of nuclear-fuel rods through New Caledonian territorial waters. Didn't they realise the things were bound for the reactors they were helping to build? FLNKS leaders had even come to New Zealand to see if they could build a smelter in the South Island, proposing that they export the ore from New Caledonia and we — nuclear-free New Zealand — export the finished product to Japan.

I was vilified both in the regional media and in public for calling a spade a spade, and told that as a white, nonindigenous woman I had no right to criticise black, indigenous leaders. What bollocks! Greed and corruption are neither colour nor race specific.

15

'Why is it called the Beehive?' the dishevelled man asked, referring to the New Zealand government building. We were sitting in his garden.

'Perhaps because it looks like a hive,' I answered. I was paying him a visit in my capacity as a mental-health professional. I'd been working in mental health for a few years, since the birth of my two younger children, Naawie and Woody. I was now qualified, but knew that being a professional didn't automatically give anyone the ability to form a rapport with people who were unwell. I'd met a lot of doctors, psychiatrists, counsellors and social workers who knew diddly-squat about how to treat someone with a severe mental illness. They didn't understand the language of madness.

'Look, there's the prime minister!' The man pointed to a large bee busying itself at a small flower. He'd been in deep thought for a while before speaking, and I'd gone into the house to make us a cup of tea.

I felt at home working with people in altered states, and knew I was able to help navigate a distressed person through a mind storm. It was hard yakka, though, engaging with people with acute paranoid schizophrenia, and those who were suicidal. The phone calls would come in the early hours of the morning, often waking the whole family. Then there were the hours of talking — steadily, gently — trying to de-escalate the extreme hypervigilance, the quasi-electrical energy of the paranoid state, bringing a person slowly back to baseline. Not to mention removing the weapons and the drugs, admitting people to hospital, calling the police, wiping blood from the walls. I could handle the blood — it was the stories of tortured childhoods and perverted family relationships that distressed me the most. I suppose you could call it 'people-whispering' — stilling the raging minds and walking alongside them through the nightmare, bringing them back from the brink.

'They keep telling me to shut the door.' The man said it in a cheery way, as if discussing a family member's bad habit. We were sitting in a Ponsonby café, drinking coffee and discussing voice-hearing. He laughed. 'Shut the door! Shut the bloody door, they say. Pretty crazy, huh?'

'Don't they know the door's shut and locked?' I asked. We both splurted into our coffee, cappuccino bubbles frothing.

'Fucking brilliant,' he said. 'I'll try that next time.'

I'd copied out something from a percussion workshop I'd attended. 'Make music with your life,' it read, 'a jagged silver tune that cuts every deep-day madness into jewels that you wear.' It helped me understand why, each day, I went back to work, where I clashed hugely with the fear-based practice model inherent in the system, the one built round containment, suppression and castration.

'No one brings you flowers in a psych unit.' The woman spoke with her eyes lowered. 'If I'd been in cardiology they wouldn't have left me lying on the floor so long when I had that seizure, saying I was acting out.'

'Neuroleptic malignant syndrome' is a fancy way of saying 'dangerous side effect from antipsychotics'. Here's what can happen: something called dystonia (a posh word for jerking), breakdown of the muscle tissue, drooling, seizures, heart and kidney failure, and more. It isn't acting out: it requires acting on, immediately. What was it about the mentally unwell, awash in their own vulnerability, that caused people to fear and avoid them? I had experienced it myself and knew what it felt like.

'We've got five manics in there today,' the nurse said. 'Be careful.'

I'd been cleared to enter the intensive-care ward of the psychiatric unit and was waiting for the electronic door to open. A familiar smell greeted me; it lingered from the use of injected sedatives, sweated from the pores of distressed individuals struggling to breathe under the weight of several burly nurses pinning them to the ground. A woman was perched on the arm of a soiled couch wearing only a G-string and heels. 'Isn't this what all you men want?' she yelled, lipstick smeared across her face. Figures with bloated bodies paced the corridor in their regulation nightgowns or pyjamas; others ran back and forth, naked, until restrained. Several were jammed into a tiny smoko room, rummaging through the old tin cans used for ashtrays, looking for butts. Walls had been punched

229

in and equipment smashed; bedding was strewn everywhere. The clinicians were holed up in one small room in the centre of the unit, exiting only when necessary. It was like walking into a war zone.

I stood and stared at the laminated poster. It was a drawing of the *Rainbow Warrior*, beneath the words 'You Can't Sink a Rainbow'. It was the only thing on the wall that hadn't been vandalised. 'Givvus an automatic, love,' a woman lisped through missing front teeth, sidling up to me. I noticed the homemade tattoos on her fingers, small pinpricks of blue ink under each knuckle, spelling out the word L-O-V-E.

'Sorry, I don't smoke,' I replied. I asked her what she liked about the poster, why she thought it was the only thing that hadn't been touched, destroyed.

'It's about hope, innit? Hope that things will change. I mean, that's all we got, the likes of us.'

Since the Stockholm Conference in 1972, 15 per cent of forest in the Amazon catchment has been destroyed, and world governments are still refusing to do anything about it. We know the current destruction of forests has put wildlife under the greatest pressure of extinction since the dinosaurs were wiped out. We are destroying potential cures for many illnesses as I type this. There goes another one . . . and another . . .

Our global economy is still unable to ensure corporate responsibility — or liability — for the production of toxic chemicals and pollutants. We know the world is running out of fresh water, and when you consider that only 2.5 per cent of the world's water is fresh in the first place, and that only a fraction of that is accessible, it's scary. Two-thirds of humanity faces a future without fresh water — on a planet with water across 70 per cent of its surface. Meanwhile, the United Nations has said the world community is unable to cope with the frequent natural disasters now occurring because of the havoc caused to the planet's weather patterns by global warming. Over a quarter of a billion people are currently in need of emergency food aid because of famine and crop failure.

The billions of dollars donated worldwide to environmental groups haven't done much to alleviate any of these problems. Most donations have gone on salaries, meetings, travel, phone bills and coffee. I know I'm being facetious, and — sure — they've managed to get a few laws changed, but are things fundamentally any different? Environmental organisations have been subsumed by the corporate, capitalist system;

they're part of it now. Those billions they have at their disposal are, for the most part, invested in banks whose interests clash directly with their own expressed goals. I can't help but wonder what a truly iconoclastic uprising could do with that kind of dosh. Make sure as many people as possible had access to clean running water, a roof over their heads, electricity, sanitation and free health care and education would be a good start.

In the 1990s I was elected to the board of Greenpeace New Zealand, at the same time as I was on the board of FoE New Zealand. Shortly after I joined the Greenpeace board, a directive came through from Greenpeace International saying that activists should not serve on the organisation's national boards. Lawyers, financiers and corporate high-flyers were fine, but activists were a no-no. This was about the time that the newly appointed CEO of Greenpeace International featured on the front of *Time* wearing a suit and tie. I was a bit embarrassed about it all, to be honest. I knew his annual salary, minus expenses, could have housed, clothed, fed, schooled and educated thousands of underprivileged children a year, and brought tangible change to hundreds of communities. Hell, he was paid more than our own prime bee.

Each of us has a fundamental right to freedom, equality before the law, adequate living conditions, and a life of dignity and wellbeing free of discrimination, colonial oppression, foreign domination, racial seg-regation and apartheid, and to a world that respects and improves the environment in which we all live. It's what we, the people of the world, consented to 30 years ago at Stockholm. And nearly 45 years ago, in the Universal Declaration of Human Rights, we agreed that everyone is born free and equal in dignity and rights, and that ignoring or despising these rights results in barbarous acts. Maybe such declarations, treaties and charters, all the legislation and paperwork produced at conferences, summits and conventions — maybe all these mean absolutely nothing when push comes to shove. You just have to look at how the multi-nationals behave — especially away from home — to know that none of the good work has yet been incorporated in any global business plan.

I don't know about you, but I feel more than a ghost of loss in all this. Our collective psyche has become flawed by our consumerist obsession, our Pac-Man approach to devouring product and spewing and shitting waste. Our desires and preferences must change at the emotional level, that which dictates our choice and use of resources. Ask yourself the question: would you go without to ensure an equity of resources? Would you downscale your lifestyle, get rid of your toys? Be honest. Would you do it voluntarily, or would you compromise, strike a deal, meet halfway? We need to reclaim our global heritage before the rainbow disappears entirely, on a planet of no water, behind a sunless haze from burning fossil fuels. We need to be concerned with the coherence of existence. We need to get with the programme before it's too late.

Go and lie on your back in the forest, on your own. Listen to the wind in the trees, to the birds, the insects and the other animals around you. Feel the invisible cloak of belonging surround you, balance you. See the colours, shapes and textures of Creation and be inspired. Savour the depth of your understanding. Is the world so full of weeping that nothing can be done? Hear the rhythm calling you, eliciting a response — growing louder, stronger, the suffusion of humanity's pulse. Lock on. Don't be scared. You'll know what to do. You'll know how to journey well. There can be no other path.